The Journey of the Magi

The Journey of the Magi

MEANINGS IN HISTORY
OF A CHRISTIAN STORY

Richard C. Trexler

PRINCETON UNIVERSITY PRESS
PRINCETON, NEW JERSEY

Copyright © 1997 by Princeton University Press
Published by Princeton University Press, 41 William Street,
Princeton, New Jersey 08540
In the United Kingdom: Princeton University Press,
Chichester, West Sussex

Library of Congress Cataloging-in-Publication Data

Trexler, Richard C., 1932–
The journey of the Magi : meanings in history of
a Christian story / Richard C. Trexler.
p.   cm.
Includes bibliographical references and index.
ISBN 0-691-01126-5 (alk. paper)
1. Magi—Cult—History.   I. Title.
BT315.2.T74   1997
232.92′3—dc21   96-39399   CIP

This book has been composed in Galliard

Princeton University Press books are printed
on acid-free paper and meet the guidelines
for permanence and durability of the Committee
on Production Guidelines for Book Longevity
of the Council on Library Resources

Printed in the United States of America
by Princeton Academic Press

1   3   5   7   9   10   8   6   4   2

For Tom and Henry

———————————

CONTENTS

ILLUSTRATIONS

ACKNOWLEDGMENTS

MY INTEREST in the magi started in the 1970s with my friendship with Rab Hatfield, who had recently opened up the subject to a social-historical interpretation. Edith Cooper, Randall Kritkausky, and Michael J. Rocke did some digging into the subject during my graduate seminar in 1980. In the next decade, several scholars made more than passing contributions to the work, among whom Paul H. D. Kaplan, Randolph Starn, Jean Wirth, and Erik Zürcher stand out. The Center for Advanced Study in the Visual Arts (the National Gallery), the John Simon Guggenheim Memorial Foundation, and the Wissenschaftskolleg in Berlin gave me the institutional backing to write up the results of my research. Finally, several colleagues at that Kolleg read parts of the text for me: Robert Darnton, Wolfgang Kemp, Ora Limor, Klaus Schreiner, and Susan Trainor. All contributed to making this text better than it was, and I much appreciate their input.

The Journey of the Magi

INTRODUCTION

These magi . . . are also called kings, because at this
time philosophic men of wisdom ruled.
—Nicholas of Lyra[1]

EACH HOLIDAY season, newspapers, television, and planetaria bring us up to date on the star of Bethlehem. We are told what is new about this old "star," that marvelous astronomic event said to have announced the birth of Jesus of Nazareth. The star (or comet or planetary conjunction) is reborn, as is the child: a heavenly event that seems ever new as we would be renewed.

Most people today, including many Christians, suspect the story of the star because they know that the arrivals, or epiphanies, of many famous leaders, and not just Jesus, are associated with such unnatural manifestations of the heavens.[2] Moderns would say that on its face, the Christian story has no more claim to belief than do these others. Either all such stories should be believed, or none.

And yet, despite it all, the human need to "follow a star" that will not dupe them makes the storied transformation of the heavens at Christmastide, and the birth of Jesus that is said to have accompanied it, ever new for many people. Gathered together beneath that star, we see the events of the sacred birth through our own lens. We construct the crib, as well as the actors around it. Christians have historically built into the nativity scene, as they have into other powerful sacred images, their own social and political experiences. This they continue to do, in order to render themselves emotional in the presence of those images. That is not so obvious in the story of the star, for it was by definition beyond human manufacture. But as we mix in with the first devotees at the crib of Bethlehem, we enter the realm of social and political experience. We are told by one source that shepherds appeared first, by another that their very opposite, wise men called magi, had the honor. The star of Bethlehem speaks to our metaphysical self; shepherds and wise men involve us in the hands-on sociology of the sacred.

Look again. The whole of life seems to be at the crib. Simple shepherds recognize divinity in this helpless infant, as do the animals, emblems of a farming population. Then come the magi, shown either as kings or as intellectuals, the very antithesis of the shepherds' ruddy simplicity. These aristocrats bestow upon the infant a type of diplomatic recognition as king by reverently offering gifts. In turn, this offering hints at the presence of still another social group at the crib, the merchants. Who else had gathered together the gifts of gold, frankincense, and myrrh, if not them? Solomon indeed speaks of frankincense and myrrh as "the merchants' powders."[3] And who were experts at exchange if not traders? The implicit merchant presence at the crib is still more clear when the magi and Mary actually exchange gifts at the crib, as they sometimes are said to have done.[4] To this day, Christians, in arranging these crib scenes, place the infant in a recognizable social order of herders, farmers, courtiers, and merchants that pairs and polarizes country and court, riches and poverty, simplicity and complexity.[5]

Precisely this social and experiential range, legitimated by the wise and powerful magi near the center, permits Christians to be moved by this innocent child. This plasticity is nowhere more evident than in the identities that Christians have given to these evangelical wise men over the centuries. No Christian icon has permitted Christians to so form and reform their own social, cultural, and political order and experience as has their story and image. The present work studies the political sociology of the magi in Christianity from their appearance in Matthew until the present. It aims to discover why and how the magi, journeying to and around the crib, have been so assiduously emulated by later societies.

An important beginning on this road comes from the apostle Paul, who recognized that the legitimation of Christianity had to come from persons with no vested interest (like the magi). "It is necessary to have witness from outsiders," he wrote a colleague.[6] In effect, where there are no magi, no god or divinity can become apparent. And so it was that from shortly after the infant's birth, certain outside secular powers are said by Christians to have recognized Jesus' legitimacy as king and God. Indeed, the magi's *journey* to and *adoration* of Jesus together form the one and only "Christian" heraldic event in the New Testament. Its clear purpose was to legitimate the infant in the *saeculum*. By extension, the social oppositions we observe in the total scene at the manger themselves seem God-given, a part of the "natural" social order apparently maintained by the sage and powerful magi. Foreign wise men determined that the Bethlehem events were significant; they, not the shepherds, made space for Christianity.

Later rulers have maintained and widened that space. For centuries, Christian adults and children, both clerics and laypersons, have acted out the story of the magi and the shepherds in festivals, putting the pieces of their social universe into place around crèche and altar. They have been social engineers constructing a social order. When modern crèche builders place the star over the scene, they seem less to let heaven shine upon earth than to have transformed into astral terms the social and political universe they have constructed.

It would be wrong to think that the socially balanced crèche of today is what the evangelists described. But the mistake is not new. Consider, for instance, the manger scene in an adoration of the magi painted by Joos van Cleve around 1525, which hangs in the Dresden Gallery. In the lower right corner, the evangelist Luke sits painting what is before him.[7] That might seem unexceptional, until we realize that Luke never described such a scene in his Gospel. Writing independently of Matthew in the latter third of the first century, Luke told the story of the shepherds but not the magi, while Matthew, independently of Luke, tells of the magi but not the shepherds.[8]

The painter, and his patrons, got it exactly backward, for Luke knew nothing of magi. The later image of the magi and the shepherds sharing the same barn with Mary and Joseph actually results from early Christian bishops deciding that both gospels were divinely inspired. It took centuries befor Christian storytellers imagined the magi and the shepherds actually meeting each other.[9] But once they did, it was evident that overlapping the tales of Luke and Matthew did provide an aesthetically more unified notion of the significance of the birth and manifestation of Jesus than did either one alone, all without shaking the obvious medieval truth that it was the magi who indeed legitimated the infant's pretensions.

Indeed, Matthew's and Luke's accounts agree on only two points: that Jesus was born in Bethlehem and that this was confirmed by outsiders. According to Luke, Mary and Joseph traveled to Bethlehem from their home town of Nazareth, where they found no room in the inn and so sought out the stable, where the infant Jesus was born and soon celebrated by shepherds. Matthew on the other hand says that the couple lived in Bethlehem, so that the magi "entered into the house" there and not into a barn, to worship a child and not, as it appears, an infant.[10] The separately tracked stories continue after these visits. According to Matthew and him alone, King Herod feared the child because he was said to be king of the Jews. Herod ordered the *massacre of the innocents*, but Mary and Joseph eluded Herod by a *flight into Egypt*. Alas, only Matthew has it this way. The Gospel of Luke never mentions Herod and knows nothing of a massacre of innocents or of a flight into Egypt. More prosaically, he has Mary and Joseph see to the infant's circumcision locally, before the family returned to Nazareth, where Jesus grew up.[11] The infancy narratives do not complement each other. As scholars have always recognized, they in fact contradict each other.

Further contradiction is found within Matthew's own story. The arrival of the magi in Jerusalem was the talk of the citizenry. A marvelous star appeared over the house in Bethlehem, so presumably the people of this village five miles from Jerusalem witnessed the spectacle of the illustrious magi come to see the infant.[12] Yet no contemporary writer mentions these events. Herod feared the birth of a king of the Jews, yet curiously, he did not follow the magi to find the child, as he might have. Worse, once the magi had avoided Herod by going home another way, this prince ordered a massacre of innocents because his spies could not determine which house the very public magi had visited. It all sounds suspicious, so much so that by the 1960s belief in the magi was a litmus test to determine if one were a conservative or a liberal in matters biblical.[13]

Some learned commentators may still try to discover the "true story" amid these contradictions. Yet quite separately, Christians' behavior around the crib built the magi into central representations of their social, political, and even natural universes, for around the crib, it was clearly they who represented secular force and authority. More important, in time the actions of these devotees ever reshaped the magi, as they did their own societies. Essentially, medieval Christians Europeanized a Near Eastern tale. Then Europeans and the people of the Americas reshaped the image once magian gold was found there. Nor has this process of reshaping the magi been limited to tribal or to so-called European popular cultures. During the French Revolution, enemies of the crown viewed these "three kings" and all the customs associated with them as a monarchist plot, and they substituted a republican cult in their place.[14] Nor, as shall be seen later in this book, have the magi been just a tool of the rich. Aristocratic though the cult appears on its face, European peasants and black slaves in the Americas have at times donned magian crowns and threads before rising up against their oppressors.[15]

Though the following work does not pretend to be a history of the magi cult, its organization is roughly chronological in character.[16] It aims to describe in time the relation between the arrangements around the crèche and the social and political organization of Christian societies. In the six chapters that follow, certain political, social, and cultural structures are seen to evolve for which the magi story provides a discourse. My interests revolve around these structures and discourse. Chapter 1 deals with the magi in Roman times till about A.D. 800. During this period the magi image becomes fundamentally political in shape and content. The Roman festive theme of triumph passes to the Christian world in the persons of the magi. The notion of the magi as diplomats reaches back to this early time. The association of the magi with the Constantinian church will attract our attention, since this first Christian emperor followed the magi in pursuing a sign in the heavens. Finally, the gifts of the magi emerge already in the early Christian story as tribute or taxation.

Chapter 2 surveys the magi as they appear in Europe from Char-lemagne until the arrival of their alleged remains in Cologne (800–1164). Our emphasis in this chapter is the theatrical fortunes of the magi, for it is in this period that they take to the stage. The Byzantine emperors led the way, playing the sun or star as they received ambassadors and handed out offices; having their wives play Mary when they bore the first child and then staging adorations around this scene; and finally encouraging the birth of a nativity drama, these rulers provided the inspiration for sev-eral Western adoration practices while creating their own indigenous ap-proach to the nativity. The chief western mediaries for these influences were the Ottonian emperors: They too took to playing the sun or star, yet unlike the Byzantine rulers, they imagined their polities as themselves ruled by the magi, who were by now considered to have been not just intellectuals, but royals. At this point, the chapter turns to the early magi liturgical plays in Western churches and to their social content. The prominence of Herod in these early plays is emphasized, and thus a secu-lar thrust at the inception of the theatrical tradition of the magi. It was as much at Herod's as at the infant's court, it seems, that contemporaries learned how to pray, how to greet, how to give.

Chapter 3 considers the period from the late twelfth century until the year 1500. Real European kings began to play the role of one or more of the magi in outdoor festivals, even as some of the Italian republics took to legitimating themselves by turning their republics into kingdoms for great magian pageants. In this process, such real magi/kings, if they were to represent their whole polity, needed among their two fellow magi/kings not just mature white faces but also ones that were young, effemi-nate or female, even black. Thus the second part of this chapter studies the emergence of an exotic magus among the three kings, who is dis-tinctly young, or black, or effeminate, standing in a polarity over and against the established world of solemnity represented by the first and second kings. An image of the magi that represents the whole of a society emerges, even its excluded or liminal forces.

The conquests of the Americas in the sixteenth century furnished enor-mous new fields where, relatively unchecked, Europeans could impose their own behaviors and social organizations. Chapter 4 shows what a significant role the story, the drama, and the images of the magi played in this "civilizational" undertaking. Part 1 describes how on the eve of the explorations, the magi story helped shape the European imagination of the world outside, and then subsequently, how Europeans cast the dis-coveries themselves in magian terms. The Europeans, in short, found in the Americas the places whence at least one magus had come with all his riches to Bethlehem. Then these pages turn to their most significant task, which is to describe the use to which the Europeans put the dramatic processional images of the journey and adoration of the magi to reorganize the inhabitants' space and time into Christian ones. From Peru to Guatemala, then on to Mexico City and even to far-off Huron country, native Americans found themselves constrained into a new path toward a new goal to pay their old respects—and taxes—to a European god.

Returning to Europe, chapter 5 documents a radical reversal in the public personas of the magi during the early modern period and the ancien regime. At a crack, royals ceased to play the magi publicly, and the slack is taken up by new social groups. Even as aristocrats and bourgeoisie play the magi in large private banquets, there appear at their doors on the eve of the feast of the kings (5–6 January) the representative "kings" of early modern Europe, the beggar bands of boys with paper crowns on their heads, asking for alms in exchange for a song and a good wish in the new year. The central part of this chapter is the important social theme of the magi as traveling beggars in early modern Europe. Thus at its base is the curious reversal in the social image of the magi. Who are the magi now? Are they those good bourgeois who gift the child beggars at their doors, or are they the princes who take up collections for a poor child on Epiphany? Are they the crowned children themselves, or the retired soldiers or day laborers who, in this preindustrial era, also appear at the door wearing a paper crown and threatening those who would deny them not so much gold or frankincense as simple bread and wine?

The last chapter of this book is in the form of an epilogue sketching the magian presence in modern societies. Two modern German visionaries reveal a new romantic image of the "childish" magi. One of these women is provoked to visions by playing at the crèche. Alternately, theosophists and numerologists popularize a modern urban vision of wise men hidden away in distant India and Tibet. There the magi are at home in the terrestrial paradise, where they await the arrival of tired and perplexed adorers from the West. They had come to rest. The journey of the magi was over.

Chapter 1

THE STAR ARRIVES

For almost two millennia, western Christians have heard the gospel of the magi on 6 January, the feast of Jesus' "epiphany," a word that means "appearance" or "manifestation," "revelation" or "coming out." For almost that long, the faithful in most of western Europe have thought that these wise men arrived at the crib on that same date, the twelfth day of Christmas, when Jesus was thirteen days old. During the Middle Ages, 6 January and the previous evening were also called the feast of the kings, when Balthazar, Melchior, and Caspar had their annual moment in the sun. Let us say something about the origins of this important festival.

The early Christian feast may have descended from a pre-Christian celebration in Egypt on the evening of 5 January that commemorated the sun god Aion's birth to a virgin. This feast featured the blessing of the Nile, whose water was said to turn to wine. Our first record of the Christian feast of the epiphany occurs among eastern Christians of the early second century, who celebrated on that night and (perhaps with something of a hangover) on the following morning of 6 January.[1]

The themes of the Egyptian rite are important because they overlap those of early Christian celebrations. The early church in Jerusalem celebrated the birth of Jesus on 6 January, not the magi.[2] Other Eastern Christians chose that date to recall John's baptism of Jesus in the Jordan, when Jesus really "came out." The celebration of other events was assigned to this date as well—the marriage banquet in Cana, at which Jesus turned water into wine, and Jesus' multiplication of the loaves and fishes. To these narrative evocations of the early Egyptian celebration may be added a ritual one: On 6 January eastern Christians baptized newcomers and blessed holy water.[3] So far in the East we find no mention of a celebration of the magi.

Some time after Constantine recognized Christianity in 313, the western church decided to strike out on its own and to celebrate the birth of Jesus on 25 December, a date probably chosen to draw some of the crowds that were out celebrating the Roman saturnalia.[4] By the end of the fourth century, most eastern churches had adopted this date for the feast of the nativity. Significantly, they included the magi in their commemorations of that date. In the same eastern rites, however, 6 January remained the more important feast, celebrating the baptism of Jesus (i.e., his epiphany, or coming out) along with the other biblical events just listed, but not the magi. To this day, Armenian Christianity only celebrates 6 January.

The western church celebrated these same memories on 6 January, with one important variation: it relocated the celebration of the magi's adoration of Jesus from his nativity to 6 January. Thus eastern Christianity considered the baptism of Jesus as his epiphany but from the time of Augustine of Hippo (d. 430), western Christianity, while it also recorded the baptism of Jesus on that day, identified Jesus' epiphany with the arrival and adoration of the magi before Jesus. In the West, the magi eclipsed the baptism of Jesus as an occasion for celebration.

Thus were born the twelve days of Christmas. In the West, the magi— their journey, gifting, and adoration—became the center of Epiphany celebrations in an explosion of fifth-century sermons and treatises on their story. Jesus did not "manifest" himself when he was born, for there were no witnesses to the nativity per se. Nor did Luke's humble Jewish shepherds provide sufficient witness. The advent of the wise men, potentates from the East, and Mary's unveiling of the child to them became Jesus' epiphany. Based on this liturgical calendar, it came to be said that the magi had seen the star on 25 December and had arrived in Bethlehem just thirteen days later, on 6 January.

Now hear Matthew's words:

> When Jesus was born in Bethlehem of Judea in the days of Herod the king, behold, wise men from the east came to Jerusalem, saying, "Where is he who has been born king of the Jews? For we have seen his star in the east, and have come to worship him." When Herod the king heard this, he was troubled, and all Jerusalem with him; and assembling all the chief priests and scribes of the people, he inquired of them where the Christ was to be born. They told him, "In Bethlehem of Judea; for so it is written by the prophet: 'And you, O Bethlehem, in the land of Judah, are by no means least among the rulers of Judah; for from you shall come a ruler who will govern my people Israel.'"

> Then Herod summoned the wise men secretly and ascertained from them what time the star appeared; and he sent them to Bethlehem, saying, "Go and search diligently for the child, and when you have found him bring me word, that I too may come and worship him." When they had heard the king they went their way; and lo, the star which they had seen in the east went before them, till it came to rest over the place where the child was. When they saw the star, they rejoiced exceedingly with great joy; and going into the house they saw the child with Mary his mother, and they fell down and worshiped him. Then, opening their treasures, they offered him gifts, gold and frankincense and myrrh. And being warned in a dream not to return to Herod, they departed to their own country by another way.

Matthew continues. After the magi departed, an angel told Joseph to flee with the child and his mother to Egypt, where they would remain until the death of Herod (4 B.C.). This fulfilled a prophecy, Matthew says, and it protected the infant from Herod who fell into a rage "when he saw that he had been tricked by the wise men" and ordered the massacre of the innocents. So as to eliminate Jesus, ". . . he sent and killed all the male children in Bethlehem and in all that region who were two years old or under, according to the time which he had ascertained from the wise men."[5]

Who were these mysterious, obviously rich visitors? Matthew's very imprecision tantalized early Christians, indeed, the faithful to this day; no one, of course, has shown the same interest in Luke's poor shepherds. The magi were from the East, they interpreted stars, they traveled, and then they gave gold, frankincense, and myrrh as presents to an infant. That is all the curious have had to go on. Yet over the centuries, every vital statistic about the magi and their journey has been worked out from these sparse leads, from Old Testament stories that were seen to announce elements of the Jesus story, and from the visions of Christian mystics. These details have been widely represented in literature, in the arts, and in festivals. In this chapter, I shall describe what was discovered about the magi in these early centuries when they first passed the gates into the Christian imagination. My next goal is to understand the social and political context into which they were first received. Finally, we shall study the use to which early Christians first put the magi saga of travel, adoration, and gifting.

To determine the background of the magi, early Christians used three discrete approaches. The first was to emphasize their astrological skills in reading the meaning of the star. This suggested to some commentators that the magi came from Chaldea or the Mesopotamian valley, whose intellectuals were famous on that score.[6] In this reading, their adoration of the child showed that religion had superceded astrology as an occult tool.

A second approach was to exploit the word "magi" itself. The magi were from Persia, many assumed. They were the people or priesthood of that name in a part of modern Iran, whence came the word "magic." Because this area of Medea had long been ruled by the Persian king of kings, it was easy to imagine that subjects of that great king recognized Jesus' royalty long before Constantine did. They did this not by setting off on their own for Bethlehem; rather, they went on legation to find the child on the orders of the Persian king.[7] In this reading, Persia proved itself wiser than Rome. In its time, this political approach was quite as important as the symbolic interpretation of the Persians' adoration, which was that magic, as well as Persian Zoroastrianism and Mithraism, had been delegitimized by this "true religion."[8]

Both these readings obviously served the elect Christian clergy in its struggle with contending priesthoods. Whether Chaldaic or Persian, the magi came from an area to the east, which lay in the grip of the forces of darkness. Yet a third approach suggested that the magi came not from the east but from the south and that they were rulers more than intellectuals, thus representing many lands rather than one. More than the other approaches I have mentioned, this one searched the Old Testament for confirmation.

The Christians' conviction that Jewish and even gentile prophets had foretold Jesus' birth meant that they were also the primary sources of information on the magi. Matthew himself knew that Jesus was fated to be born in Bethlehem of a virgin.[9] So early Christians like Origen (ca. 185–254) found it child's play to determine, for the whole Christian tradition, that the star had been forecast by the Mesopotamian outsider and "magus," Balaam.[10] "There will come a man out of [Israel's] seed," Balaam had said, "and he will rule many nations. . . . A star will rise from Jacob, and a man will stand forth."[11] To learn more about the magi, one had only to discover the prophetic texts that foretold their journey.

The first biblical passage lending itself to such a forecast was put forward by Tertullian (160–220). He thought that Psalm 72 obviously had the magi in mind because, like Matthew, it features foreigners bringing gifts and submitting themselves:

> May the kings of Tarshish and of the isles render him tribute,
> may the kings of Sheba and Seba bring gifts!
> May all kings fall down before him, all nations serve him![12]

To the present day, this passage, early adopted into the liturgy of the feast of the epiphany, has remained the classic Old Testament forecast of the magi. Countless Christians learned from it that the magi were "as good as kings," as Tertullian himself first suggested. Some then surmised that they came from the area of the Red Sea.[13] The mention of Sheba engendered the idea that the famous queen of Sheba had prefigured the magi's visit to Jesus when she made her journey up the Red Sea to visit Solomon in Jerusalem,[14] as well as the possibility that at least one of the magi, like her, had gifted the gold of Ophir.[15]

The general thrust of Tertullian's choice is more important than these details, as a comparison with earlier notions of the magi's origins makes clear. Those who thought the magi came from Persia or Chaldea saw them as intellectuals, sent as legates of the king of kings to Bethlehem. Tertullian, on the contrary, imagined them as quasi-monarchs who represented different kingdoms and commanded their resources. The notion that, far from harboring the philosopher's stone, the lands of the magi hid economic resources conveniently controlled by monarchs would interest medieval commentators and would fire the imagination of future explorers and conquerors.

Early commentators could not have dreamed that Christianity would one day command these resources. Their purpose was simply to fill in the sparse Matthean picture of the magi, and in that pursuit they next searched out passages in the Old Testament that mentioned foreigners bringing the particular gifts brought by the magi. There is a source that twice mentions frankincense and myrrh—products of varieties of balsam trees commonly imported to Judea from the Red Sea—but which our exegetes do not bring into relation with the magi story. This source is the Song of Songs:

> What is that coming up from the wilderness, like a
> column of smoke, perfumed with myrrh and frankincense, with
> all the fragrant powders of the merchant?[16]

In the gorgeous "behold you are beautiful, my love" passage, Solomon, after describing his beloved's eyes, hair, teeth, lips, cheeks, and neck, turns to the woman's breasts:

> . . . like two fawns, twins of a gazelle, that feed among the lilies.
> Until the day breathes and the shadows flee,
> I will hie me to the mountain of myrrh and the hill of frankincense.
> You are all fair, my love; there is no flaw in you.[17]

It is not difficult to divine why these passages were so rarely pressed into service as harbingers of the magi.[18] The eroticism of the Song of Songs has always embarrassed solemn readers, and Matthew himself was presumably interested in the magi's frankincense and myrrh as offerings for divine services not as aphrodisiacs. Another reason exegetes did not refer to these mentions of myrrh and frankincense is that the former passage calls these aromatics "the powders of the merchants." Church commentators had something else in mind for the magi than to cast them as crude merchants who only bought and sold wares.

To assume that the magi were intellectuals or rulers was one thing. To suggest that they might have been spice and drug merchants, as the class of magi were in fact sometimes understood to be, was clearly unworthy.[19] Actually, some scholars now believe that the first gift of the magi was not gold but a third spice, the error having arisen from a bad translation of Matthew's lost Aramaic original into the Greek Septuagint. *Zahab* ("gold") is in fact listed along with frankincense and myrrh in surviving commercial documents from the Red Sea area.[20] Matthew may therefore have imagined figures somewhat akin to the snake oil salesmen of the American heritage: healers who peddled occult wisdom with their goods.[21] But the magi did not emerge as merchants from the musings of exegetes.[22]

Instead, early students selected the other biblical text that mentioned their gifts as the most significant prophecy of the magi, and it indeed emulated the pluralistic, aristocratic, Arabian focus of Psalm 72. When we look back over two thousand years of magian history at the end of this book, we will be in no doubt about the triumphal role this Isaiahan passage has played in ascertaining the meaning of the magi:[23]

> Arise, shine; for your light has come, and the glory of the Lord has risen
>   upon you.
> For behold, darkness shall cover the earth, and
> thick darkness the peoples; but the Lord will arise upon
> you, and his glory will be seen upon you.
> And nations shall come to your light, and kings to the
> brightness of your rising.
> Lift up your eyes round about, and see; they all gather
> together, they come to you; your sons shall come from far,
> and your daughters shall be carried in the arms.
> Then you shall see and be radiant, your heart shall
> thrill and rejoice; because the abundance of the sea
> shall be turned to you, the wealth of the nations shall cover you.
> A multitude of camels shall cover you, the young camels of Midian
>   and Ephah;
> all those from Sheba shall come.
> They shall bring gold and frankincense, and
> shall proclaim the salvation of the lord.
> All the flocks of Kedar shall be gathered to you, the
> rams of Nebaioth shall minister to you; they shall come
> up with acceptance on my altar, and I will glorify my glorious house.[24]

In an unmistakably triumphant mode, Isaiah 60 pictures kings and whole nations moving from diversity to unity, and from darkness to light. Accompanied by great retinues of men and animals, they wend their way to submit themselves before the altar of Israel, to become the Christian altar. In a narrow sense, Isaiah confirms the southern origins of the magi. But his poetic vision makes far greater claims. Through the blinding light of his verse, Isaiah suggests a cosmic vision of philosopher-kings. They come to the infant "from the ends of the earth," terminology used by the ancients to vaunt the power of their kings.[25] Precisely this global reading was then classicized by Augustine.[26]

In his book *An Inquiry into the Nature and Causes of the Wealth of Nations* (1776) Adam Smith recognized that in truth the merchants, not

the pompous kings, were the ones who brought together Isaiah's "wealth
of nations" from around the globe. But for the early Christians, who
heard from their preachers that the magi's gold proved that Jesus was a
king, their frankincense that he was a God, their myrrh that he was the
doctor or savior of souls, the great processions of Psalm 72 and Isaiah 60
could only have evoked images of the Roman imperial triumph.[27] The
magi would indeed be the continuator of this political form of legitimation through the Middle Ages.

We turn now to the experiential world of the early Christians. Embit-
tered by the Jewish establishment's rejection of the young cult and fearful
of persecution by the Roman Empire of which they were all subjects, the
leaders of the young church soon saw its future as linked to the gentiles
(non-Jews). Indeed, Matthew probably already thought of the magi as
representing that gentile world.[28] Augustine would establish the notion
of the magi as the "firstfruits" of the gentiles,[29] while Luke's Jewish shepherds, converted over time into the polar opposite of the rich, intelligent
magi, soon stood for all Jews. When had the Jews received such a legation
as that of the magi to Jesus, asked Augustine triumphally.[30] Even the
queen of Sheba had come only to hear Solomon, not to adore him as the
magi adored the king of the Jews.[31] In what follows we shall try to charac-
terize the broader political and social experience of early Christians in the
areas of parades, gifting, and banqueting.

Early in the twentieth century, Franz Cumont and Guillaume de
Jerphanion interpreted a set of important Roman monuments originating
in Salonica, Greece. A fourth-century sculptor, in decorating the church
of St. George with figures of the magi arriving before Jesus, had directly
copied figures of non-Christian foreigners in eastern clothes submitting
to Galerius (d. 311) from that emperor's nearby triumphal arch.[32] Here
as elsewhere, these stock figures of the Roman triumph bear no clear sign
of high station; they are simple prisoners of war or legates of a foreign
power submitting itself to Rome. Building on that archaeological observation, Cumont made several comparisons of early magi representations
to Roman triumphant sculptures of this sort and came away with no
doubt. Formally, the early Christian magi in art were little more than
translations of a secular motif of Roman triumph that was now made to
show the triumph of Jesus.[33] This triumphal motif, in which the glory of
a host is emphasized by the submission of his guests, was not new with
the Romans, and it has by no means vanished from the scene today.

Thus the triumphal Old Testament texts identified as the prophetic
source of the magi found their corollary in the visual sphere, where
Roman panoply, perhaps even a particular triumph, was used to anchor
this magi vision in the Christian consciousness. Albrecht Dieterich was
the first to suggest that the oft-described visit to Nero of the Armenian

1. *Pope John Paul II welcomes a prelate*

prince Tiridates in A.D. 66 had been a model for Matthew's description.[34] Accompanied by a train of "magi" and some three thousand Parthian riders, Tiridates did not appear to be subject to the Romans. He seemed to be making a triumphal entry himself, comparable in a way to the emperors' own ritual of ceremonial entry, or *adventus*, into Rome.[35] Yet appearances were deceiving. The Armenian's purpose, one writer said ironically, was "on his own to offer a triumph over Armenia" to Nero.[36]

It was crucial to Rome's assertion of authority that it seem to rest, indeed that it at times be generated by, the free submission of outsiders to the *pax romana*. In countless pictures of the magi, these subordinate figures, more than the virgin and child, appear to be the center of attraction. This is how it was with Tiridates. Accounts of the episode indicate that he seemed triumphantly equal to Nero, when actually he was subjecting himself and his land to the Roman. Arriving in Nero's presence amidst enormous panoply, the Armenian prostrated himself before the ruler of the world, as he would before Mithra, he said. In a subsequent banquet, Tiridates, called a "magus" (presumably along with the magi in his retinue), initiated Nero into the Mithraic religion in the midst of "magical dinners."[37] The whole Armenian contingent then returned home by another way. So did the evangelical magi.

Jean Gagé makes it still easier to see this event as a possible inspiration for Matthew. Nero was a devotee of the sun, indeed Sol's incarnation, says this author.[38] He lived in a "house of gold"—the metal of the sun—where he researched ancient treasure troves that once uncovered might finance a new golden age. In Gagé's view, Nero wanted to use Tiridates's Eastern magi to make gold. An eternal "feast of money" might be possible, like the one King Herod's grandson had celebrated at Caesarea at the time of Nero's predecessor, Claudius.[39] What did not occur to Gagé was that a millenium and a half later, explorers and conquerors would still be seeking the same metal: the gift of gold of the evangelical magus.

Whether or not Tiridates's or similar Roman triumphs inspired Matthew is not very important in this context, and there are other candidates for such inspiration.[40] What our description of the event is meant to demonstrate is that the magi's entry into Jerusalem and Bethlehem was comparable to the entry of Roman rulers and their subjects, and the structural fact that in his triumphs or advents, an emperor's authority depended on the seeming freedom and honor of those who submitted to him or of their legates. That might seem improbable in what was, after all, a representation of military humiliation, but was a sine qua non of subsequent imperial rule, when emperor and subjects had to be "brothers." This exchange network of the ceremonial welcome was mirrored in a second reciprocity allowing early Christians to imagine their own magi: the phenomenon of giving gifts.

Because the magi gave what must be called diplomatic gifts to the "king of the Jews," our sketch of contemporary Roman gifting practices should begin at that level. This lens reveals the early Christian comprehension of the magi's gifts. Who could be surprised that what were called "gifts" were in fact often tribute? The kings of Psalm 72, and thus by extension the magi, "brought gifts," which in the psalm is equated with "render[ing] . . . tribute" to their king. Countless Eastern potentates or their legates, as well as Roman officials returning from mission, brought home "gifts" from grateful allies: exotic animals of the East, wagons full of food in containers of precious metals, and most significantly the golden wreaths called *aurum coronarium* that were offered to the Roman sovereign. Thus we see that constraint on factual subordinates was an integral part of diplomatic gifting in this age, a constraint that might be acceptable because it also brought the benefits of the

Roman peace. Having been triumphantly received, such crowns were quickly assessed, their value being entered in account books by imperial bureaucrats before they were melted down. The *aurum coronarium* was central to imperial authority, and after being adopted as a headdress by Julius Caesar, it became one of the standard attributes of the Roman emperors.[41]

Like us, the Romans may have been more willing to accept the deceit that diplomatic gifts were voluntary, where such an appearance might be deemed necessary to world order, than to tinker with the institutions of domestic giving. Yet even in this more private realm such equivocations ruled, if we are to believe the early Christian social critics. After all, did not the Bible say that no one should present himself before God with empty hands?[42] And was it not customary in all kingdoms to give gifts at the birth of a now or future king?[43] The need to feign sincerity extended from the top to the bottom of social giving. As in other cultures, norms and sincerity were always at war with each other.

In the Roman world, domestic gifting was especially prominent in the late December saturnalia, when the sun was reborn, and on New Year's day, called the calends of January, a feast that by the fourth century extended till 5 January and had begun to absorb the festive vocabulary of Saturnine celebrations.[44] Originally, some difference in the character of the gifting on the two feasts may have existed. Gifting during saturnalia was a means of inversion, of "turning the world upside down." In Ovid's time (d. A.D. 17), gifting on New Year, on the other hand, centered on the *exchange* of gifts between more discrete social units like families and business partners, as well as on the new consuls' incense offering to the divinities on the Capitoline hill. Such New Year's gifts, called *strenae*, originally consisted of old coins, which were thought to embody good luck for the coming year.[45]

From early times, Roman social commentators recognized that, though the rich might be encouraged to be liberal toward the poor, on the whole such gifting redistributed wealth upward. The grains of precious frankincense that the poor man was told to give his superior, irrespective of what the latter gave him, obviously represented the greater sacrifice.[46] Still, the dominant ideology was that in so doing, the weaker giver balanced things out by participating in the joy of the more powerful receiver. Ideally senators "offered" their emperors gold crowns (*aurum oblaticum*) and plebs gave them *strenae* to celebrate a military victory or some private imperial joy, like the birth of an heir. Just as ideally, the recipient then reciprocated liberally, Tiberius for example being said to have returned gifts given him on New Year's day with fourfold *congiaria*, as imperial gifts were called.[47]

The reality was that *strenae* to the Roman emperors were not usually personal gifts. In the reign of Tiberius's predecessor Octavian, for example, the Romans brought gifts of coins to the Capitol, and they did so even when the princeps was away.[48] Nor were they given only for reasons of state. The same Tiberius, Suetonius complained, wanted *strenae* to dower his daughter.[49] Such gifts also might be bestowed to prepare for future undertakings like the expedition of armies, whose success, along with the ensuing peace, was understood to be a future gift of the emperor. The reality was that these *strenae*, which had probably always been an expected part of festive behavior, became assessed, levied, and recorded taxes in a polity that might theoretically be free of them.[50]

As we have seen, savvy social commentators like Suetonius used the ambivalence between gift and tribute, between free will and constraint, to denounce certain rulers. Yet we have no reason to think that the average Roman did not understand these fictions, violently as he might respond to the revelation that he had been tricked and his generosity taken advantage of. We should rather see the Roman as participating in a ruse so as to generate sentiment, and prevaricating in the hope of a greater, almost transcendant return: the eternal *pax romana* or at least the ongoing avoidance of harm. Though the magi gave freely, they too, as we shall see, received in return.

A third general Roman social context that helped early Christians to comprehend the magi and their gift giving was the Roman banquet, where food was the object that mediated a discourse on the character of equality and inequality, as the magi also mediated such a discourse. In this setting the host obviously appeared to provide food as a gift, not as tribute. He might say, as once did the emperor Caligula, that he wanted all his guests to be equal, just as the process of ingesting food and expelling waste is equal.[51] Yet Roman diners often established a dining hierarchy that regulated the consumption of the food. One common feature of Roman banquets was the election or appointment by the diners of a "king of the banquet," or king of drinking (*rex bibendi*).[52]

The results of such elections could be as perplexing as Eastern savants or potentates giving precious spices to a carpenter's son. True, participants at such banquets sometimes elected their actual ruler as the king of the dinner and placed the crown of the *rex bibendi* on his head, thus continuing the real political order in the banquet hall. Yet on other occasions, Roman rulers are found electing the most humble person at the table as their ruler for the banquet. He received verbal honors and toasts, and, not unusually, his "subjects" made him deep prostrations.[53] Such inversions of the real social order, creating new inequalities to accomplish the equal business of consuming food, were the background against which etiquette might require that everyone be a king for an evening. We hear of one dinner at which the same Caligula, so as to flatter real subjects, wanted everyone to be a feigned or real king and to wear a crown.[54] Thus in Roman society, highly dynamic rites of election and coronation temporarily inverted and seemed to equalize social orders.

From the time of the earliest church fathers, Christian moralists provided sweeping criticism of mainstream gifting and banquet practices. Their own love feasts, or "agape," at times were suffused with deep feelings of mutuality, as the celebrations of small, voluntary organizations often are. Early church leaders proclaimed a qualitative psychological difference between the dynamics of the gifting and the banqueting that occurred inside their conventicles and what occurred outside them. Outside was deception, or "false festivity"; inside was real gifting and the meal of eternal life.[55] Maximus, bishop of Turin (380–470), added a class analysis. Is it not unjust, he asked, that in such public festivities, it is actually the inferior who gives to the superior, who has plenty. The pair might call each other friends, but the duplicity was evident: "[One] greets [a 'friend'] with a gift before greeting him with the fraternal kiss. Just think how much such a kiss is worth! A purchased kiss, all the less valuable the more dearly it is bought."[56]

Yet these attempts to identify a "real gift" or a "real banquet" among competing spaces and objects did not work because the faithful themselves understood the political and social function of the *strenae*, as well as the attendant deceptions. Trying to convince an urban audience that they should not go to the seasonal banquets after leaving church, Augustine in one sermon made fun of country people who left tables laden on calends to insure abundance during the year.[57] In another sermon, he cried to his listeners: "[The gentiles] give *strenae*. You should give alms."[58] Yet Augustine was no fool, as this playing with words reveals. He knew what his hearers would say. "When I give *strenae*," he has one of them retort, "I myself receive them."

To which the preacher responded: "What! Do you receive nothing when you give to the poor person?"[59] Yet listeners understood the political and social function of church "alms" as well; they knew that the equivocation between gift and tribute was present within the churches as well as without. The earliest liturgical records indicate that negligent Christians were told not to come "with empty hands" to the altar to receive the bread and wine.[60] The notion was that since the offerant received back the same bread and wine he offered, it was theft not to offer it. Christians were also ordered to give alms to the poor, that is, to the widows and orphans of deceased members. Yet as the faithful well knew, the use of these gifts went further. Alms and offerings supported the growing ecclesiastical establishment, which deserved to be paid for its work.[61]

Returning to the gifts of the magi, the author of the unfinished gloss on Matthew, the *opus imperfectum*, recognized that alms were indeed the essence of the gift of myrrh. "For as myrrh keeps the bodies of the dead from corrupting," he said, "so good works serve to keep Christ crucified perpetually in the memory of man." He too told his readers not to come before God empty-handed.[62] Others understood the gold as alms. "[God] accepts as [magian] gold," Augustine had told his listeners, "what we give as alms." This theme has resounded down through the ages.[63] Still other commentators, like Fulgentius (468–533), however, saw the gold of the magi not as alms but as tribute. In seventh-century Spain, money collected at communion was then ritually distributed to the clergy in the presence of the laity.[64] These gifts further supported the expansion of Christianity, just as the gentiles' gifts to their rulers underwrote future goals. The insistence on "freewill giving" was, and is, a rhetoric that is part of the cost of community.

Thus the intense feeling palpable in some early Christian eucharistic meals did not inhibit participants from viewing the latter like other banquets, as part of their everyday world. Here too those faithful in a position to do so might send their offerings to the altar with servants rather than show themselves personally submitting to the clergy, those bankers for the Lord. Inversely, as at other banquets, offerants might use the occasion to show off their liberality.[65]

As if to confirm that the Christian banquet was not inherently different from the dynamics and forms of gifting in general society, eucharistic breads of the sixth century were called "crowns" and as late as the eleventh century were still shaped like them.[66] Nor did the adoption of the small, circular host in that later century end the association to general societal giving, for these hosts were calculatedly made to resemble coinage, and coinage had long been the standard gifts or tribute of the gentile festival.[67]

Predictably, objects like these also became gifts of the magi in the scores of early Christian paintings and sculptures to which we now turn. In previous pages, I have intimated how early Christians would have perceived the magi by anchoring the social foundations of their story—triumph, gifting, and feasting—within Roman society, using mainly written sources. Now we turn to the magi in early art, an even more important source than writings for studying Christian imagining about their wise men. As if to say that magian giving was no longer encountered in the real world, a sixth-century celebrant cried that "no longer are gold, frankincense and myrrh offered" as the faithful flocked to the altar with their gifts on epiphany.[68] Yet in the universe of visual art, legions of cultural artifacts continued to use the image of the magi for different purposes, including the solicitation of gifts and tributes.

The association of the magi to the gentile world is key to interpreting much of this art. It serves as a beacon for understanding the gentile Constantine's (and his sychophants') turn toward Christianity, and it was after all his recognition of Christianity in 313 that prepared the way for that religion's triumph. But first some background on the magi in early art. An early concentration of magi representations is found in the Roman catacombs. Overwhelmingly, these paintings date from the time of Constantine until the mid-fifth century. Used by early Christians to bury and remember their dead, these caves were fitted out with burial niches and tomb walls covered by paintings that occasionally commented on the persecutions that had claimed early martyrs. Among narrative scenes, that of Shadrach, Meshach, and Abednego, the three "children of Judah," was especially popular. Like Christians, these servants of a Chaldean monarch had suffered martyrdom rather than adore a royal statue.[69] Another popular theme was the apocalyptic figure of the Good Shepherd and of the heavenly banquet that hard-pressed Christians looked forward to. They were among the oldest and most popular paintings.[70] But the magi's journey to Mary and Jesus soon enough became the most popular infancy scene in Christian art, and it remained so for centuries. In the catacombs alone there are more than a dozen pictures of the magi preserved till the present day.[71] But the Christian dead soon came above ground, and a great many of their sarcophaguses featured representations of the magi.

Whether carved or drawn, these representations have certain common features that distinguish them from the magi in the crèche scenes to which moderns are accustomed. True, they are usually, though not always, three in number. But differing from more modern magi, their race and dress, and even their age, are mostly identical.[72] As noted earlier, their "Phrygian" bonnets, pantaloons, and shoes are little different from those worn by the eastern emissaries so common in Roman imperial art, but where we can compare them on the same monuments, they are also not differently dressed than the three martyred Jews of Babylon with whom they are often coupled.[73] This identical clothing almost certainly means that, like multiple heralds or legates who then and later wore identical clothes, they were thought to represent one and not different kingdoms, just as the martyred Jews were servants of the one Babylonian king. Certainly at the symbolic level, the significant title *magorum beata legatio* refers not to "other" authorities, but to one legation from *the* other ruler.[74]

The figures of Mary and child furnish a second common feature in these early paintings and sarcophagal sculptures of the magi. With few exceptions, Mary greets the magi seated on a chair or throne. Often she holds a young child rather than an infant (which, when represented, has all members tightly bound in swaddling clothes). A crib is rarely present, but when it is, it is separate and away from the persons involved in the adoration.[75] This is a pompous diplomatic reception rather than a sentimental one, and the type definitely precedes the earliest representations of the magi being received by Herod, which became a focus of thespian diplomatic pomp during the European Middle Ages.

The third common feature of these early works is that the magi are shown in similar, when not identical, procession toward Jesus and his mother, not in a static state before them.[76] Occasionally they are led by an angel that is often identical to the Victory figures of Roman triumphal art. Later catacomb paintings occasionally show them at rest after arriving. But they are standing erect, not bowing in obeisance.[77] Their movement toward Jesus, not adoration from a fixed position, represented the international recognition of Jesus, as such movement did of the Roman emperors. As Cumont has demonstrated, processing toward a ruler with gifts was a type of submission.[78]

While the absence of prostration remains a significant feature of magian works in this early period, their gifting showed the adoration of which Matthew spoke. This emphasis on gifting is a fourth common characteristic of early Christian magi representations. All the magi approach the quasi-enthroned mother and child, their covered hands usually holding plates that contain the gifts themselves.[79] In an early poem, the Spaniard Prudentius (d. ca. 410) labeled the very containers of these gifts "golden," so we should not pass them by.[80] Since deepest antiquity, at Roman receptions and at early Christian eucharistic services, the containers were often more valuable than the bread and wine, candles, honey, and milk that they might contain. In the Middle Ages, the gold of the chalices and boxes usually dwarfed the magian presents themselves.[81]

A fifth and last common feature of these early representations is that, in keeping with the implications of Matthew's narrative, the first magus, as far as we can see in these often damaged works, always offers gold. This would never change. Clement of Alexandria (d. ca. 215) had already imagined that the magi brought the golden wreaths common to Roman imperial representations, so it is not surprising that such wreaths, when not gold coins, appear on the plates with impressive frequency.[82]

When we consider these presents of gold together with the food products that also are discernible among some gifts, we begin to have some idea why the magi were so popular, especially in early funeral art of the type found in the catacombs and on sarcophaguses. The Christians who paid for these representations wanted to show that, like the magi, they had made gifts to Jesus through his church. This fundamental association between what had launched the church—the magi's gifting of Jesus—and

2. *Adoration of the Magi*

the salvational giving that was as a consequence expected of all Christians
will be one leitmotif of this work.

   The carryover from magi to faithful happened in these monuments.
Some sculptors actually incised numbers on the magi's bags and plates,
almost certainly to stipulate the extent of the testator's charity. Numbers
from eleven to sixty-five (as on the gift of the second king represented
in figure 2) can be read. With Wilpert, I take that to mean as many
gold coins.[83]

   Thus these early Christian magi sarcophaguses can give us specific information on testamental charity, and they display an ideology toward
such gifting that has a long history ahead of it. In several of these works
the boy Jesus reaches for, even grasps, the testamental gift of the first
magus, as he continues to do in adorations of the magi fifteen hundred
years later.[84] This was not just any child being attracted to the glitter, as
would later be argued. As we have already seen, the infant was conceived
as a poor person accepting alms for the poor, and that of course meant
the church as that infant's vicar acting for the same poor. Incontestably,
these early representations of the magi not only address Jesus' own death
through the gift of myrrh, but the deaths of his followers as well. These
paintings and sarcophaguses prove that the testator had been charitable
to a measurable extent and to a greater or lesser degree claim that the
testator will be found worthy of salvation through the agency of the child
who reaches out to accept the gold.[85] The grasping infant makes the gifts
acceptable to Jesus and his church.

   At a time when Jesus' passion was still far from codified in Christian
funeral art, this hope or expectation of salvation largely explains the magi's
popularity.[86] By showing their charity to God, the testators might win his
grace; by showing it to humans, they moved viewers to pray for their salvation. Some sarchophaguses (fig. 3) actually show the deceased in their
togas as part of the magi's train, at times armed with their own gifts, "as

3. *Adoration of the Magi*

if they too want to approach [the child] to adore him," in Wilpert's words.[87] What they want is salvation. They hope to obtain it by imitating the magi, as preachers like Ambrose and Augustine told them to do.[88]

Driving home this message of "I give so that you give" (*do ut des*), as do such representations, we see that the epiphany of the testator is also in play in these many adorations, the veil over his portrait at times being drawn back just as any god's.[89] In such *imaginae clipeatae*, witnesses saw the testators themselves apotheosized in the heavenly life their gifting had hopefully insured. The intention of a significant number of early Christians was to show that their gifts were like those of the magi. The young Jesus could have returned no greater gift to such magi than salvation.

These personal expectations of wealthy Christians, which we view in early Christian funereal art, were obviously never far from the political and social imagination. When we ask what the powerful faithful expected to find in the heaven they so earnestly sought, for example, we see in early Christian art heavenly banquets in which, though all were said to be equal, the existing hierarchical social order is flawlessly reproduced. The same is true of early scenes of the Second Coming, where the twenty-four crowned seniors of the Apocalypse, if not the magi themselves, head a tightly ordered heavenly society.[90] Bliss was obviously unimaginable apart from the forms of the existing political imagination, and whose but the ruler's imagination has ever counted for more? According to one story, Constantine (d. 337), the first Christian emperor, had miraculously ascended to heaven to lead the nonstop parade that was heaven.[91] Before he did, however, he provided proof (if any was needed) that we imagine heaven through the eyes of authorities like himself. Like the magi, this firstfruits among domestic rulers also saw a heavenly vision, and again like the magi, Constantine would be said to have fulfilled biblical prophecies.[92] The connections between these sky gazers deserve our attention.

In the few scenes of the magi viewing the star that may predate Constantine, the form of the magi's star is twofold. Far the most common is a six-pointed star; in rare cases one encounters the superimposed Greek

letters iota and chi (✳), the first letters in the Greek word for "Jesus"
and "Christ."[93] After 312, however, both the star and the (✳) encounter
competition from a superimposition of the letters chi and rho, the first
two Greek letters of the word "Christ" (☧). This celestial sign, or *chrismon*, evokes Constantine's stellar vision, called the *labarum*, which led
him to support the Christian God and the Christian church. The tale is
familiar. At the Milvian bridge, God caused a celestial symbol to appear
that, once reproduced on the soldiers' staffs, flags, and shields, made
them invincible. According to Eusebius, who says he had the story from
Constantine himself, the ruler first saw a stellar sign in daytime. It was a
cross aflame with the Greek words for "in this sign conquer" (Latin: *In
hoc signo vinces*). In a vision that night, Constantine saw the decisive labarum: within an *aurum coronarium*, or wreath filled with precious
stones, appeared the chi rho (☧), and beneath this were imaged Constantine and his sons.[94]

For hundreds of years, this sign of the cross, as well as the labarum,
were thought to bring victories to Christian armies. The call "In Hoc
Signo [vinces]," sometimes abbreviated to the initials IHS, would serve
a similar purpose for the crusading Latin armies. Yet that was not all.
Constantine's vision of a heavenly object, though it was not called a star
in the sources, reshaped what the magi saw, and this without any indication in the sources that Constantine followed their cult. Writing at the
turn of the fourth century, the poet Prudentius described the star of
Bethlehem as the "royal flag" of Jesus, mounted above his crib.[95] Here
the crusading mentality of centuries to come is prefigured.

This reimagining of the magian experience is apparent quite early in
art. We recall that in the catacomb of SS. Pietro and Marcellino, the
magi first glimpse the star not as a star, but as the superimposed first
letters of "Jesus" *and* "Christ" (✳). Though this sign is called "pre-Constantinian" by experts, it may also refer to the sign Constantine saw according to Lactantius's variant account of the vision.[96] There is a figure in
the catacomb of Ciriaca that points to the post-Constantinian monogram
(☧) as to the star.[97] Rossi, Wilpert, and De Waal identify the figure as one
of the magi by his clothing, but Kehrer thinks it is a prophet.[97] The difference is unimportant for our purposes. In Rossi's words, "Who does not
see a manifest allusion to the monogram of Christ which appeared to
Constantine in the sky, even if it is wrapped in the biblical veil of the magi
who point to the Star. . . . How can this not allude to that famous prod-
igy of Constantine, whence came the triumph of the church in the
Roman Empire?"[98]

Evidence from the sarcophaguses strengthens our reading of Constantinian magi stars in a convincing fashion. On one side of the tomb of
Flavio Giulio Catervio, the three Jewish boys mentioned above point

(with no biblical justification) to the chrismon (✳) surrounded by the *aurum coronarium*, or laurel wreath of victory. On the opposite side of the sarcophagus we see, above the magi, the variant sign ⸆, that is, the sign of the cross with the superimposed Greek letter rho.[99] This latter sign is not the Constantinian emblem, but in all these figures the magi point increasingly to Constantinian *letters* rather than to a star, a notion *not* encountered in any magi apocrypha. The magi are in a sense made to see the coming as much of Constantine as of Jesus.

The practice continues, becoming ever more politically charged. Thus the Constantinian chi rho proper appears on the 643 Ravennese sarcophagus of Isaac VIII of Armenia, the second known tomb to devote one whole face to the representation of the magi.[100] This monogram does not replace the star, which stands behind and over the mother in its standard six-pointed form. Rather, the Constantinian monogram appears on top of Jesus' nimbus, in the first magus's line of sight to the star. In short, the magi see the star through Constantine's own celestial vision.[101]

The appearance in this context of the Constantinian monogram, made up of the first two letters of "Christ," over the figure of Jesus might seem to do no more than identify the child as savior. Yet a closer examination of some contemporary written evidence shows that more was involved. Not long after Constantine's death, the Syrian scholar Ephraim (d. 373) asserted that the magi were princes who had actually seen an angel in the star, one presumably shaped like a human.[102] Probably not much later, followers of Ephraim, in the so-called Book of Seth, determined that the star as seen by the magi, who were in this later source said to be a secret society come from "the beginning of the orient, near the ocean," was "almost in the form of a little child, *with a picture of the cross above him*."[103] Certainly converting the star to a human figure helped explain how the magi had known its meaning from the outset. And the combination is close to what is shown on our Ravennese sarcophagus. I suspect that the story that the star of Bethlehem had a human form comes from the Constantinian vision, in which the emperor saw himself and his sons beneath the labarum.

Either in human form or in the form of letters, the star of Bethlehem, and therefore the magi themselves, have been made to forecast Constantine. Less directly, they also forecast the victory of Christendom, for the Constantinian monogram they at times saw is a discretely military emblem (it won battles) and so refers indirectly to the words in Constantine's vision: "In Hoc Signo Vinces." On some monuments, these words are written out alongside the monogram.[104] When we then recall that all the representations we have studied come from the burial tombs of individual Christians, we see that these testators were attaching themselves to the vision of the heavens held by the first Christian ruler, and they were rereading deeper history through the letters of Constantine's labarum.

In sum, as little as we can make out about the society of living offerants around these dead men's graves, and as little as the magi in art themselves change in these centuries, the social-organizational vocabulary of the magi was constantly being enriched. Beginning as outside legitimators of an upstart sect, the magi, imagined as the potentates of the Other or as his legates, now were made to journey after the imperial star of Constantine and thus to have foreseen the victory of the Christian church and the day when the powers of this world would come to do homage to the Roman pontiff. This statement about power did, of course, have a lasting pious expression as well. The association of Constantine at prayer and the magi in adoration would remain an irresistible theme in medieval art.[105]

Less than a century after Constantine, in 417, the ecclesiastical writer Orosius took the association of the imperial and Christic epiphanies one step further. Orosius assigned cosmic significance to the fact that Octavian had staged a triple triumph for himself in Rome on one 6 January, "or on Epiphany," he wrote, "when we . . . observe the Apparition or Manifestation of the [fulfillment] of the Lord's Promise."[106] This monarchical triumph of Augustus had brought with it the closing of the gate of Janus and the proclamation of the Roman peace, Orosius noted. Among other premonitions, that event had also been preceded by Octavian's celestial vision of a halo around the sun.[107] Again, this association of the Roman triumph with Jesus' triumph in the adoration of the kings would become a commonplace association in medieval and Renaissance literature and art.[108]

The imperial future of this universal church to which the monarchs of the world would one day journey is heralded in a Roman monument that arose in just these years in the wake of the Vandal sack of the city in 410: the church of Santa Maria Maggiore, certainly the major pictorial assertion to date of the authority of the Church of Rome. The huge triumphal arch that separates its nave from the choir and apse, with the name of its commissioner, Pope Sixtus III (d. 440), at its summit, commands our particular attention because of the manifold presence of the magi. Santa Maria Maggiore is one of the few papal monuments in which the magi are made to contribute to papal glory. In Phrygian dress and looking the part of emissaries, they are shown standing erect before Herod. In another scene, again erect, they offer their gifts to the enthroned Jesus, who is surrounded by the Christian angels of victory.[109] To the offerants who in this and later centuries processed under the triumphal arch to bring their gifts to the altar, the message is scarcely muted. The magi bring their gifts to the child and his vicar, whose name crowns the great arch.

4. *Adoration of the Magi*

Noting the derivation of this church arch from the Roman imperial arch, André Grabar has demonstrated that the mosaic program, rather than representing a narrative order, shows the recognition of Jesus as "emperor" on the top register, the submission of kings on the second level, where an imperial Jesus sits on a throne—apart from Mary—surrounded by the magi, then the offerings of the barbarians on the third, where the magi appear before Herod, and finally, the requisite Roman "trophies" on the lowest level, here manifested by the Christian faithful shown as sheep.[110] Grabar notes as well that in this triumphal scene, neither the adoration of the shepherds nor the birth of Jesus finds a place.[111]

The triumphal meaning of the magi's dual presence in this work is given a special edge by another triumphal representation associated with them. Opposite the magi's adoration of the triumphant child on the second level is an apocryphal story concerning the flight of Jesus' family into Egypt. As told in the Pseudo-Matthew, the Roman governor of Egyptian Hermopolis heard that the 365 gods in its temple fell to the ground when the family arrived to lodge in the town of Sotinen. He then arrived with a large military contingent to fall down and worship the infant. Affrodosius was convinced that Jesus was "the god of our gods," who had to be worshiped to avert destruction. "Then all the people of the city believed in the lord through Jesus Christ," the narrative concludes.[112] In our mo-

saic, we see Jesus on the move with Joseph and Mary not sitting in immobile majesty as in the opposite mosaic. He comes to the Egyptians at
Sotinen, rather than others coming to him in Bethlehem.[113]

Viewed from either side of the arch, the stories' meanings were not
difficult to comprehend. First, the young Jesus had been worshiped not
once but twice, by non-Christian legitimating forces: by outside magi as
he sat immobile and by an inside Roman imperial representative (one
who far predated Constantine) on his entrance into Egypt. Had not Orosius written that Octavian himself had seen a vision of Jesus' ultimate conquest? As shown by this *adventus* of Jesus in Egypt, the child legitimized
the local Roman social order as much as vice versa, for that order would
not continue to exist, the story has Affrodosius recognize, without being
reconstructed around the altar of the child. It is as though the designer of
the program wanted to show Jesus, and in his person the apostles and the
Roman church, legitimizing political and social orders at the earliest
point possible in its life. Here an apocryphal nobody like Affrodosius was
made to serve that purpose, long before the very real Constantine, master
of the world and maker of the universal church, came on the scene.

This complementary triumph/advent of Jesus on different sides of the
arch of Santa Maria Maggiore provides our first visual evidence of two
different models of the evangelization of the world. In the one, the powers of this world are in charge, people like the magi or their lord, or like
Constantine. In the other, as at Sotinen, the infant Jesus himself, and by
extension his apostles and church, is seen as the decisive force.

The use of this weak apocryphal tale to assert church power over state
power shows fairly early in the history of Christianity how problematic
the story of the magi was for any pope, who, like the infant Jesus, de facto
depended on outside approbation. Down through history, the see of
Rome would not develop the cult of the magi to the extent that many
secular kingdoms and republics did. With good reason! These rulers
would at times use the cult of their magian "brother kings" to assert their
control both over Rome and over their local churches.

So it is not surprising to find early churchmen attempting to weaken
the magi's role as secular legitimizers of the Christian God and church. In
the *opus imperfectum* of the fifth or sixth century, the magi are said to
have evangelized and imposed Christianity only *after* they had been baptized by the "apostle" Thomas, that is, by proper church authority.[114] In
the seventh century Jacob of Edessa defended the dominant Eastern story
that "[the magi] are not three, as the artists depict them, but twelve
princes."[115] Having the magi prefigure the twelve apostles, was another
attempt to subordinate them to the apostolic succession, or clergy, "as
if," Abelard would brilliantly state, "already in these first fruits of the gentiles were presignified the first apostles of the disciples of Christ."[116]

In the papal basilica of Santa Maria Maggiore, which from an early time had a cult built around relics of Jesus' crib, triumph was therefore paid both to a child struggling for authority and to one who already claimed it.[117] Yet as Christians, even in their new Constantinian threads, never forgot, the triumph of those coming to an altar was (is!) a condition of the triumph of him who was at the altar. Magi had to triumph if their Lord was to do so. This tension between splendor sparkling on the move and splendor that to be eternal has to glow immobily would remain one of the classic social and cultural negations acting on the Eastern successors of the Roman empire in the West, which came to an end in 476.

Nowhere is this tension so clearly seen, nowhere in these early centuries may the magian behavior of the living be so tactilely sensed, as at Ravenna, on the east coast of the Italian peninsula. There in mid-sixth century, the Byzantine monarch Justinian (d. 565) commissioned the completion of one of the most telling of magian monuments, just before his defeat of the Goths and well in advance of the Lombard conquest of the area at the end of the century.

In the long nave of the church of Sant'Apollinare Nuovo, whose wall mosaics date to 561, the faithful move about within a heavenly space created by great mosaic processions on those same walls. On the right on entering, a long line of male martyrs sweeps us into their procession toward the altar. At its terminus on that wall, the awful adult Jesus sits enthroned to receive the processants; originally he bore a book with the inscription, "I am the light of the world."[118] To our left, a procession of female virgin martyrs also orients us, this time toward Mary with child at that procession's terminus. Like the adult Jesus opposite, this mother and child are surrounded by four victory angels; also like the God opposite, Mary and the infant receive the crowns, or *aurum coronarium*, offered by each martyr. But different from the male martyrs in this total representation of Jesus' second coming, the females are led by the three magi, who, as so often, rush to present their gifts to the infant (fig. 5).[119]

This is a heavenly procession, not an earthly one, a representation of Jesus' second coming, or epiphany, when all the world led by the church's martyrs would offer their crowns and their goods for the heavenly banquet. Yet there is also history all about, both ancient—in the martyrs' memories and in the Bethlehem scene with magi—and contemporary. At the rear of the procession on the inside entrance wall of the church once stood a representation of the patron Justinian and his Ravennese bishop, as at its head stood the magi.[120] Led by the first potentates to convert to the living God—the gift-bearing magi of Matthew who are here as elsewhere optimal for such eschatological representations—the procession concludes with its hero, the Roman emperor.

5. *Adoration of the Magi*

The devotees beneath are also enveloped in this eschatological magian space. A century before the dedication of Sant'Apollinare, a Ravennese bishop had called out to his flock:

> Since the time of Christ's birth has come . . . we all come to adore him. . . .
> We offer gifts, because an offering is always publicly made to a new-born
> king. . . . Here the magus proves it who, loaded down with gold . . . , bows
> before the crib of Christ.[121]

Through the work of Otto von Simson, we may well reimagine this sixth-century pageant. The women beneath the female martyrs, the men on the right side of the aisle beneath the male martyrs wend their way, or at least their offerings make their way, toward the altar of sacrifice, as do the martyrs. Simson's recreation of the feast of the epiphany is especially powerful.[122] On this day devotees heard the gospel of the magi and knelt so as to imitate their adoration. The offertory of the mass on this day was none other than Psalm 72, the tale of the kings of Tharsis and the isles, of the Arabians and Saba who offered gifts. To the sound of an offertory hymn, the faithful imitated the magi by giving or carrying their gifts along basilical floors referred to as "streets of gold,"[123] which in some other churches were covered with mosaics of harvests and banquets that encouraged the laity to give alms.[124] As they journeyed, the priest said, "Graciously regard, O Lord, we beseech thee, the gifts of thy Church, in

which are offered now no longer gold, frankincense and myrrh, but . . .
Jesus Christ thy Son our Lord. . . ."[125]

What the liturgy spells out on epiphany is no less evident during the
rest of the year. This ecclesiastical theatre, in Simson's words, directly as-
sociates the gifts of the faithful to those of the magi in a cosmic procession of earth and heaven. Leading their emperor from west door to eastern heaven, the faithful, through his and their offerings, will anticipate,
perhaps stimulate, the resurrection of the dead at the Second Coming or
Epiphany.[126] By prefiguring this celestial activity through their giving and
by prefiguring heaven's sexually distinct divisions through their social organization in church, these Christian laity may protect their city from the
invaders.

Few will dispute Simson's conviction that these mosaics pictorially represent certain theological ideas or that they embody liturgical canons of
the time, all of which he carefully lays out. But certainly Sant'Apollinare
Nuovo was more than a theatre or stage for arcane discourses. We need
to receive from these pictures what normal contemporary viewers may
have seen or heard from their preachers. As the magi in sarcophaguses of
the age drew attention to the past charity of individual testators, so this
program in Ravenna elicited material contributions from the living.
Among other things, Sant'Apollinare was a theatre, a powerful spatial and
narrative inducement, to surrender and redistribute property. First the
Ravennese gave to the church for God; in the future they would receive
God's gifts, or *congiaria*. Ambassadors from earth, the magi introduce us
to the imagined organization or sociology of heaven. The mosaics of
Sant'Apollinare show a heavenly hierarchy that the social order of the
devotees must mirror.[127]

How seemingly diverse and yet how fundamentally similar is the appearance of the magi in that other mind- and eye-entrancing Ravennese
monument, the Byzantine imperial chapel of San Vitale. All appears at
rest in its choir mosaics, done between 546 and 548.[128] From the oval
apse at the eastern terminus of the choir, the resurrected young Jesus
looks down and to his right to hand over the imperial laurel to Justinian,
that is, to crown him. The emperor Justinian is thus to our left, accompanied among others by a warrior whose shield bears Constantine's labarum
(☧). Then to the apsidial Jesus' left is the equally famous figure of the
empress Theodora (d. 547) opposite her triumphant husband. Seven
women stand to her left and rear, two male clergymen on her honorable
right. She bears a gift. These clergy do not receive her gift, which passes
directly to Jesus, just as Justinian on his side reaches a gift directly to
his apsidial lord, past his archbishop. Byzantine historians have recognized in this act the ceremonial occasions in Byzantium when these rulers
did precisely offer such gifts in public.[129] In the absence of any procession

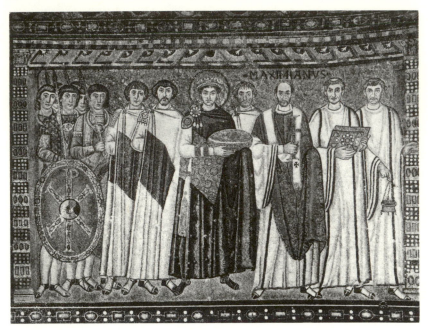

6. *Justinian and Courtiers*

of saints of the type found at Sant'Apollinare Nuovo, here Justinian and
Theodora, the living power, seem to proclaim that the mere dignity of
the imperial offerants by itself insures the legitimacy of that lord and his
saints.

Patronized by Justinian, these choir mosaics are the oldest representations showing the Byzantine emperors, indeed perhaps any identifiable
Christian lord, offering gifts to the Christian divinity.[130] In bypassing the
clergy while presenting their gifts, they are certainly representative of
Byzantine notions of so-called caesaro-papism. Almost a priest himself,
the emperor held his power directly from God and had the responsibility
to supervise the church. In the Western church, to the contrary, the
notion had already been enunciated that God had given humanity two
separate swords, one to the pope as spiritual lord and the other to the
emperor as temporal lord. Small wonder, that in Byzantine ceremonies
these emperors emerged, as we shall see, as incarnations of the divine
power almost on a par with Jesus.

Yet let us not imagine that here or elsewhere works of art merely state
a particular theory of authority.[131] We see that these mosaics make a
forceful political statement: Justinian and Theodora built the church by
their offerings. They sound a thunderous moral injunction: As the rulers
offer for you, so should you offer in church for their memories. They

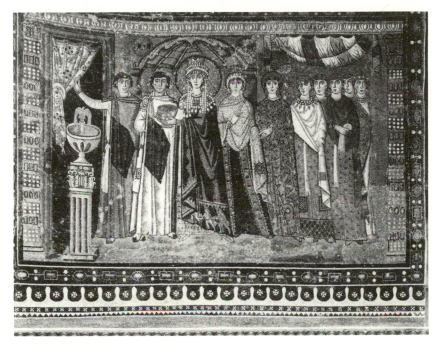

7. *Theodora and Courtiers*

announce an unmistakable understanding of exchange: The greater those who give gifts are made to appear, the greater becomes he or she who receives them, and consequently the greater these imperial offerants become, *in saecula saeculorum.*

These statements can be read from the mosaics without attention to detail. The necessary divine legitimation that these two rulers, husband and wife, claimed in making such gifts is also readily visible. As we have noted, the guard to Justinian's right bears a shield with the Constantinian monogram, recalling for us the "fact" that not only the founding Christian emperor, but the magi themselves, had seen that sign in the sky. With that in mind, it was easy enough to look to one's right and discover that on the hem of Theodora's opulent gown were stitched the three magi, also bearing their gifts to Jesus. Thus two living monarchs, husband and wife, play the role of the three magi.

In the years just before the erection of San Vitale, Abbot Caesarius of Arles (d. 542), for the first time in the West, noted that contemporaries called the magi "the three kings."[132] The same notion of princely magi appeared in the East around this time, although, as we shall see, the Byzantine state in its domain would suppress any idea that the magi had been royals. Still, the mosaics of San Vitale warn us not to overemphasize the question of the magi's royal or nonroyal status. We have insisted that the magi were commonly viewed as ambassadors of a monarch even if they were not said to be kings themselves and that quasi-royal status of the herald or ambassador is obviously present in the magi at San Vitale, where, for the first time, particular rulers are represented as "imitating the magi." The magi on Theodora's gown are clearly not royals, but because Justinian and Theodora are, the latter stand there like the magi who offered to Jesus. As inserted into mosaics that are a discourse about power, Matthew's San Vitale magi are for the first time shown speaking for specific secular rulers who make their own solemn, all but motionless pilgrimage to the youthful divine Lord. The historic mission of the magi was to speak of power, whether they were royals or not. How they did that is what needs emphasizing.

It would not be that long before Western as well as Byzantine monarchs would also play the magi. In the visual sphere, however, Justinian and Theodora doubtless take pride of place. They were indeed the first "magi" seen wearing imperial or monarchical clothes. This was not done without revealing a fundamental problem about monarchical magian representations, to be sure. While the magi are three, these royal magi are two, husband and wife. Yet neither this pictoral problem of sovereign dualism nor that of placing the Godhead centrally between odd-numbered magi would inhibit either the Byzantines or the great abbots, popes, and monarchs of the West. Think about it. In the *adventus* of San Vitale, the magi, though they had come from outside, now serve to shape our image of inside power. The magi are both the Other and a presence constituting the legitimate Inside.

The two centuries that followed the construction of San Vitale and Sant'Apollinare witnessed the end of the ancient world and the first tortuous steps toward the medieval civilization that was to succeed antiquity. Various invaders swept over Ravenna, as over the rest of Europe. Greco-Roman culture withdrew to the East, while the Mediterranean Sea became an unreliable means of travel for the old centers of the Roman empire. Marauders at times bivouacked in the Ravennese churches as they did at times in those of Rome, perhaps even emptying out the magian sarcophaguses to bury their own dead, as happened elsewhere in Europe.[133] No more than the modern tourist, who von Simson thought gazes uncomprehendingly at the decorations of these empty stages at Ravenna, could they have fully understood the monuments that we have described.[134] Who would have guessed in those dark days that these fragile images of the magi would survive and that their progeny would become the prime social-organizational icon of Christianity during the European Middle Ages? Yet survive and flourish they did because the story speaks to any society's fundamental task of creating and maintaining legitimacy by exchanging values both within and without its borders.

Probably all societies and polities have similar narratives, for the outside must always legitimate the inside. Perhaps as early as the third century, a Chinese story told of the emperor Ming's (A.D. 58–76) dream of a "golden man."[135] As interpreted by an imperial courtier, Ming's dream meant that a deity named Buddha dwelt in the "western regions" and that an embassy should be sent to bring the man and his doctrine to China. Ming sent the ambassadors, who returned from their journey to the west with Buddhist scriptures and missionaries. Certainly the Chinese fabricated this story to make the emperor responsible for the coming of Buddhism, which in fact had already entered China without his intervention. As the story of the journeying magi legitimated Christianity, so Buddhism in China was legitimated by the story of the embassy of the emperor Ming.[136]

Thus gates and borders have to be crossed or breached to bring the truth and manifest or legitimate it at home. In the Middle East, we find the magi story itself used to demonstrate this same truth to those outside Europe, including non-Christians. We recall the story that the magi had actually been sent west as envoys by the Persian or Parthian "king of kings." This already implied that in a type of return triumph, the magi did in fact come home with the good news of the birth of the infant, a story soon elaborated in various apocrypha.[137] Such Eastern stories, which showed that the truth from Bethlehem had passed deep into the ecumene, of course helped legitimate the many Nestorian Christian communities across this vast space, some of which survived until the European conquests of these parts many centuries later. But just as fascinating is the evidence that non-Christian groups maintained magian memories to their own legitimating ends. The story went that Mary had given Jesus' swaddling clothes to the magi as recompense for their gifts. Once they proved fireproof, the Christic rags are said to have become a Zoroastrian relic and to have served to legitimate that religion against outside attack, including attack by Islam. Nor is that the end of it. In the twentieth century, the American geographer Jackson found the inhabitants of Persian Urmiyah, said to be the birthplace of Zoroaster, proudly showing off the alleged tombs of two of the magi in the town's Nestorian church![138] One religion can easily charge itself with the memory of another, thus building a type of institutionalized border crossing into their relations.

One final story demonstrates the border crossing legitimation that is at the root of the magi story. A marvelous Greek letter of 836 tells us that when the Persians under Chosroes invaded Palestine and took Bethlehem in 614, they found the magi among the mosaics on the outside facade of what they said was Constantine's Church of the Nativity, on the spot, that is, where Jesus was said to have been born.[139] The same scene also greeted Western pilgrims, and they had returned home with ampoules of sacred oil as mementos of their "holy land trip," which often featured representations of the magi, perhaps the same as were on this facade or in the apse.[140] To their surprise, the Persian invaders found these magi's dress identical to their own, so they spared the whole basilica. We may doubt the story but not its foundation, which is that the magi, like Ming's ambassadors, regularly mediated relations between as well as within cultures. The Western pilgrims came to the crib and took back the magi, who had come on their own; the Persians found their own and thus spared the foreign temple. They were both validated by what they saw at this church.

In these same centuries, so often dark and obscure in the West, savants across the ecumene, but perhaps especially in the East, were elaborating the simple tale of the magi into a richly textured myth that will be the subject of the concluding pages of this chapter. According to this myth, much that was of note at the moment of the adoration was said to have existed since the time of Adam and Eve, and all such significant materials would live on until the end of time. In the process of mythification, these enriched wise men from the East came to harbor within themselves several characteristics of the classic medieval magi in the West, and these identifying marks obviously need to be mentioned. Alongside such individual narrative creations, the new unified theory of the magi is quite as fascinating because it assigns to the magi a significance that is human, not merely Christian, in its import. This universal import keeps whole cultures looking for the star.

The groundwork for an ecumenical vision of the magi was laid by Augustine of Hippo (d. 430) who intimated that the three magi represented the whole gentile world. The classical names attributed to these men—Balthazar, Caspar, and Melchior—appeared in the same fifth century, but they did not come into common usage for another half a millenium; the truth was that none of the three had any individual identity.[141] In England the Venerable Bede (d. 735) sharpened Augustine's generalization, stating that "mystically, the three magi signify the three parts of the world, Asia, Africa, Europe."[142]

This same Bede also, however, introduced into the West a powerful historical idea that already had roots in the East. He stated that the magi could also signify the three sons of Noah, who were the fathers of these continents' races (*humanum genus*).[143] What the theologian Bede took for signification could in other hands easily be historicization. Not only might the magi be the descendants of these sons of Noah, they might also be of different ages from each other. This notion was soon seized on by one of the first writers to actually describe the three men, the so-called Pseudo-Bede. In this influential but never canonical reading, Melchior was old and bearded, Caspar was a beardless youth, and Balthazar was fully bearded, either he or his beard being "fuscus," or dark.[144]

However, it was probably in the East and not the West that the magi were first shown in art as an elder, a man of middle age, and as a beardless youth.[145] Such representations in turn stand in close relation to a marvelous written tradition that we have already introduced in the person of the eastern writer Ephraim, who states that the magi saw a human image in the star.[146] A comparable story in the so-called eastern Chronicle of Zuqnin, which was terminated in the eighth century, shows *twelve* magi seeing distinct things as they gazed at the one star. Between them they saw what we call the ages of man: one saw a child, another a youth, the third a "humble and ugly and afflicted man," a fourth the crucified Jesus, etc.[147] Obviously, each magus had seen his own age in the star.[148]

In subsequent centuries, western as well as eastern artists would take to representing the magi as Everyman, that is, as all three male generations. In the next chapter I will show that in doing so, they made the magi into emblems not only of the cooperation but also of the competition that ever unites and divides male generations among themselves. The magi were not simply an event, they were rather a deep historical image showing that force of eternal generational cooperation and competition at work.

Alongside such cosmic generations, mostly eastern writers developed a still more powerful myth in the tale that the magi had brought to Bethlehem samples of all the wealth of nature, wealth that had always existed and could ever reappear in future times. Different from the animal riches that Noah gathered into the ark, the objects that the purveyors of the present myth were most interested in were mineral in nature, gold first and foremost. The theme was originally found in the so-called Book of Seth, son of Adam. Already referred to in the fifth- or sixth-century *Opus Imperfectum*, this lost book of the East says that the three gifts of the magi came from a treasure cavern that had been filled by Adam himself from the wealth of paradise.[149] The magi's gold especially was thus prelapsarian in origin and had to be understood within a cosmic historical context. Coming from paradise, over the centuries it too was made to reappear at many world-historical moments. Abraham had had it. Alexander the Great had possessed the gold before the magi gave it to the infant; already in this age the story spread that the gold given the latter then reappeared in the thirty pieces of silver Judas got for betraying his Lord.[150] And so on. As we shall see in the next chapter, some medieval and modern churches claimed that their chalices were made from the same gold. Thus Jesus was only one recipient among many world-historical persons both older and younger than he who endlessly recirculated these predominantly mineral riches of the earth. Perhaps it is not so surprising that one of the apocryphal eastern stories which regularly found its way into western art would be that the magi found Mary and the infant not in a house or stable, but in a cave or grotto where such minerals existed.[151]

The reverse of this bestowal of eternal gifts on the infant was the notion that in exchange, Mary and the infant had reciprocated by gifting the magi. One such gift was Jesus' aforementioned fireproof swaddling clothes. Another important gift that the magi received was a marvelous stone that could cause fire and blinding light, as well as control nature and polities. For hundreds of years to come, the magi would be thought by some to have thrown this stone into a well after consulting it.[152] In still another tradition the gift was a type of bread, perhaps meant to be associated with the Last Supper or the Real Presence, or the future multiplication of the loaves and fishes.[153] A final story has a comparable import. In this one, the magi took a painter along with them to Bethlehem. We are told that the picture that he painted of the virgin and child later became the centerpiece of an Iranian temple.[154]

Some of these narrative developments traceable to the fifth to tenth centuries made their way into the broader apocryphal tradition and into art, but many others remained within distinctly localized traditions that have only been identified by modern scholars like Monneret de Villard and Leo Olschki. Their significance here is less their details than their thrust, which is to show that the story of the magi was assuming a position as a mythic narrative about fundamental realities: the shape of the cosmos, the classification of its peoples, the generational characteristics of humanity, the sources of wealth in that universe, natural treasure as the stuff of history, and the concept of history as a constant recirculation of significant objects. The one major omission from this list, it would appear, is any commentary on the division of the sexes. The story, indeed the cosmos, appears as a male thing.

The reverse of this characteristic of universality is, of course, narrative specificity, and it is not altogether absent in the East. Thus in the very earliest of that area's sources, we find evidence that the magi were kings, indeed rulers of listed realms.[155] Yet in a slightly later tradition, they are not kings but wise men, and the official Byzantine tradition would have little room for magi royals, as we shall see. I will argue that, contrary to the East, where the myth I have described mitigated against a notion of individuality, the West will seek its own way, developing visions of cooperation and tension among the magi themselves.

This rich narrative tradition, mainly from the East, exploits nothing more than the potential of the Matthew story itself. In one last tale from this region, the wise men are said to have offered gold, frankincense, and myrrh so as to determine just what the child's status was. They meant to test the infant. He would take the gold if he was a king, the incense if a priest, the myrrh if a doctor. Thus as humans are wont to do, the magi meant to classify the child. Confounding them, Jesus took all three.[156] He, along with the magi who exchanged with him, were to be cosmic centers.

Little by little, elements of this cosmology evolving around the magi spread across Western Europe, most obviously in the ruminations of the Venerable Bede and those influenced by him. At the same time, bits and pieces of what was to become the classical magi tale and image in the medieval West also made their way across the Mediterranean. It would be surprising, for instance, if Caesarius of Arles, a city with a colony of Syrians, had been unaware of the Eastern stories of the magi's royalty. Certainly, the Spaniards who in time retold the tale of the just-mentioned test the magi gave Jesus obtained it from no other source than the East.[157] Just as surely, western pilgrims also returned from the East with that region's tales of the evangelical magi.

The literary tradition survived, and even in the artistic realm, these centuries had not been a complete wash. A seventh-century fibula representation of the magi found in a grave near Minden in Germany suggests a continuing association of the magi with individual mortuary practices.[158] Then in the famous altar of duke, later king Ratchis of the Lombards (in Cividale, ca. 737) the angel, still evoking the Victory of antiquity as do the palms on the adoration panel, leads the three magi to Mary and Jesus who, seated on an arched throne, seem to recommend the first magus to the viewer.[159]

Even the behavioral tradition survived, the rulers of Europe not having forgotten that the magi were, after all, the first "Christian" diplomats. Indeed by this point in time, 5 and 6 January, the feast of the magi, had begun to serve as the optimal date for diplomatic ceremonies involving princes. I refer to the events surrounding the donation of Pipin and the coronation of Charlemagne.

In 753 Pope Stephen II had fled Italy for France, hoping to win the backing of Pipin, whom Stephen's predecessor had recognized as the first Carolingian king of the Franks, against Aistulf, king of the Lombards and successor of Ratchis. As the pope approached the royal pfalz at Ponthion (Chalon-sur-Marne), Pipin first sent his son, the future Charlemagne, out some distance to meet the pontiff. Three miles from Ponthion, Pipin, his queen, and a host of other Frankish dignitaries themselves greeted the papal *adventus*. According to the papal source, the king descended from his horse and threw himself prostrate on the ground. Raised up, he then led the pope's horse back in procession to the pfalz oratory as he sang the praise of God.[160] One sat down alongside the other. Then the pope, covered in ashes and wearing a hair shirt, "having given many gifts to the king and the optimates" according to the Frankish source, tearfully asked Pipin to help the See of Peter by taking the Exarchate of Ravenna from the Lombards and rendering it to the pope. Pipin agreed.[161] This was the promise that came to be called the Donation of Pipin, which formed one basis of the temporal authority of the papacy.

But when did this momentous meeting take place? According to the papal life of Stephen II, the date of the meeting between the two powers, of the ensuing procession, and of Pipin's promise in church was "the sixth day of the month of January, on the most holy solemnity of the Apparition of the lord god and our savior Jesus Christ."[162] Is it significant that this particular feast was chosen for the meeting? Is it merely fortuitous that the Frankish account of the meeting gives no date when it pictures Stephen being received (*susceptus*) by Pipin in the pfalz and says nothing about Pipin coming out to meet the pope, whereas the papal source, which emphasizes the feast of the epiphany and its solemnity, shows Pipin receiving the arriving pontiff (*adventus*) by moving toward him on foot? In the former account it is the pope who gives the gifts, and in both accounts it is Pipin who makes the promises whose issue is the gift, or Donation of Pipin.

By the conclusion of this work, the reader will have no doubt that the feast of the epiphany often served as the occasion for many diplomatic receptions, and thus one that was commonly used for international gifting. In some cases we shall review, it will be clear that the magi were the conscious image within which such diplomatic activity was organized. The princes of this world emulated their magian ancestors. That having been said, however, it is impossible to state definitely that this was consciously so on the feast of the epiphany, 754. It is but the first of many such diplomatic events I have encountered that were celebrated on the epiphany. We pass now to another such event, the coronation of Charlemagne in A.D. 800.

The event was simple enough. With his own hands, Pope Leo III crowned Charlemagne with a precious crown.[163] Then he was thrice hailed by those present in St. Peter's with the words, "Life and victory to Charles, crowned by God [as] the most pious Augustus, great and pacific emperor." Finally, the pope anointed the son of Charlemagne. The historical significance of this event needs no emphasis. With this act, the Roman Empire was recreated in the West, and it is from the imperial title of Charlemagne that the designation of medieval Germany as the Holy Roman Empire ultimately descends.

Perhaps the one aspect of this event that has not received due attention is the fact that it took place on Christmas Day. Yet we shall find it difficult to ignore that date once in the next chapter we examine the Byzantine rites on December 25, rites which, as Charlemagne and the pope well knew, celebrated the nativity *and* the magi. Did Charlemagne emulate a magus during this festivity? Some scholars believe, for instance, that the crown Leo put on Charlemagne's head was the very one Charlemagne had just removed as a sign of humility.[164] In one eastern tradition of the time, the magi indeed "took [their] crowns and put them under [Mary and Jesus'] feet, because he would reign eternally."[165]

A further thin link to the magi deals with Charlemagne's gifting. The official life of Leo III follows up the description of the coronation by enumerating a large number of precious gifts that the new emperor bestowed on altars like "the basilica of the holy mother of God *ad praesepe*" ("at the crib"), that is, Santa Maria Maggiore.[166]

We dare not, need not, press the matter further. After all, Charlemagne's court intellectual Alcuin himself had compared the angels' announcement of Jesus' birth to their presence at the election or coronation of this same pope.[167] Imagine the new emperor entering Santa Maria Maggiore on Christmas Day, proceeding past the great triumphal arch of that church dominated by magian scenes and arriving before the very crib of Jesus, and *not* thinking himself a modern magus. In his person, the Roman triumph passed to the Middle Ages, and the main actors in these advents would soon become, and remain, the three kings.

Chapter 2

THE TRUE LIGHT SHINES
IN THE DARKNESS

THE YEARS from the coronation of Charlemagne in 800 until 1164, when bodies said to be those of the magi were solemnly installed in the archepiscopal city of Cologne, witnessed the slow emergence of Europe as a political and cultural entity. Charlemagne having established himself as a competitor of the eastern Roman emperor, his successors in the West emulated the marvelous Byzantine court rituals before that empire fell to westerners, if only briefly, in 1204. With the end of the Germanic migrations, the new Europe burst outward: in the Crusades against the Moorish civilization of Iberia, in violent attacks on Moslem Palestine attempting to regain the "Holy Land," and finally in no less frightful Crusades against Christian opponents like Byzantium but also against dissenting elements within the new national states themselves. The establishment of the exotic magi from the East in the western commercial emporium of Cologne became an important symbol of this warlike, expansive European society.

We shall see that no more than the Byzantine rulers, who had long used the magian story in their arsenal of legitimating images, did the Cologne prelate Rainold von Dassel know the names of the three magi whose bodies he so solemnly brought to this Rhenish crossroads city in 1164. Indeed, he gave as little indication that their royal status was particularly important. The truth is that at the end of this second chapter, the magi, whose names, royal status, and even personal appearances were only at this time becoming widely known, would still not have a cult. Indeed, no significant cult ever grew up around an individual magi, nor were they either popularly or officially canonized as a group. Few prayers are known to have been directed to them at this time, and only slowly did they assume the function of protecting travelers.

Our study of the function of the magi in ancient society and art has shown, however, that the absence of cult or even of individual personalities does not imply an absence of social significance. Even as faceless messengers, they were important to early Christian life and society. In the period we now examine, the same facts obtain. Nameless magi stand at the beginnings of European liturgical and popular drama during this period. Their gold will precede their bodies as a relic in Europe, just as their bodies preceded their names on the altars of Cologne. No less important, we shall see that as Europe organized itself for the first time, the iconography of the magi reflected and informed the expansionist, imperial crusading thrust of the age.

BYZANTINE MAGI

While Liutprand of Cremona was in Constantinople in the fall of 968 at the behest of the Holy Roman emperor, Otto I, he witnessed a procession featuring the emperor on his way from the royal palace to the church of Haghia Sophia. Along the way, choirs cried out to the ruler, "Look, there comes the morning star."[1] Liutprand was not impressed by their comparing the emperor to the planet Venus, or rather to Jesus as in the star of the magi, which was thought by some to have been Venus. He considered the emperor himself unworthy, and he was well aware that the Byzantine empire of his day was not that of Justinian and Theodora.

Long under attack by the Moslem "infidels," who would force its submission first to the Latins between 1204 and 1254 and then conclusively to the Turks after 1453, Byzantium the more stolidly preserved its fabled imperial rituals and thus its claims to the Roman inheritance and world dominion. Indeed during Liutprand's lifetime, the emperor Constantine Porphyrogenitus (905–959) brought together in his *On Ceremonies* descriptions of the rites of the imperial household, some of which are directly associated to the visit of the magi to Bethlehem.[2] In what follows, we shall see that Byzantine rulers followed Constantine, Justinian, and Theodora in using the nameless magi as part of a symbology of power, and that in turn, the Byzantine court seems to be the inspiration for several later western customs.

All the direct references to the magi in the *De Caerimoniis* occur in the chants of the feast of Christmas; we recall that it was then and not on 6 January, which continued to be reserved for the celebration of Jesus' baptism, that the magi were remembered in the Byzantine rite. The setting for these evocations was the procession of the emperor and his train to and from divine services in the church of Haghia Sophia, which was imagined by the neighborhood choirs that greeted them as the march of the star to the cave in Bethlehem. One choir bellowed as the imperial train approached, "The star moves toward and illuminates the cave, to show the magi where is the master of the sun!"[3] Thus the emperor was the star of Bethlehem, leading the magi, that is, leading his subjects.

Arriving at Haghia Sophia, the emperor removed his crown for the length of the ceremony, which included the emperor's bestowing of gifts of gold on the altar. After being re-crowned by the patriarch of Constantinople on leaving the church, the emperor encountered another group singing, "Heaven sends the star to direct the magi to the birth. The earth prepares the cave to receive the author of all things! But may [Jesus] himself, having taken our [earthly] flesh from the virgin, guard in the [royal] purple your royal power, crowned by God!"[4] We recall that on Christmas day in the year 800 the Romans cried out that Charlemagne had been "crowned by God" after Pope Leo had crowned him, as was the Byzantine emperor when re-crowned by the patriarch.

Clearly the Byzantine emperor was represented as the star, not as a magus. He leads the wise, rather than being led by them. A third and last magian chant of Christmastide that heralded the emperor's approach to his palace on his return from Haghia Sophia further establishes that this stellar emperor was conceived as a triumphant military figure, just as Constantine had been. Here the choir cries, "May the giver of life raise up your power in the whole universe, [O] sovereigns! May he force all nations to offer gifts to your royal power, as [he so forced] the magi!"[5] Thus perhaps for the first time, the magi were explicitly viewed in a context that was quasi-diplomatic as well as military.

This unbiblical concept of the magi as forcibly submitting to Jesus may, in turn, help explain why Byzantine art before the Latin conquest of 1204, so different from Western art, rarely shows the magi as kings, even though the notion of magian sovereigns itself came from Syria and even though Byzantine theologians argued that they were kings.[6] In the wake of this general absence of magi kings in Byzantine art, it is not surprising that in this same tradition, the magi are rarely if ever thought prefigured by Psalm 72 or Isaiah 60, with their references to eastern kings.

This obviously did not prevent an exquisitely political understanding of the magi motif. Some illuminated manuscripts from Mount Athos may not show the magi as princes, but they do tell an Eastern story, which is that the Persian emperor Cyrus the Great (fl. 546 B.C.!) sent his magi to gift Jesus[7]; needless to say, it was child's play for a Byzantine to imagine Persia submitting to a Byzantine emperor in a similar fashion. It again proves more important to see the magi's position within a political universe than to dwell on whether or not they were royal.

Although the Byzantine rite did not evoke the magi in the calendar of feasts after Christmas, that tradition did carry out ceremonies which, once transposed to the West, would be associated to the feast of the epiphany and thus to the magi. We learn from the *De Caerimoniis*, for instance, that on the calends of January in the years around 927–930, at least, the emperor diplomatically received three groups of foreign dignitaries or ambassadors and exchanged gold gifts with them.[8] The exchange of gifts on calends being a long established Roman domestic custom, here we find evidence of an exchange of gifts involving the diplomatic corps on the same day. In the West, the diplomatic reception of ambassadors on Epiphany would prove attractive to westerners in later centuries.

More directly relevant to our inquiry were the several activities on 6 January, the so-called Byzantine feast of lights, which, the experts assure us, did not commemorate the magi. It was customary on the eve of this feast for the emperor to promote someone to the high office of *magistros*. The candidate approached the emperor and prostrated himself at the imperial feet, to then be raised up to receive the tunic and belt of office, in exchange for which the new official again lowered himself, this time to kiss the imperial feet.[9] This ceremony is reminiscent both of coronation and of knighting in the West, rites that were often performed on Epiphany and commemorated, as we shall see, in a magian pictorial format.

The promotion having taken place, the emperor proceeded to Haghia Sophia on this eve of Epiphany with the same ceremonies—and thus presumably with the same magian acclamations—that were employed at Christmas. There he took part in the blessing of the water, the ecclesiastical highlight of the eastern feast of the epiphany. Then in the presence of other officials, the emperor and the patriarch thrice drank that blessed water around a sacred table.[10] Although the ceremonial acclamations apparently have not been preserved, they certainly included a toast like, "Long live the Emperor!" or "The emperor drinks!" exclaimed as the emperor drank the water. In contemporary toasts elsewhere in Europe we find the corollary, and in the future Epiphany cry, "Le roi boît!" we may find the evocation of such Byzantine toasts.[11]

On the morning of Epiphany proper, the emperor once more made his way to Haghia Sophia, again laying down his crown on entering the church, again being re-crowned by the patriarch before marching back to the palace to the acclamations of the crowds. The same military character pervaded these processions as was remarked on the feast of Christmas. Thus it was imagined that through Jesus' baptism in the Jordan on 6 January, God had broken the head of the dragons, so an epiphanic choir rang out in greeting, "May he crush the head of the barbarians at your [sovereign] feet." "May he exalt and augment the force of your power for the prosperity and glory of the Romans!"[12] The Byzantine emperor was then originally, and thereafter repeatedly, recrowned in a context that emphasized his triumph over the enemies of the state. In the West as well, coronation ceremonies would emphasize the military duties of the crown.

We have reviewed the imperial Christmas ceremonies in which the magi were evoked, and other court rituals on the feast of lights that in the West will take on a magian character when celebrated on that day—if they did not already have such a character in Constantinople. One other celebration in the Byzantine rite that directly involves the magi was occa-

sional rather than calendrical. This is a ceremony attending the arrival or
epiphany of an heir to the crown, that is, the birth of a future emperor.
Celebrations of this sort had been common from the beginning of the
Roman imperial line, and Byzantium was no different, except that it consciously integrated the Christian theme of the birth of that religion's firstborn king, just as early Christianity had been conscious of the Roman rite
when it shaped the celebration of king Jesus' epiphany.

Constantine Porphyrogenitus' *On Ceremonies* tells us that on the
eighth day after the birth of the firstborn male, the infant was solemnly
named in a ceremony in the vestibule of Haghia Sophia. After being carried back to the empress-mother at the palace, the child was dressed in
gold cloth and placed alongside his empress-mother, who wore similar
clothing.[13] At this point the provosts began the formal presentation of
different personages to the mother and child, beginning with a group of
magistrates. Having come out, the child for the first time met the imperial servants he would one day command.[14]

Following on the heels of these magistrates, the provosts presented to
the child two groups of women. First came the wives of high officials
and senators, and then the widows of men of that status. The text reads
at this point:

> All these [women] congratulated the empress on her happy parturition and
> blessed him. They rendered due reverence to the infant and [then] each
> bestowed upon him a small gift which testified to their benevolence toward
> the newly-arrived guest . . . whatever each had brought with her for his
> fascination and delight."[15]

After these women came the rest of the male magistrates. They
"blessed the empress with adoration, and gave congruous cult to the firstborn infant through pious promises and such good words as, we said
above, were customarily directed toward the emperor."[16]

Though the magi are not mentioned in the texts describing this rite,
and though the donors are women, scholars have long been confident
that this behavior was meant to mirror the magi presenting gifts to Mary
and the infant.[17] Their opinion has been strengthened by a document
only recently brought into relation with the image of the gift-giving
magi. A gold medal minted about 324 in Trier shows Constantine's nim-
bed empress Faustina seated on a throne with a child in her lap. On either
side, personifications of Felicity and Piety salute her, while at her feet an
angel brings her the *aurum coronarium*. Certainly Deckers is right that
the occasion for this medal was the birth of Constans to Faustina and
Constantine. Doubtless this author is also right to have juxtaposed this
medal to a representation of the magi before Virgin and Child found on

8. Left: *Empress Fausta between Felicitas and Pietas*. Right: *Adoration of the Magi and Shepherds*

a sixth-century oil ampoule. Surely Byzantine women, and perhaps court men as well, were imitating the magi in ceremonially gifting the imperial mother and child.

Thus the texts of Constantine Porphyrogenitus confirm in writing what the Ravennese mosaics show in images: the Byzantine rulers used the magi as a part of state representation, and they did so on certain dates and occasions. As important as the utilization of the magi story by royals will be to our story, however, their activities are but one aspect of our overview. Their trickle-down manipulations of biblical history only touch the surface of the use of the magi in Christian history. We saw early on that individual Christians no less than rulers associated themselves to the magi so as to win a place in heaven. Now at this juncture, a Byzantine source allows us to espy how the *dramatization* of the magi story will in the coming millenium permit the elaboration of deep problems of Christian self-definition.

It is quite probable that when the imperial cortege entered the church of Haghia Sophia on Christmas, its members witnessed a partial dramatization of the Bethlehem events they celebrated. This dramatization had roots in Byzantine culture that were quite apart from, and perhaps antecedent to, the imperial protocols. Syrian hymnody of the fourth and fifth centuries already contains dialogues introduced and mediated by a narrator. Then in the seventh century, the patriarch of Jerusalem Sophronius (634–638) supposedly authored an impressive group of twelve Nativity hymns dramatic enough to lead authorities to speak of a Byzantine "Nativity play." In them, actors playing Joseph and Mary, as well as a chorus representing "the people," discuss and resolve the puzzling phenomenon of a virgin birth.[18]

The cycle begins with the narrator appealing to Bethlehem to prepare the manger for God incarnate . . . much as the imperial choir demanded similar preparations when the emperor appeared in the street on Christmas.[19] By the third hymn, the core problem of the cycle surfaces: Joseph, astonished and disturbed, asks Mary to explain how it is that she has hidden herself in a cave and is hastily or unexpectedly giving birth. Clearly he thinks Mary had secretly conceived by someone else. He denounces her for bringing sorrow and shame upon him instead of the honor and joy due him as a spouse.[20] Not until the penultimate hymn will Mary satisfy Joseph that the boy has God as his father.

Thus the essence of this drama, perhaps performed before the emperor himself, was the husband's conviction that he had been cuckolded by his wife.[21] This is not the last time that Christian dramatists will struggle with the unnaturalness of Jesus' virgin birth, though such reflections present a stunning contrast to the pomp we encounter in the *De Caerimoniis*. For at least a millennium, the improbable character of the virgin birth, and the fool that story seemed to make of Joseph, would continue to fascinate the Christian mind.[22]

Thus another role that the magi will play in the unfolding Christian story of the infant birth begins to emerge: their glossing of the relation between masculinity and generation in light of Joseph's non-fatherhood. The magi are not dramatis personae in this Byzantine play, to be sure, as they will be in the *officia stellae* of the West, but they are mentioned three times by Joseph and the chorus in significant ways. The fourth hymn describes their being led to the cave to adore Jesus, who, the fifth hymn says as if describing the emperor himself, "holds in his hands the boundaries of the world."[23] In the sixth hymn, an ecstatic Joseph reveals the nativity mysteries, including the magi's adoration, and in the last hymn of the cycle their visit is listed among the wonders of Bethlehem. In this presentation I see emerging a dramatization of Joseph's perplexity: far from being ridiculed by other men for allowing his wife to bear someone else's child, Joseph witnesses eastern savants throwing themselves at the feet of the wondrous male child, like the most effeminate of dependents. Thus in these hymns the magi could bear witness that not just living men like Joseph could produce a male child, but that their gods or churches could do it as well.

Our conventional image of Byzantine court culture does not include scenes of clerics playing the parts of cuckolded males in the midst of divine services in church. It is much too serious for that. And thus our image of this world also has little room for the raucous behavior that was in fact part and parcel of Byzantine church life, as might be expected in a culture that so directly faced the sexual and gender imponderables of the Christian story. Stingy as it is, the Byzantine evidence hints at riotous celebrations in the churches and squares of Constantinople precisely in the season of the Twelve Nights, and precisely evoking the raucous Christmas behavior we shall later encounter in the Twelve Nights of the medieval West.

One of the first documents regarding the festive life of Byzantium is contained in a prohibition of the Council of Trullo or Constantinople dated 692 against dancing and transvestism during the calends of January. These practices are condemned as deriving from the pagan age. While clerks are especially sanctioned when practicing them and the synodal fathers say they want to banish them "from the city of the faithful," these acts are not explicitly said to have been performed in church.[24]

The same is true of the first detailed evidence of such holiday misbehavior, from the reign of the emperor Michael III (842–867).[25] This emperor organized a festive company, in which his captain of the guard played the "patriarch" while the remaining eleven companions played archbishops or "metropolitans," the emperor himself mimicking the archbishop of Cologne. All dressed in ecclesiastical robes. The troupe went through the streets to the tune of rough music behind their "patriarch" mounted on an ass—as had the apostles behind triumphant Jesus on Palm Sunday, and as, in the future, would the emperor himself playing Jesus on Palm Sunday.[26] Presumably in church, the company burlesqued the distribution of communion, using a chalice filled with mustard and vinegar instead of bread and wine. Outside, they mocked the real patriarch of Constantinople on encountering him in procession.

Perhaps the most interesting part of their mockery was the emperor's feigned consecration of each of the companions as prelates.[27] It is not clear if Michael's deposition of prelates upon the conclusion of the farce festivity, which is mentioned by other sources, was practiced on real prelates or only on the companions. But it is certain that the established clergy and its liturgy, especially the liturgy of coronation or consecration, were the objects of their scorn. As we shall see, mock coronations and consecrations became a standard feature of Epiphany in high medieval western Europe.

The behavior of this imperial troupe was condemned as an execrable excrescence by a church council following Michael's death, but it continued largely unabated. Trying to explain why the great churches of Byzantium themselves were the scenes of such irreverent festivities during their lifetimes, the Byzantine historian Scylitzes (fl. 1081) on the one hand, and the canon lawyer Balsamon (ca. 1140–1195) on the other, both blamed the clergy itself, especially Theophylact, the patriarch of Constantinople from 933 till 956. According to Scylitzes, this prelate, a mere sixteen years old on assuming office, had such a consuming passion for his stable of two thousand horses that he profaned the ceremonies of Holy Thursday with them. It was Theophylact, said Scylitzes, who was responsible for the enduring custom of dancing, laughing, yelling, and brothel songs that were still in his time part of the celebration of the "splendid and solemn festivities" that belonged by right to God.[28]

A century later Balsamon emphasized that these "excesses" were associated with festivities of the ecclesiastical calendar, especially the Twelve Nights. They were done, he specifies, "by clerks on the feast of the Birth of Christ and on the Feast of Lights" (Epiphany), "in the most holy, great church" of Haghia Sophia.[29] These activities included clerks playing women, dressing as soldiers, monks, or four-legged animals, all "in order to bring laughs to the spectators."[30] Balsamon added that until the patriarch Luke put a stop to it, such indecorous theatrical undertakings were also done "in sanctorum notariorum festo," "by the notaries, instructors of the adolescents."[31] It was wrong, Balsamon said, to defend such spectacles by saying that they were ancient Roman customs. Even though his remark merely repeated the sentiment of the already mentioned rubric of the Council in Trullo of 692, Balsamon insisted that these dubious rites had been initiated not in ancient Rome, but by the patriarch Theophylact.[32]

In all likelihood, the Twelve Days had been marked by spectacles annoying to the highest prelates from their inception in the fourth century, just as the Roman feast of the calends and the Egyptian feast of epiphany had been broad social celebrations before Christianity. Certainly such practices continued at the time of Balsamon. What is so noteworthy about the record we have described is how hermetically separate the different forms of behavior were kept in the sources. The clergy had its serious liturgy, which it described without reference to any of the clergy's popular liturgies, and the emperor Constantine Porphyrogenitus wrote a textbook on ceremonies that neglected to say anything about his predecessor's and contemporaries' festive mimicry.

Our best guess is that in reality, these different worlds merged with each other. This was not a world of festivity that pitted what some might call "popular culture" against "elite culture," but one where (indeed led by a stellar elite) a whole society confronted the unnatural mysteries that bound a clergy, in part by allowing festive groups to mock the solemn object of the feasts—virgin birth, resurrection, and the like. It is such a universe that we now attempt to view in the West, from a similar perspective. It insists on the social divisions at the base of festive presentations, and it rejects dividing society on psychological bases.

THE STAR IN THE TENTH-CENTURY WEST

Since the publication of James Frazer's *Golden Bough*, it has been traditional to view many European customs as rooted in agrarian life, even if these customs are almost always found originally in the records of towns and courts. Most scholars have therefore followed Frazer in viewing the election of a seasonal king, a very old pre-Christian habit indeed, as a fertility rite at home in the villages of an overwhelmingly rural Europe.[33] This is a matter of no little import for our work, for as we shall discover, the three kings or magi of the Bible became part of the festive life of Christian Europe—people began to play the magi—in some relation to the ancient practice of electing and crowning seasonal or festive kings, a practice which, as we have seen in Byzantium, easily operated separate from the story of the evangelical magi and from an agrarian economy.[34] After all, Jesus was, so to speak, elected king by the magi. Even today, electing a boss or leader for a particular job or feast is as much an urban as it is a village custom. These are social processes. Relating such processes to a story, like that of the magi, comes afterward.

We are emphasizing the story of the magi as it reflects social processes. Our task is to find out what festive or artistic representations of the magi describe and reflect, not to delve into the origins of the elections of real or play kings. In our examination of Byzantium, we found the emperor playing the star and, in the streets, either leading the magi or forcing them to their knees before him and Jesus. On the other hand, we found actors in church confronting the question of the virgin birth, which the magi, alone among lay biblical figures, could persuasively assert to have truly happened.

As we turn now to western Europe, we seize upon an image that, properly understood, will give us a clear picture of what it is we have to re-create. It is an intimidating frontal painting of the Christian Savior, which from the sixth century was carried about Rome on August 14, its feet washed by the clerks after having been kissed by the laity. From the twelfth century onward, copies of this original appeared across Lazio and received the same treatment, being dipped in the river at Sutri to wash this Savior's feet.[35] Thus in these obscure ages of limited political order in the West, the faithful preserved their center. It is the task of these pages to show how, over time, such citizens surrounded these Saviors with painted adorers, evidence of more stable frames of reverence. Painted adorers afforded nonstop prayer, something no living Christian could accomplish.

Bearing in mind the image of this kissable Savior, we shall examine the picture of the magi that men of power in western Europe developed in these centuries, even if we have to use sources like breviaries, which were limited in circulation, and were mainly meant to flatter powerful men. Only then shall we turn to the more overt picture of the magi that was emerging for all to see in the liturgical dramas of the central Middle Ages. The magi of the courts and the town churches were not terribly unlike, when their bodies were brought to Cologne in mid-twelfth century.

The first stage in the formation of a medieval imagery of triumph in western Europe is ascertainable in the art of Charlemagne and his successors. This new triumphalism does not employ the magi, who infiltrate that world of triumph only toward the end of the tenth century. Thus when Charlemagne had the church of San Vitale copied in Aachen he did not, as far as we know, adopt that chapel's magian theme. Instead, its cupola, as well as several other Carolingian monuments, were dominated by the Apocalyptic twenty-four elders laying their crowns before the Lamb of God, a motif that was closely associated to the magi in antiquity as a triumphant motif.[36] The famous arch of Einhard (biographer and confidant of Charlemagne), with the inscription "Ad tropaeum aeternae victoriae sustinendum," also bypassed the magi in favor of the twenty-four royal elders, in representing Louis the Pious, son of Charlemagne, as the triumphant new Constantine.[37]

Yet the essence of magian iconography—a representation of triumph in time related to eternal triumph—is as characteristic of Carolingian iconography as any magi representation. Thus in the Codex Aureus made for emperor Charles the Bald (d. 877) we see on the right of facing folios a representation of the elders around the Lamb of God and the star of Bethlehem, an image of celestial triumph that draws the attention of this emperor, who is seated in triumph in the left folio illumination (fig. 9). The latter's triumph is emphasized not only by the baldachin above and by the courtiers to either side of the ruler, but by two crowned women bearing horns of plenty to the emperor—common symbols of submission long since associated with the magi. This is clearly a variant on the theme of the *aurum coronarium*, the emperor gazing over to Jesus as upon another ruler, both being adored.

If we pursue this abstract Carolingian image of the nations or tribes submitting to the western emperors into the Ottonian art of the late tenth and early eleventh centuries, we soon discover linkage with the magian imagery of the high Middle Ages. In fact, the Ottonian rulers' favorite fashion for representing their military triumph, or even statist authority, was to picture the submission of the German provinces to them. Thus in a Bamberg manuscript, Otto II (d. 983), seated in majesty in the right folio, is approached on the left facing folio by four labeled imperial provinces, four crowned women bearing not only horns of plenty, but other objects also found in magi representations, including what seems like an offering of gold pieces.[38] In a Chantilly ruler picture of

9. *Charles the Bald in Majesty*

Otto II, this gift is given by the four women in the form of golden apples.[39] Several authors have pointed out that these representations of
nations submitting to an empire are closely related to Ottonian magi representations and were in some cases prepared by the same workshops. In
Deshman's words, an image of the magi like that in the Codex Egberti
(fig. 10) was a "deliberate parallel to the crowned personifications of
provinces."[40] The distinguishing mark of several of these magi representations of the late tenth century is that the magi, like the heads of the nations, are for the first time, and forever more, crowned. In art, the magi
are now the three kings.

In the West, this coronation of the magi had been a while coming.
Thus in the Stuttgart psalter's illumination of Psalm 72, done in the tenth

10. *Adoration of the Magi, Codex Egbertus*

century, the magi still wear their Phrygian bonnets to the Adoration.[41] It is true that the "kings of Tarshish and the Isles" are shown crowned already in the ninth-century Utrecht psalter, but they adore an adult, not infant, Jesus. Long the classic Old Testamental premonition of the magi, the figures of Psalm 72 seem to have first inspired images of the magi as kings.[42] Yet only in the later tenth century, that is, in the mid-Ottonian age, are they shown crowned in scenes of the adoration itself, some four centuries after Caesarius of Arles had first written that they were usually called kings. Our evidence for these early crowned kings at adorations takes us across the channel, to England.

From the beginning, we have emphasized that the question of the magi's royalty is less important than the fact that even as legates, they always spoke for power. This approach is particularly justified when we examine what is one of the earliest representations of crowned magi in an Adoration. In the benedictional commissioned between 971 and 984 by Aethelwold, bishop of Winchester and confidant of the Anglo-Saxon

King Edgar, the second and third crowned magi, still shown with the traditional Phrygian leggings, offer traditional bowls from customarily veiled hands. The gift of the lead magus, also crowned, is what is significant. According to Deshman, he presents to the child three overlapping diadems, symbols since antiquity of rule and triumph.[43] While neither such diadems nor crowns will become important figural gifts of the magi in the coming centuries, it is still important that the classical diadems are preserved in an early presentation of the three kings. The central theme of triumph, here emphasized by Mary and the child seated beneath a triumphal arch, has clearly survived Christian antiquity. So has the association of that triumph to the celebration that occurs on 5 and 6 January. In the Winchester benedictional, Jesus' magian epiphany stands to the left of the facing page's representation of the baptism of Jesus. In that baptism of Jesus, angels descend to invest Jesus with royal diadems and scepters, while a dove anoints him.[44] This is strikingly similar to the coronation imagery we encountered in Byzantium for the same, nonmagian, feast of the baptism.

Deshman notes further similarities between the Byzantines and these German and Anglo-Saxon artists and rulers. Especially interesting is that all these national rulers avoided being personally identified with the magi themselves: in both Ottonian and Anglo-Saxon royal art, Deshman shows, it is the ruler who is portrayed as the *imago Christi*, much as the ruler of Constantinople was compared to the star Jesus. The 973 coronation *ordo* of Edgar says that this king was anointed by Jesus himself, and it refers to the new king holding the "scepter of the Saxons, Mercians, and Northumbrians," while another contemporary document speaks of the fear in which Edgar was held by "the kings of many people."[45] Thus as of the year 1000, the magi, now increasingly crowned in the West, might be thought of as subsidiary royalty subordinate to the *basileus* or *augustus* of different realms. This was certainly in keeping with the old concept of the magi as legates. Still ahead lay the day when kings would willingly play the role of individual magi.

This introduction to the development of magian images in medieval Europe is, of course, an important aid in comprehending the political science of the age. The magi are now conceived as expressions of a total political order. Since they are also now commonly represented at different ages, they cannot be said to lack social significance either. However, almost all the images I have described thus far could have been seen by very few persons indeed. The works we have touched upon were generally the products of ecclesiastical sycophants seeking to please their royal patrons. Most of these manuscripts would have been considered hopelessly profaned if they had been seen, let alone touched, by the common people of the towns or villages of Europe.

Such elitism is not our concern, however. Our task is rather to describe deep political and social structures that help explain the popularity of the magi theme over the centuries. Given this goal, such monumental images of the magi as we have examined to date have little value unless their intellectual content can be shown to overlap with more widely visible images, such as those available in Byzantine processions, dramas, and games. Fortunately, these sources do exist, in the early history of European drama. By examining the texts of the so-called offices of the star or plays of the magi, which were witnessed by the general public in or just outside of churches, we may gain a good idea of how the magi entered into the social consciousness of Europe.

OFFICES OF THE STAR, GAMES OF THE MAGI

Before acting became a profession, plays were performed by local groups that came to the drama with a social cohesion and group identity already in place. Then as now, involvement in performances, as well as the narrative contents of the dramas themselves, might affect the social identity of the players. Indeed I will argue that the magi story had just that impact on the players, and from a relatively early point.

Early evidence of magi theatre may be found in a book illustration dated 814 (fig. 11) that shows an adoration, that is, the wise men bearing their gifts through a church nave to the virgin and child at the altar.[46] Such motions in temple spaces will become standard fare in medieval theatre. The setting is not surprising, and scores of later paintings will show the kings proceeding to the west façade (when not to the altar) of a church, where Mary, Joseph, and the child are figured. Indeed the earliest form of these plays is called "liturgical drama," meaning among other things that they were made for performance in church. We must, however, wait until the end of the tenth century to find fragments of written magi plays.[47] The texts of some nine *officia stellae*, or liturgical star plays, survive from the eleventh century and nine more before mid-twelfth century. In this same half-century a nonliturgical magi play in a living language (Castilian) was written. All this before the magi came to Cologne in 1164.[48] At this date, with many texts extant of this most popular of Christmas stories—usually comprising the story of the magi and of Herod, and often the story of the slaughter of the innocents as well—we can determine to some extent the social groups that came to play the magi at Christmastide. Let us first use some external documentation to study these groups, then turn to the dramatic texts themselves for the same kind of information. We ask the obvious magian question, Who gave gifts to whom?

11. *Adoration of the Magi*

The most characteristic quality of such protodramatic groups is that they were young and thus of dependent status. This quality was manifest in their behavior. During Christmastime as well as on other festivities, such groups extorted payments from their superiors to do things they otherwise could not, or, inversely, not to do things they otherwise would. Thus a sixth-century bishop of Dôle in east central France, who could persuade older males (*homines*) but not "the little ones" (*parvuli*) to stop celebrating 1 January in the accustomed fashion of banqueting and gift giving (*strenae*), paid small gold coins to these *parvuli* to abstain from their "sacrilegious custom."[49] The gold coins paid to the monastic children of St. Gall in the early tenth century during Twelve Nights were probably not much different from those at Dôle, even if the lords in the latter monastery reported them as spontaneous gifts they gave the children for good behavior.[50] These coins were in fact more like concessions under threat to dependent groups during festive periods.

Forerunners of the classic medieval charivaris, such exchanges amounted to contracts between social types. Organized under their own "king" and law, the oblates at St. Gall, like so many Charlemagnes or Rolands defending their castles, had the right to seize and hold for ransom guests of the monastery who invaded their quarters during the three "days of the students," which began on the eve of December 28, the feast of the innocents.[51] Till the end of the Middle Ages and beyond, the election of play monarchs and the seizure of hostages against ransom would remain associated with these days.[52] Perhaps even before the term *officium infantum* referred to the play of the slaughter of the innocents, it indicated such paramilitary *ludi* of a more directly social character.[53]

If these payments were used to rein in marauding *parvuli* in a sixth-century hamlet and to control the children of a tenth-century monastery, it is not surprising that they were also coin of the realm in later cities, where the liturgical drama was in place. By the time of Jean d'Avranches, or of Bayeux, archbishop of Rouen (d. 1079), the different statuses or dignitaries in cathedral churches had divied up the Twelve Nights into "offices" that seem to have had a theatrical profile. For example, deacons and priests, dignitaries who tended to hold fixed-income benefices and to be committed to ecclesiastical careers, had rights to celebrate respectively the vigils of the feasts of Stephen and John the Evangelist on 26 and 27 December. The town children, who as choirboys or altarboys were perhaps in minor orders and thus called "clerks," but obviously had no benefices and no group commitment to a life of religion, had their *officium infantum* on the eve of 28 December, feast of the innocents.[54] It is uncertain how early these children came to play either the shepherds or innocents of the Christmas story. What is clear is that by the twelfth century, in England, Italy, Germany, and Spain, their *officium* often included the pompous appointment of a "boy bishop," complete with regalia, who was in charge of his peers for the length of the office, usually till New Year's Eve.[55] Significantly, this boy bishop was at times called the "bishop of alms" because he *and his court*—at St. Paul's in London each courtier imitating one real cathedral dignitary—begged in their regalia.[56] Here we find impersonation, a group of children paid for representing the mien and behavior of others. The ambivalence so common in the charivari, where those whose extortion is clear and resented do insist on earning their keep by providing a service or amusement for their fare, is quite apparent.

By the end of the twelfth century, recompense for either performing or not performing an *officium* was made to all the ecclesiastical orders and to children.[57] Yet the payments made to the subdeacons will prove most important for our concerns, and the most problematical. When Jean d'Avranches wrote in the late eleventh century, it was not clear if the subdeaconate, third in dignity among the seven holy orders and made up largely of older adolescents—called "young toughs" (*fortes et iuvenes*) by Guillaume Durand (d. 1296)[58]—was a major or a minor order. Though close to the altar, its members remained closely associated to lay status and least committed to a clerical life. Perhaps for that reason, d'Avranches does not mention them, nor does he refer to the feast of 1 January, with which they would soon be associated. Rather, after considering the feast of the children, or innocents, d'Avranches jumps to the "office of the star" (*stellae officium*) on Epiphany and mentions the significant fact that on its eve, the laity banqueted rather than fasted.[59]

A century later subdeacons were considered to be in major orders, and in his liturgical work that often copies d'Avranches, the Parisian master Jean Beleth (fl. 1180) does describe their role in Twelve Nights. Depending on the diocese, says Beleth, the subdeacons celebrated their feast "on Circumcision, . . . on Epiphany, or on its octave" of 13 January.[60] Why this variety? Beleth saw it as related to the character of the days or of the order of the subdiaconate. He says, "We call [the subdeacons' feast that] of the fools [*stultorum*].'"[61] This feast of fools, usually (if not always) associated with the subdeacons, would remain popular in France for centuries.

Beleth's *stulti* are certainly the same as the *fatui* whose feast the archbishop of Paris was trying to reform at the turn of the century. We learn from this latter prelate's correspondence that on the eve of 1 January it was customary for the subdeacons to lead their "lord of the feast," who elsewhere bore the title "king" or other sovereign title, to and from the cathedral in procession or parade. This lord received his staff of authority over the subdeacons at the point in vespers when the phrase from the Magnificat, "He has deposed the powerful from their seats and has exalted the humble," was intoned.[62]

Now the archbishop thought he could stop the raucous practices the subdeacons associated with these rites (the feast was elsewhere called "of the ass" presumably because the lord of the subdeacons rode into church on one) by recompensing all those who traditionally profited by it. He ordained that the noncanons, or unbeneficed cathedral clergy, be given three pence per annum and that the choir boys receive two pence per

annum if all were found present for the solemn ceremonies of this day . . .
and thus absent from their wonted festivities. If the activities of the circumcision resumed their old "enormity" and lack of order, he said, the
payments would be canceled.[63]

As Chambers recognized, distinctions not only of status but of age and
class or economic interests were involved in such distributions. The archbishop offered the carrot and the stick only to those who were not cathedral canons and thus did not have a regular income from the church.
Many were the unbeneficed, salaried "mercenaries" at all levels, from
choir boys to priests, who sold their services in these medieval cathedrals,
and many were those who tried to create a market for themselves.

While there were doubtless cases where the authorities themselves performed the dramas because they increased attendance and thus incomes
that supplemented their prebends—like the priests and deacons who
dramatized the feasts of Saint Stephen and Saint John Evangelist—there
were probably many more clerical actors who were hired from among the
choir boys or altar boys to the same end. Perhaps in some instances the
plays were more remunerative than regular services. At Rouen, for example, the bishop limited acting in such plays to those who had first regis-
tered for services in the choir.[64]

Thus the theatre of Chrismastide became a significant income source
for *parvuli* in age or status, who might be called "clerks" but often had
no intention of pursuing an ecclesiastical career. But just how popular
were these early dramatic efforts? Gerhoh of Reichersberg was master of
the boys in an Augsburg monastery in 1124 when he penned his criticism
of the monastic life, and he painted a picture of the churches filling up for
such dramas and festivals. Dormitories and refectories were empty, he
wrote, "except on the rare feasts, when they represented Herod. . . ."[65]
Certainly the urban church choir was just as soon a stage for earning such
income, whether in the form of a stipend or a banquet. I think we shall
not be far wrong in imagining groups of children before and youth after
calends, "clerks for a day" playing "kings for a day," surging onto these
stages from the city streets.

Thus in the two weeks before Epiphany, different ages and statuses
contended among one another, marking off turf through their creative,
more or less intimidating behaviors. Such behaviors often featured the
assumption of princely regalia and titles by dependent groups and the
bestowal of often extorted "gifts" upon such "kingdoms." To a certain
extent, much of this behavior is best understood from a sociological view-
point rather than from the angle of Christian dramaturgy. Thus Durand's
"strong-armed youth" celebrated the feast of the circumcision as a way of
announcing that after the Last Judgment "there would be no weak age:
no *senectus*, no *senium*, no impotent childhood."[66] His casting of the

calends, or the feast of the circumcision, as the property of one generation is significant. His typical notion of the elderly and children as compa-
rably helpless, and of both these generations as dependent on the sexually
mature *iuvenes*, speaks for itself.

Yet certainly the story of 6 January, when mostly mature magi knelt
before a mere infant, emphasized something else, namely generational
differences. It goes without saying that the story of the magi lent itself to
a liturgical representation of several such primary social tensions. To understand the magi plays of this age is in part to comprehend how such
exchanges of bribes came to be acted out as the gifts or tributes of the
magi and how such generational tensions came to be mirrored in the
magi of different ages.

That having been said, I would dispute the notion that Epiphany
merely took over the rites of the older calends, or that the *officium stellae*
on that feast was just a summation of all previous calendar activity of the
Twelve Nights. Despite the statement of Jean Beleth, as repeated by Guillaume Durand at the end of the thirteenth century, that the subdeacons'
feast of fools was sometimes done on the Epiphany or on its octave a
week later, for example, most of the synodal attacks on the feast of fools
during the Twelve Nights mention the circumcision or calends of January, not the Epiphany. The question was: How could Epiphany, which
involved the adoration of the infant by decent people, be decently celebrated after the disorders of calends?[67] As we shall see, the theatre surrounding the Epiphany was an object of independent criticism by the
twelfth century. Clearly, much more information will be necessary before
we have a clear picture of the social reality behind the early magi plays.

To understand the process involved in the emergence of magi theatre,
we must begin by resisting the temptation to assume that magi theatre
was a clerical creation that spread from churches to the laity outside. As
we have already seen, the quasi-secular character of the "clergy" that performed it should discourage such polarizing notions. Second, one of the
oldest magi plays is in fact in a vernacular language, and its prototype
could be as old as the oldest Latin fragments. The Castilian *auto de los
reyes* is not, as was once thought, merely a translation of a Latin church
drama. Crucial elements of its story rather descend from older French-
language poems or even (nonextant) dramas, and that points to performances by and for the laity.[68]

The singular story line in this vernacular *auto*, in fact, points toward a
sociologically lay, as much as an ecclesiological comprehension of, the
magi. In the liturgical dramas, the kings always give their three gifts in a
consciously symbolic manner: aware of their historic roles, they simply
express Jesus' undoubted kingship, priesthood, and humanity by their
gifts of gold, frankincense, and myrrh. The kings of the *auto* and the ver-

nacular poems, on the other hand, give gifts for a purpose we encountered earlier in an apocryphal Eastern story: the magi offered their gifts to test Jesus' divinity.[69] Thus not only do these early vernacular representations have roots in part distinct from the liturgical drama; they also understand magian gifting as a dynamic social activity rather than as the pure expression of a clerical doctrine.

In the medieval town or village, where it was usually the most imposing public building, the church was the common stage and *sopra altare*, the customary place for the dynamic or reciprocal exchange of gifts and tributes between humans, as well as between humans and divinities through their clerical agents. Innumerable medieval contracts made the payment of annual rents to lords and the reciprocal expression of the latters' duty to the payees fall due on major feast days, including the appropriate one, the Epiphany.[70] In turn, on high feasts like the Epiphany great lords, desiring the tenfold reimbursement promised by the Bible, often, in Beleth's words, "offered precious utensils to the church on the altar or in other suitable places."[71] Obviously, this raises the possibility that sculptures or paintings of the magi might record such noble charities, much as did ancient sarcophaguses. They might precede this act by humbly placing their crown on that altar or on the ground at the entrance to the church, to receive it back from God's vicar after the ceremonies, as we have found the practice in the East to be. Epiphany was precisely a common and appropriate feast for legitimating not only such "gifts" to the churches but also tributes and taxes paid to the secular estates.

As we saw earlier, placing gifts on the altar was an ancient practice of the Christian laity. Processional offerings of this type among the general laity ended sooner in the East than in the West, where, interestingly, they died out at about the time the liturgical drama, including the epiphanic offerings of the magi, appeared. We can say almost casually that the magi must have been among the first altarboys to pass around the collection basket to a now immobile audience. When we ask ourselves at what point within divine services the liturgical play of the magi first appeared, Karl Young's opinion that it was first performed during the offertory of the mass on the feast of epiphany remains largely uncontested. In late medieval Rouen, for example, it remained inveterate custom to perform part of the *officium stellae* at the offertory of the mass. Thus it is particularly significant that the staging instructions for one version of the Rouen play call for churchgoers to make their offerings during a pause in the play.[72] This use of the play to attract offerings from the audience on Epiphany is also clear in the play from Besançon, where the collection was made during the gospel, before the offertory of the mass. There clerks dressed as the three kings took their turns reading Matthew's Gospel from the pulpit, each singing out their respective gift—"Gold!" "Frankincense!" and "Myrrh!"—when they came to those words in the Gospel.[73]

The fact that the earliest liturgical plays of the magi seem to have been performed during mass does not preclude the performance of vernacular plays at other times, for example, on the night before the Epiphany. We simply lack the evidence to get a sense of the range of opportunities involved. But it is significant that most of the liturgical plays soon came to be performed during the night before Epiphany as well as on the solemnity itself. It is as if such plays on the vigil were meant to compete for audience with existing laical plays or other activities that de facto kept exhausted revellers from attending services on the solemnity itself, like the long established banquets of Epiphany eve.[74]

Showing how imbedded in lay life were those children and subdeacons among the clergy who performed these plays, we have warned against viewing this competition as merely matching "the church" and "the laity." The point is that, whether done at the offertory of the mass or at vespers the previous evening, the representation of the three kings offering gifts was comprehended in relation to society's own exchange procedures, including the bribes and extortions or constraints that factually lay behind "gifts." As the general laity's processional offering declined, its dependent groups continued to represent society's exchanges in coming centuries. Soon real kings, not just clerks, will be found playing the magi.

The extent to which the arts were used for outright political as well as social purposes in medieval times has become increasingly clear in recent years. In 1099 a bishop denounced the French king for commanding the election of a boy as a real bishop, "as if this was the festival of the boys."[75] How unavoidable in this age to imagine Christmas scenes in which fake boy bishops entertained real bishops, who were but boys! Thus social commentary spilled into the political sphere. We know that the papacy used formal pictorial art against Frederic Barbarossa—as in a twelfth-century Roman painting of almost magian proportions in which Constantine leads the pope's horse—and that that emperor's friends directed at least one extant theatrical production against the papacy.[76]

The idea that the *officia stellae* might directly evoke contemporary political reality, as much as had Ottonian magian art, has also been broached in recent years. Certainly the story of Herod, inextricably tied to that of the magi, lent itself to such dramatization, he being the biblical figure the Middle Ages most commmonly associated with princely tyranny. Recently Walther Lipphardt has argued that in a 1070 Freising play, perhaps the oldest complete play telling the Matthew story, it is the figure of Herod and his court that predominates, at the expense of the magi or even of Mary or Jesus. In Lipphardt's view, the latter personages, the

more solemn and churchbound, increase in importance only as the significance of Herod declines. Lipphardt has a straightforward political hunch
about this situation: in the midst of the investiture struggle between Emperor Henry IV and Pope Gregory VII, late eleventh-century churchmen
used Herod to embody the mad and violent character of the Salian emperor. In Henry IV, the archetypal enemy of reason and God and the
slaughterer of the innocents lived again.[77]

By positing that the "Herod play" in some manner of speaking preceded the *officium stellae* or stood at least on an equal footing with it,
riotous theatre thus competing with the gravity of the magi, one may well
account for the fact that play kingdoms made up of young "fools" were
those who did the play in church. Magi plays featuring "Herodic insan-
ity" would well fit the madness of the militant subdeacons and lesser
clergy.[78] One thing is certain. In all the texts, the part of the story "representing Herod as the persecutor of Christ [and] the killer of little ones"
seems the element most likely to have attracted interest, while those involving Jesus and Mary, indeed perhaps the magi as well, seem everywhere largely devoid of fun and dramatic content.[79]

In what follows, I will patch together one drama from the texts of the
several plays put on in church in the late eleventh and twelfth century in
such a way as to draw attention to the social data in the texts. The court
of Herod being "ready," as directions might require,[80] the three crowned
kings with their greater or smaller entourages were to enter the church
"with gravity"[81] through different doors, as if approaching Jerusalem
"each from his own region."[82] At Besançon, a younger chorister with a
staff was to precede them, while an older one followed them.[83] Their
proper names never being given in the texts, the kings usually encounter
each other in the nave, under the first of what may be two distinct stars
hanging from separate wires suspended in the church.[84] With no sign of
the antagonism or fear that will surface in a later tradition of the play, they
salute and kiss each other. The text may prescribe that the king to the
right kisses the one on his left, and then the middle one busses the one to
his left, and then the far left one kisses the first king, on the extreme
right.[85] As far as can be determined, they are all crowned on entering the
spectators' view, and thus already carry their staffs, with which they will
point to the star.

They do not always have their gifts, however, when they appear on the
scene. At Győr, the magi begin the play by taking the vases containing the
"mystical gifts" from the main altar; only then do they proceed toward
Herod. No part of the Matthew story itself, this detail reminds us that
such parts of the magi's regalia often came from church treasuries, those
repositories of previous patrons' "precious utensils . . . offered to the
church and . . . placed on the altar or in other suitable places" at the of-

fertory of a major church feast, like Epiphany.[86] Such a play would thus recall the charity of previous patrons, just as a play where the magi bore new gifts might first establish a patron's philanthropy. Innumerable paintings of the coming centuries would show that vessels used in divine services were also used to contain the gifts of the magi.[87] But rarely has it been noted that viewers would certainly have associated some of these objects with philanthropists. The manifestation of such precious metals, already in the *officia stellae*, was an ongoing reflection of the exchanges being made in such communities.

Now the magi move toward "Jerusalem," that is, the court of Herod, whom we find at Győr "seated crowned on his throne in the middle of the church."[88] As we have seen, in many plays Herod was from the start, and indeed almost to the end, the center of attraction, so that some authorities prefer to call this play that of Herod rather than of the magi or of the star. The play from Bilsen in Belgium is one of those that highlight the majesty of Herod and his setting, instructing the "sect of boys" to "splendidly" begin the play by marching to the seat of King Herod, singing his praises as eternal king of the world:

> Eia dicamus!
> Hunc regnare decet et regni sceptra tenere:
> Regis nomen amat, nomen quia moribus ornat.[89]

Here at Bilsen, Herod stands to greet the flatterers, who in real life are those in his "sect" or brigade, only then to learn that an infant king, Jesus, will eclipse him. Yet in the Freising play (ca. 1070), these same lines of text are sung at the *end* of the action, when Herod leaves the stage after giving the order for the slaughter of the innocents.[90] Since he has long since been told of Jesus' royal future, it is as if crime pays!

Students have always been perplexed by these Herod-oriented texts from Győr and Bilsen,[91] but Stumpfl, developing Chambers and in turn seconded by Drumbl, would seem to be right in his view that both dignities, the Herod of the play and the king of fools who presumably played that monarch, were meant to be honored by the laud.[92] In these two plays, the chorus salutes the leader of the social groups responsible for staging the dramas, or at least their Herodic components.

In several of the early plays, there is a long interval between the time the residents of Jerusalem first sight the approaching magi and the time the latter depart for Bethlehem. This long Jerusalem period is dominated by generally nonbiblical actions which, in my view, the dramatists developed to teach both actors and audiences proper greeting rituals. Crucial to this pedagogy is the messenger or the legate or one of the soldiers of Herod, a figure who repeatedly salutes the three kings and Herod as they transmit first one and then another piece of information. Thus we hear,

"Long live you, King, forever," as one soldier, genuflecting, greets Herod.[93] Herod then gives diplomatic instructions to his legate: he wants to know "who [the kings] are, why they have come, because of what rumor they need to see us."[94] At Compiègne, that legate then greets the first of the magi, "O most outstanding king, to whom fear should be shown by doing reverence!"[95]

Etiquette prescriptions dominate the texts as the magi now enter Jerusalem and approach the throne of Herod, preceded at Rouen by Herod's legate, who will present them.[96] "*Salve*, king of a strong people and lord of the world," cries the first king to Herod, who as soon kisses him before seating him on his right.[97] Herod then seats the two other kings, who speak "gibberish" rather than the Latin of the first king. One sits to the right of the first king and the last on Herod's own left.[98]

There follows at Rouen a scene in which each king rises from his seat and, genuflecting before Herod, shows and explains to Herod the gift he has brought for Jesus (in none of these Latin plays do the magi gift Herod themselves).[99] Herod now requests from the Jewish high priests information regarding prophecies that might fit what the magi are saying. These priests, who at Fleury sit with Herod "dressed as youth" (*in habitu iuvenili*) obtain in the same play from their "bearded" scribes or "jurisprudents" confirmation from the latters' books that indeed, a king *was* expected to rise in Bethlehem.[100]

A remarkable denouement occurs at this point in the early play from Bilsen, and in it alone. Whereas elsewhere Herod may be distraught over the news that a king was to arise in Bethlehem, a violent Herod at Bilsen, upon hearing that message, imprisons the kings and seizes their gifts.[101] Rare though this moment is, it certainly evokes the kidnapping and ransom motif we found at St. Gall in the early tenth century during the Twelve Nights.[102] It emphasizes, as does the Castilian auto, that the gifts were not predestined for the babe. Still, the Bilsen play does then pull back. The royal *armiger* persuades Herod to release the magi and their gifts, so that, again underway, the magi might reveal Jesus' location to Herod, for Herod too now wants to go to adore Jesus. Princely sagacity wins out.[103]

At this point the magi, after bowing to Herod in the Laon play, leave Jerusalem for Bethlehem, led by another star on a second wire. We may note again that the exchanges between the magi and Herod in these early plays only rarely involve references to gifts; rather, the exchanges involve the formalities of greetings, and their meeting offers an extraordinary occasion for teaching good manners. It is worth repeating: the encounter between Herod and the magi is the only event in the New Testament of a royal, heraldic stamp, and it is the more important for that, for it is in such settings that one learns to behave in a princely and thus efficacious fashion.[104]

The magi soon arrive at "the crib," which, before taking on its modern shape, was just the main altar of the church, on which at Győr and elsewhere sat a wooden statue of Mary and Jesus (Herod was all but wooden!) that received the magi's gifts and reverences.[105] This statue was then borne off in procession to conclude the drama. Presuming that such a statue did not have articulated or movable arms to accept the gifts, such a piece of wood did not invite much in the way of behavioral interchange, and the plays give few instructions on that score. Yet the ones that are given are significant because they are echoed in contemporary literature and art.

In two different versions of the Rouen play, the first king is told to prostrate himself before Jesus and offer his gift to him before the other two do so.[106] The magi in the Bible did prostrate themselves, of course, and a type of prostration called "proskynesis" is in fact the devotional position assumed by many a "first king" among the magi adoring Jesus in medieval art, the second being close to, and the third king usually still far from assuming that prostrate position. By mid-twelfth century, incidentally, paintings and sculptures, but never plays, almost uniformly show the oldest king as first in line and the youngest last in order. There are, of course, variant behavioral instructions in other plays. The Laon text has each king in order first genuflect on one knee (*genuflexo dicit*) and then bestow his gift,[107] while the Besançon play calls for the kings to place their gifts on the altar from a kneeling position, perhaps in unison.[108]

Such variations are not nearly as important as the pedagogical principles that are involved. We may suspect, but we cannot be certain, that the meeting of Herod and the magi—all brother kings—was staged so as to teach students how to behave in such courtly circumstances. Further, with the help of a sermon from about 1130 we can demonstrate that some curates used the adoration of the magi in such plays, and consequently artistic representations of the same theme, to teach proper devotion before the divinities.

Julien of Vézelay's (ca. 1080–1160) Epiphany sermon invited his listeners to imitate the magi. Some seven hundred years earlier Ambrose had built a sermon on the same theme, but Julien was more concrete than his predecessor. He called on his flock to imitate the way the magi prayed.[109] Explaining that the magi taught a certain form of religious behavior (*quiddam divini cultus*) that was alas ignored by Christians, who behaved all but reverentially in church, Julien glossed Matthew's words, "they fell down and adored him," with the imperative, "You, do the same"![110]

He continued. Perhaps it was too much to ask his listeners to imitate kings like Solomon and David. Though preoccupied with courtly duties, the former is known to have knelt on both knees for the length of a very long prayer, while the latter on one occasion lay prostrate with his stomach touching the ground. But the magi did provide a worthy model, Julien insisted. The preacher seems to have been recommending that those adoring the crib use the position called proskynesis. Still more significant, he leaves no doubt that by the early twelfth century, the magi in plays and in art taught the faithful how to pray.[111]

A second behavioral instruction for the magi's adoration comes from the aforementioned play from Besançon. In this play the kings appear with capes hanging from their shoulders and *capelli cum coronis* on their heads.[112] They are told to "offer upon the [main] altar . . . their gifts with crowns."[113] In no other play of the time do we find this instruction, yet this practice as well was recommended to players by another contemporary authority.

The famous mystic Elizabeth of Schönau died on 18 June 1164. In that same year the alleged bodies of the three magi were brought to Cologne. An early biographer described a vision of the magi that had appeared to her, the first by several religious figures which, well into modern times, would flesh out details of the magi story.[114] Two details in this vision are particularly interesting. Elizabeth saw the three kings first taking off their crowns and offering them to Jesus, who takes them and then returns them to the monarchs.[115] Second, the first king gave Jesus a large gold coin that seemed to bear a royal image.[116]

Elizabeth's vision is strong evidence that when this tale was written, at about the time the so-called bodies of the magi came to Cologne, some magi plays used imperial coins as the magian gift of gold. Still more relevant is that on this evidence, it could not have been uncommon for the thespian magi to place their crowns on the altar, as the Besançon play alone documents them doing. We have little problem imagining what significant social procedures this action will have mirrored in some cases. In Besançon, for example, where at a later point the participation of three different city churches in magi plays and in a civic banquet is well documented, it is easy to speculate that the kings of the clergy of these different churches, while playing the magi, were also surrendering the crowns of their seasonal authority in Besançon on the altar.[117] Nor do we have trouble imagining that the kings whom Elizabeth visualized were more than festive lords in a play, whose mock authority would expire with the Epiphany. Her models were doubtless real kings who, as we emphasized, throughout the Christian ecumene now could be seen on feast days surrendering their crowns on entering churches, to receive them back from churchmen as part of divine services.[118]

In the Adoration of the benedictional of Aethelwold we saw a crowned tenth-century king draw attention to Jesus as triumphator by offering him a group of diadems. At first glance, however, pictorial art of the middle ages never seems to have shown the kings surrendering their own crowns as they did at times in church. Yet on closer examination of countless Adorations, the procedure is in fact partially preserved. As can be seen in the figures of this book, a typical painting of an Adoration shows that the lead king has removed his crown and usually laid it on the ground at his feet. Several quite early pictures of the Adoration have perplexed scholars because the lead king is shown without a crown, though there is no literary tradition to that effect. Yet the explanation is evident enough. Here is the classical "humble" prince, not dissimilar to monarchs like Canute the Dane, who was famous for refusing to wear a crown in Jesus' presence.[119] In such unusual pictures viewers saw the "festive coronation" they knew from church life. That is, they saw the king after he had laid aside his crown but before he fetched it at the end of the ceremony.[120] The similarity of real coronation rites and the Festkrönungen of the magi meant that viewers might easily confound the interregnum of the real prince when, without his crown, he worshiped the divinities rather than ruled subjects, and the riotous reign of the king of fools.

The late Middle Ages would bring important developments in the history of magi theatre. Before all else, their journey, cast as a parade done in the streets and squares of courts and cities, would become central to the construction of political self-images. Yet by the mid-twelfth century, some of that play's central attractions for civic life were already clear. Evidently, social groups might mirror their own seasonal hierarchies in the royalty of the magi, just as they incorporated into their rites the Festkrönungen of the real monarchs of this world. The magi had now begun to instruct the faithful in courtly and ecclesiastical etiquette through the example of their behavior with Herod and before Mary and Jesus, just as they had long since assumed the task of training the faithful in charity.

Since one early vernacular play has survived, the performance of the magi play by laity, perhaps outside of churches, may be of equal antiquity with church performances. Thus careful evaluation of the first twelfth-century criticisms of the nativity theatre in churches is appropriate because these critics see matters with all-too-clear clerical blinkers.

Criticism of church theatre is almost as old as the oldest manuscripts of the plays themselves. Some criticisms take as their theme a decline from pristine purity. Writing near the end of the twelfth century, for example, the abbess Herrad of the nunnery of Hohenberg near Strasbourg (d. 1195) conceded that it was to augment the beliefs of the faithful that the ancient fathers had created an "imaginary religion" of the magi, a package of performances that stretched from the appearance of the star to the slaughter of the innocents, to be performed on the feast of the epiphany or its octave.[121] Time, alas, had produced decline rather than edification, the abbess claimed, so that in her day, priests came into churches dressed as knights—she presumably referred to Herod's knights—to drink and play in the company of courtesans.[122] Herrad was not swayed by the fact that the tales of Jesus' infancy afforded dramatic opportunities for shaping and for commenting on real social solidarities. If anything, church plays over time probably became more restrained, not less; that is, the role of Herod, prince of tantrums, probably abated over time, or was performed outside of churches, to favor the solemnity of what went on inside.

A slightly earlier critic probably had it right. Writing about 1161, before the magi came to Cologne, the reformist monk Gerhoh of Reichersberg remembered that when he had been master of the schoolboys at Augsburg about 1124, it was theatre and little else that could bring out the sense of solidarity of his monks. He denounced theatre in the church because it stemmed from priests' avarice. Apparently the clergy made money on these plays, as we surmised earlier. More significantly, Gerhoh claimed that the immoral parts actors played, especially those of Herod and his courtiers, in fact matched the actors' own immoral reality. The very zeal with which they played Herod and his court, dressing like Herod's knights (when not like his courtesans), Gerhoh intimated, showed "not feigned false but rather true insanities."[123] First, it should be said that both these accounts certify that it was the goings-on in Herod's court, and less the regalia of the three kings, that at this point opened the way to playing up secular magnificence. Second, let us again emphasize that Gerhoh recognized that the representation of actual society had not been excluded when the liturgical drama had been established in church.

THE CRUSADING MAGI

By the time that Pope Urban called the first of the crusades in 1095, scarce elements of a cult of the three kings began to surface in western Europe. According to an early twelfth-century writer, until about 1092 a chalice existed in the cathedral of Reims that contained some portion of the gold "that the three magi had offered to the lord."[124] From that early day until quite recent times, the gold of the magi, sometimes in the form of coins, can be traced as relics in different churches of Europe.[125] From about that same time as well, and with a longevity stretching into the present century, stem the occult powers associated to the names of the kings. According to a book of the end of the eleventh century, those who carry with them the written names of the three will be spared epilepsy.[126] Finally, it is about this time that the magi, no mean travelers or pilgrims themselves, emerge as the titulary saints of inns.[127] In all these roles the magi reveal an almost invariable characteristic of their cult in the future. The magi have power and personality only as a collectivity and almost never as individuals. They were not recognized as saints. There was no significant cult to Balthasar, to Melchior, or to Caspar.

Even the indications of collective cult remain, however, quite slim, and it is fair to say that in general, the faithful at the end of the eleventh century were more likely to pray like the magi than to pray to them. Yet in these very years, powerful cultural, political, and economic forces were at work that would, a century later, transform their burial place in Cologne into one of the main European pilgrimage goals. To conclude our survey of these centuries, let us examine these forces.

First, a significant psychological enrichment took place in the motivations for the kings' gifts to the child, one that may be called a movement toward realism and romance. Durand noted that in the eighth century Bede had already supplemented his symbolic explanation of the gifts with what we may call literal ones stemming from the life situation of the subjects. The venerable English prelate had said that the kings had given their gifts because Mary needed the money, because incense would sweeten the odor of the stable, and because myrrh would kill the worms in Jesus and thus strengthen his body.[128] It seems to me that this realism grew, haltingly, from the beginning of the twelfth century, contemporary to the sentimentalism of Bernard of Clairvaux (d. 1153) and predating the classical Franciscan formulation of nativity realism.[129] We see the impetus of these unaccustomed sentiments in the sermon of Julien of Vézelay mentioned earlier. The preacher wants his audience to participate in the magi's first reaction on seeing the manger scene, and so he paints a solitary scene with words of a "squalid" Joseph, a mother, with no wet nurse nor midwife at her side, covered with a *vili et plebeia veste*, and an infant in tatters. Playing to the social prejudices of his audience, which would scarcely have accepted "such a lower-class [*popularis*] child" as king, Julien thus made his listeners recognize that Mary needed the money.[130] Without it, he implies, she could not have fed herself and thus would not have been able to keep her breasts full for the infant. This realistic tendency continued, so that by the time of Francis such sentiments were no longer unusual, having become a typical part of the late medieval comprehension of the crib.

A second modification or enrichment of the image of the magi is closely linked to the early history of the crusades in the first decades of the twelfth century. Readers will be familiar with the fantastic figure of Prester John, a pure creation of the western imagination that appeared for the first time in the 1140s.[131] He was said to be a theocratic Christian pope/emperor living in the East. Perhaps it was inevitable that after the first crusade opened up the East to the gaze of the West, its wealth would obsess westerners. Figures like the Prester (that is, *presbyter* or priest), who seemed to promise fabled wealth without bloodshed, if only his kingdom could be located, would catch on.

Yet Prester John had no biblical authority behind him, so the search for the homelands of the descendants of the magi kings, who did have biblical legitimacy, would become a matter of no small importance to those seeking gold and spices. At the same, time the exotic character of those kings would be stressed in literature and especially in art, to the exclusion of Prester John, who never did establish an iconography. Again in the sermon of Julien of Vézelay, delivered between the first (1095) and the second (1146) crusades, we find an outline of this future. Certainly with the memory of Constantine's mother Helena in mind, the preacher implies that his listeners should make the pilgrimage east as faithfully as the magi pilgrims had come west. Perhaps the magi's patronage of pilgrims stems from just such a crusading context. Julien may indeed be praising those soldiers of the first Crusade who died in the East and thus went to heaven, for he links a verse from Matthew 2 that tells of the magi's passage to the west with Matthew Sill, where Jesus tells how the Roman centurion was but the first of legions of gentiles who would pass from west to east:

> Nato ergo Domino *in diebus Herodis regis, ecce magi ab Oriente venerunt.*[132]
> Venerunt isti *ab Oriente ,venient et* alii ab *Occidente et recumbent cum Abraham et Isaac et Iacob in regno caelorum.*[133]

The crusading idea that gentiles (also from the west) might be the heirs of Jerusalem,[134] even as the eastern magi had been the first gentiles to recognize the truth of Christianity, would over time develop into the notion that the western crusading monarchs were indeed like veritable magi, returning to rescue Jerusalem from latter-day Herods. Already in 1099, the Frankish leader Baldwin had himself crowned king of Jerusalem on Christmas Eve, not in that capital city, but in Bethlehem.[135] The chroniclers praised his humility, of course, but in fact it was a proud imitation of Christ, done at the place of the nativity, where once the magi had found Jesus and crowned him, so to speak. Baldwin could not have acted without awareness of the association. Whether in the realm of economic or political history, the magi would be one of the main images through which Christianity would encounter the East in the coming centuries. When the Mongols invaded Christendom in 1243 and were asked why, they responded, said Matthew of Paris, that it was to recover the bodies of the magi and to take them back east to their homeland![136]

The so-called transferal of the magi's remains to Cologne in 1164, an act of great religious and political importance, must be seen in relation to the new conceptualization of a *respublica christiana* and its polarization to the other world of the East. The ancient city of Cologne rose and prospered with the Crusades, being the central Rhenish port linking Flanders and northwest Europe to the East, its markets full of the latter's exotica.[137] Reinhold von Dassel was the city's archbishop-elect at the time of this transferral and, along with the prelates of Trier and Mainz, one of the prince-bishops of the German empire. He was the chancellor of Frederic Barbarossa and, along with the historian/prelate Otto von Freising, was charged with the development of Barbarossa's imperial propaganda. Thus he was often at odds with the papacy. Just as Dassel was Barbarossa's handyman in bringing about the canonization of Charlemagne in December, 1165, so the archbishop was instrumental in moving the alleged remains of the magi to Cologne from Milan, the last seat of the old Roman empire in the West.[138] As Dassel made clear in his correspondence, Germany had essentially become the home of gentility and the leader of Christendom, so that it was right that the Eastern magi would come to rest in his see.[139] It is not certain that the emperor himself ever conceived of the magi's residence within Germany as being politically useful, although Dassel obviously did. But within a few years, there was no doubt that their *royal* presence was to play a major role in subsequent German history. The coronation of the German kings would use the Matthew story as its liturgy, and the magi's altar in Cologne would become the first pilgrimage goal of each such prince, just as the selfsame altar, ensconced in this commercial emporium, would become one of the central pilgrimage destinations of Europe.

Chapter 3

THE PAGEANT OF THE "TWO" KINGS

WRITING ABOUT 1172, Werner von Tegernsee pictured all three magi as Chaldeans. They had come together not to follow the star, but to enter into parliament (*tagedinge*) so as to determine peacefully the borders of their empire[1]: again, the magi as structure. It was just such a meeting of the magi in the liturgical drama of St. Benoît that brought its kings to proclaim, "O admirable commerce."[2]

With that comment these dramatic kings did not mean to praise trade (or, corrosive usury), but rather the honorable, even courtly, skill of conversation, that is, the diplomacy by which the "best of men" manage to avoid conflicts among themselves and their subjects, in short to keep their polity in a steady state.

In the second part of the present chapter we shall study how the magi related to each other. In doing so, we shall discover that often two rather than three human types, two kings, if one likes, and not three, were involved in this "commerce." The pageant of the magi is in fact about one type interacting with another. Commerce, says the liturgist Durand, is where something is accepted and something is given.[3] The essence of the "commerce" these kings engaged in was the *exchange* of conversation, even as they pressed their gifts on the infant. In what follows, that noble undertaking of interactive royal behavior, that self-representational triumph societies offer to themselves, is in full public view at center court. The image that emerges is often one of polarities, not triads.

And yet, we get ahead of ourselves. The first part of the present chapter describes a capital event in the history of western Europe when, from roughly 1200 till 1500, rulers and cities presented themselves in the guise of magi to great outdoor urban audiences. The indoor liturgical dramas were not disappearing. Rather, they were being trumped in popularity by great outdoor cavalcades enacting the journey of the magi. Churchmen might hasten their own loss of popularity by excluding Herod and his court from the church proper because of their Herodian "indecency," in which case the outdoor cavalcade came to center on the magi's pompous reception outside by their brother king, Herod.

Thus primary social groups, like real kings, courts, and cities, began to represent themselves, and they did so as much in magnificent Journey as in Adoration. Nowhere is this spatial shift toward equalizing Herod and Jesus, the profanely sacred with the sacredly profane, as memorable as in

12. Master Gruamon and Adeodato. *The Magi Appear before Herod and Adoration of the Magi*

the substantial architrave that in 1166 Master Gruamon and his brother
Adeodato sculpted at Sant'Andrea in Pistoia, probably the largest magi
representation in Europe at this crucial point in the threesome's history.
At the center of the sculptural field is not the Adoration but the enthroned Herod's reception of the (named) kings! It is their cavalcade that
captures the viewer's interest. The adoration of the child Jesus is consigned to the right corner. As we shall see, this emphasis on the meeting
of the brother kings corresponds to the dynamics of processional representations in this age.[4]

About 1245, the legist cardinal Hugo opined that "it is not credible
that if they were kings, just three would come. Rather, they would be
accompanied by great retinues."[5] The age of collective self-representation
had arrived in Europe, and the magi would be a significant vehicle for
such recreations. The journey of the magi, not as *tableux vivant* but as a
full-scale ride through the city, permitted a court or a city through its
riders and horses to celebrate itself as through no other gospel story.

"THE THREE KINGS OF COLOGNE"

Frederick Barbarossa's gift of the bodies of the kings to his chancellor and
archbishop of Cologne, Rainhold von Dassel, may have been hasty and
ill-conceived, as the documents regarding this event suggest. Not so the
negotiations surrounding the canonization of Charlemagne in Aachen,
which was proclaimed on 29 December 1165, just a few short months
after the magi reached Cologne. Perhaps it makes sense to think of the
two acts as related parts of a common imperial policy, but there is reason
to believe that Barbarossa, if not the archbishop of Cologne, did not at-
tach much importance to the wise men from the East, whereas everyone
recognized that a great national king was being canonized in Charlemagne.[6] Whatever Barbarossa's thought on the matter, the relics of the
kings soon became stellar attractions of this largest and most important
trade emporium in medieval Germany. Originally installed in the old cathedral of St. Peter, they were moved to their present site in 1322. By this
time, the magi were known throughout Europe simply as "the Three
Kings of Cologne."[7]

Much had happened in the meantime to cement the relationship of the
kings with Cologne. Perhaps the most fateful was their being used for
political legitimation. By the end of the twelfth century, it was the custom
for the archbishop of Cologne to crown German kings at Aachen; thus
Henry VI, son of Frederick Barbarossa, had been crowned there in 1169.
(Eventually, these new kings traveled immediately to Cologne to worship
before the shrine of the three kings, but this became the rule only in the
later thirteenth century; Henry VI [d. 1197], never did visit Cologne).

It is at this point, however, that the magi of Cologne first exercized their power to legitimate German rulers. Upon Henry's death, and with the future Frederick II still a child, the electors of Germany decided against choosing another Hohenstaufen. The result was a double election by contending groups among the electors. Philip of Swabia, a son of Barbarossa, was one choice, Otto of the anti-Hohenstaufen Welf family was the other. The former was the more popular among the prince-electors and had the right insignia of office, but he had neither been crowned in Aachen nor by the archbishop of Cologne; Otto IV might be the less popular choice, but he had been rightly crowned in Aachen by proper prelate.[8]

One moment in the struggle between the two involved the famous shrine of the three kings. Started about 1175, the shrine was still unfinished in 1200, though its underlying structure was probably fixed. The front end of the shrine was to feature on the right a scene of Jesus' baptism, in the center Mary and child enthroned, and on the left three niches for the three kings. Thus the shrine commemorated the two great events of the epiphany. Alas, at the turn of the century the sculptor changed the plan for the left face. He squeezed two kings under one arch, so that the third arch was vacant (fig. 13). Into this arch was brought the figure of none other than Otto IV, who on the feast of epiphany, 1200, ostentatiously placed a precious gold crown on the head of each of the three magi.[9]

Though one writer has indeed called Otto "the fourth King," scholars in general seem to have remained unaware that that topos already had firm roots in Christian art.[10] Otto's presence was a continuation of that tradition, with the Welf the likelier to get to heaven because of the crowns he had financed for the church of Cologne. Let us not neglect the ruler's obvious political intention, however. Clearly, Otto aimed to weaken Philip while strengthening the legitimacy of his own claim to the crown of Germany, particularly among those who backed him in the city of Cologne. Nor can it be said that his plan went awry. When his antagonist was murdered in 1208, Otto assumed the crown of Germany in complete right and was crowned emperor in Rome in 1209.

Otto IV's successor as king of the Germans, Frederick II, did indeed come to Cologne in early August, 1215, after being crowned at Aachen. But that was his only visit during his long reign (d. 1250), and he left no record of venerating the shrine of the magi. Thus it would appear that on the whole, the Hohenstaufen dynasty showed little interest in the cult, quite to the contrary of the Welf interest. As we already indicated, not until after Frederick II would Cologne become a required first stop after the coronation. However, our interest has little to do with the cult per se and is more concerned with the political imagination shaping notions of order and sovereignty that the magi have triggered in history. From that point of view, a document of some significance has come to light that specifically links the Hohenstaufen with the magi. We find one of Frederick II's house intellectuals, Nicholaus of Bari, thinking up legitimizing metaphors based on this Christian narrative of the magi.

One of the main problems of representing sovereignty in magian form was that unless the reigning monarch was to be portrayed not as a magus but as the theocratic single star of Bethlehem itself (as in the West Otto II and III did choose to be), there seemed no convincing way to represent his total and single sovereignty as full amid several maguses. Alternately, there was no easy way to represent a sovereign couple, man and woman, in this format. We saw this difficulty in the mosaics of San Vitale, where in an offertory context whose magian base is there for all to see, the emperor Justinian on the left, accompanied by the chi rho or "star" of Bethlehem of his ancestor Constantine, is balanced on the right by the empress Theodora wearing the magi. It proved difficult to replace givers of three gifts with two living sovereigns.

The magi's inability to represent a single authority may be the principle reason why the magi simply never attained royal status in the theocratic Byzantine empire. They long remained nameless as well, uncrowned heralds or ambassadors exhibiting little or no individuality. Thus as we have seen, in some Ravennese and Roman sarcophaguses of the early period, the deceased is pictured as a fourth personage behind three such identical ambassadors, almost as if they are one, supplicating for another. This is the solution (if it can be called that) that was adopted by the Welf Otto IV. But a fourth magus of this type was scarcely in keeping with the assertive sovereignty Otto would have wished for himself. Only the dead could be satisfied with this solution.

A quite different solution to this problem of representing sovereignty in magian format was found in the West, one that allowed the reigning monarch to represent himself with all charisma. This was to represent himself as a royal who was the hereditary descendant of dead forebears. One possible solution was to picture the magi kings as three generations of one dynasty, thus converting an ecumenical image into a national or familial one. And this is what Nicholaus of Bari accomplished.

Adorations showing dynastic kin as the kings are well known in the sixteenth century among the Habsburg. But it is not generally recognized that this practice, employed as a literary device, distinguished one living from two dead magi at a much earlier point. We see it first in Apulia, in the age of the Hohenstaufen. In a laud addressed to Frederick II around 1235, Nicholaus of Bari referred to Frederick's grandfather Barbarossa and then to his father, Henry VI, both deceased. Beginning with Barbarossa the grandfather, each generation was ever more worthy than the last. "Your grandfather was great because he was Holy Roman Emperor;

13. *Shrine of the Three Kings*, detail

.Aduant tres magos colonie.

14. *Emperor Henry VII and His Wife Visit the Shrine of the Three Kings in Cologne*

your father was emperor and the King of Sicily; but the present one is the
greatest: he is Roman emperor, King of Sicily and King of Jerusalem. In
fact," Bari declares ecstatically, "these three emperors are just like the
Three Kings, who came with gifts to adore God and man, but it is this
one, the most adolescent of the three, over whom the child Jesus has
placed his happy hands and sacred little arms."[11]

The emphasis on the third and youngest magus will command our special attention later in this chapter. For now, let it be said only that Bari's
emphasis on the Hohenstaufen dynasty as a magian entity works politically by highlighting its one living sovereign. Already in the high Middle
Ages, therefore, two dead magi are imagined as legitimating a single living ruler.[12] It can be said that in this approach, the ruler is privileged over
the dynasty, the individual over the collectivity, the living one over the
dead many. Precisely such a discourse about the old and the young, and
the dead and the living, is in the background we need to understand
when we turn our attention later to this magical third king.

The years after the death of Frederick II witnessed two important turning points in the history of the magi as German political legitimators.
From now on, directly after he was crowned at Aachen, the burial site of
Charlemagne, the new king of the Romans journeyed to Cologne and
made his first German *adventus*, or triumphal entry, into that great city,
much as had the magi in their *adventus* in 1164.[13] That event was then
topped by another triumph of the archbishop of Cologne, which transpired in Aachen in 1274. In that year, the new German king Rudolf
Habsburg adopted Jesus' epiphany as the theme for his coronation, a custom that would last through the ages. To be reminded of the magi was,
of course, to be reminded of Cologne. In one fell swoop, the archbishops
of Cologne could boast an epiphanic or Colognese liturgy in Aachen, and
show that the kings crowned with this liturgy then had to travel to Cologne to touch the relics of the three kings.[14]

In the coronation *ordo* of Rudolf, which is extant, the king and queen
(if she is present) hear themselves compared to all those biblical heroes
now evoked before them, much as in a liturgical play. The appropriate
passages of Isaiah in the *lectio* indicates that the world is moving from
darkness to light, then in the gradual, Psalm 72 implicitly compares the
coronation to the arrival of those from Sheba with their gold and incense.
Presently the magi tell their basic story, partly in their own words. After
the alleluya, the new German king rises and, once having prostrated himself in the form of a cross, he swears to the archbishop to faithfully exe-
cute his office. All the aforesaid is then gone over with the king by the
archbishop in German, for the former, being "illiteratus et laicus," did
not know Latin.[15]

Later in the proceedings, the Gospel of Matthew regarding the magi was read aloud. This was followed by the offertory in which was read a phrase from Psalm 72: "The kings of Tharsis and the islands offer gifts, the kings of Arabia and Saba bring their gifts and all the kings of the earth adore him. All peoples serve him, alleluia!" In the immediate wake of these readings, the *ordo* reads, "Scepter in hand, our lord the king makes an offering, then the queen, then the lord princes: first the archbishop [electors] my lords of Mainz then Trier, followed by the other electors." In the following Secret, it is made clear that actual gold, frankincense, and myrrh are no longer offered,[16] but clearly we have here a duplication of the image of Justinian and Theodora as a couple offering their magian gifts to the infant.

The first visual representation of a German ruler visiting Cologne supplies what is failing in these words. Henry VII had just been crowned at Aachen in 1309 when, with every intention of traveling on to Rome for an imperial coronation, he made his *adventus* into Cologne and had himself recorded (fig. 14), as it were, with his queen visiting the shrine and touching the remains with the famous gold fork reserved for worthy tourists.[17] Nor was this all. Continuing his journey toward Rome, Henry, on his arrival in Milan, chose to be crowned king (*ad consecrandum regem*) of the Lombards on the "day of the kings," as was remarked by contemporaries.[18] Clearly, the feast of the Kings had by now become a favorite day, and their cities a favorite place, for the making of monarchs.

Further visual evidence allows us to demonstrate something much more important, namely, that the linkage between coronation and magi was not merely an accidental development in German medieval history. Royal coronations and the adoration of Jesus by the magi were thought of as two sides of the same coin. This double illumination (fig. 15) from a distinction of the canon law dealing precisely with coronations ("de iure nature et humane constitutionis") shows brilliantly that coronation and magi were in fact inherently linked in the latter's story. In this unified representation, the verso folio shows the establishment of the secular and ecclesiastical powers: a king, and a bishop are crowned on opposite sides of Jesus. On the opposite recto folio is a typical adoration of the magi. What lends the two illuminations their character is, of course, their juxtaposition. In the adoration, the magi crown Jesus, so to speak, while inversely Jesus crowns the kings (the first king is without a crown); in the illumination to the left, both church and state are crowned by the right kind of angels. In numerous adorations, the link between coronation and magi is right at hand.[19]

Rather than a clearly definable context in which German kings actually play magi in public cavalcades, at this point I have described the emer-

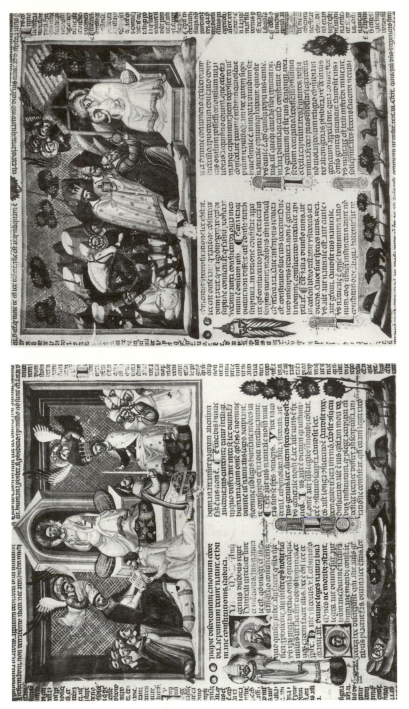

15. Left: *Coronations*. Right: *Adoration of the Magi*

gence of a magian structure surrounding the German coronations, with the ultimate outcome being a mandatory visit by king after newly crowned king from Aachen to Cologne. The cavalcades and the panoply are there, but not until a (since destroyed) painting of the emperor Sigismund (d. 1437) as one of the three magi is there evidence of a German king directly assuming the role of a magus. Still, our point has been made. A peculiar affinity made the theme of the magi, the central Christian heraldic icon, an important tool in stabilizing the image of the itinerant German monarchs. Nor was the phenomenon limited to Germany, for, in the wake of the stunning success contemporaries saw Cologne to have had with the bodies, several European principalities assumed, after Cologne, the three crowns of the magi into the coats of arms of their lands.[20]

It is to the kingdom of France that we turn our attention to witness the actual acting out of the magi drama by European royals. In a crucial assemblage in Paris in 1378, three monarchs, in order to cast their diplomatic activity into a legitimating frame, put themselves forward as magi on the last of the Twelve Nights.[21] There are faint echoes of a magian theatrical overlay in the earlier history of France. It is claimed, for instance, that Philip the Fair either at the time of his coronation in Reims (late October 1285) or, as seems more likely, on the upcoming day of the kings, 1286, heard a sermon delivered by his teacher, the Augustinian Giles of Rome, that laid out Philip's royal duties from the standpoint of the magi's good behavior. Around Pentecost, 1313, Philip invited the king of England and the young king of Navarre to Paris so that these three kings could celebrate the knighting of Philip's three sons.[22] Finally and most suggestively, according to a contemporary chronicler, the kings of Spain, Navarre, and Portugal were present in Bordeaux at the birth of Richard II of England on 6 January 1367. Specifically called "magi," they brought the infant king gifts in the manner of those monarchs.[23] But even this notice is put in the shade by the events of early 1378.

On 4 January 1378, Charles V of France received into Paris the Holy Roman Emperor, Charles IV, and the latter's adolescent son Wenzel, now king of the Romans. The contemporary importance of this meeting is signaled by the fact that its description takes up twenty-six folios of the *Grandes Chroniques* and includes many miniatures illustrating the events.[24] We rely on these miniatures for a good deal of historical information, including, as luck would have it, the description of the ceremonies as if they in a sense repeated the journey and the adoration of the magi. The chronicler does not, early on, refer to the pending feast of the epiphany by name, but there is no possibility of looking at the image of the three royals encountering each other without immediately reacting, This is an image of the magi![25]

16. *Entry into Paris of King Charles V, Emperor Charles IV, and Wenzel, King of the Romans*

Soon enough, however, the presence of epiphanic imagery in the *Grandes Chroniques* becomes literally overt. Thus on the eve of Epiphany, the chronicler has the French king Charles V take young Wenzel—the latter's father was indisposed by gout—first to vespers in the Sainte-Chapelle and then, "it being the eve of the Kings," as the chronicler informs us, to a huge banquet in the Grand Palais. According to the official heralds' reports, no fewer than eight to ten thousand knights, foreign and domestic, were present to partake in what was one of the premier gastronomic events of any year.[26] Yet it was less the size of the events that moved writers to admiration. Christine de Pisan, for example, noted how many people had praised the king for "knowing how to put so many people into such an order that there was no pressing."[27] The king, in short, proved a masterful master of ceremonies. Here again, the magi story zeroes in on a key function of any royal—his or her ability to keep people in order.

Then came the feast of the kings itself, and the emperor decided to see the French royal relics, a tourist highlight in those days. The obliging Charles showed him his private cache, and then, at the beginning of mass, sent him not only the Matthew magi text for the day, but more holy water than Charles needed (appropriate for that day, which also celebrated the baptism of Jesus). The *Grandes Chroniques* continues, "And when the Offertory [of the mass] arrived, the king had had prepared three sets of offerings, of gold, of incense, and of myrrh, to offer up for himself and for the emperor, as he was accustomed to do."[28] King Charles then asked his imperial guest if he would not make an offering at all, and the emperor responded in the negative, he being so ill that he could not walk or genuflect, as was of course necessary to a magian adoration.[29]

On being urged by the emperor to proceed as was his host's custom, Charles V did so, and the chronicler described this offertory scene step by step. Three chamberlain/knights were present, each holding a gift in his own enameled, gold-plated cup. The first gave his gift of gold to the king, who upon genuflection then gave it to the archbishop of Reims (the primate of France, who crowned French monarchs). Now the second chamberlain gave his gift of incense to the first, who then passed it on to the king, etc. Then the third chamberlain/knight gave his myrrh to the second one, who passed it on to the first, who gave it to the king, who genuflected before the archbishop and then presented him with the myrrh.[30] That evening, a large group of dignitaries watched a play showing how Godfrey of Buillon had conquered Jerusalem.[31] Such was the course of Epiphany at the French royal court, 1378. As we shall soon see, Charles V also became the first French king to have himself shown as one of the magi in an apposite adoration.

It might seem an uncertain step indeed to turn at this point from the French royal capital of Paris to the bourgeois cities of northern Italy in pursuit of the political spectacle of the magi. Yet the move will prove justified. Diffferences there were. In the fashion-dictating French court, the doings of the dynastic family made news. The charisma of a man like Charles V, the *corpus Domini*, so to speak, radiated out to those around and beneath him when he played the magus. In the great merchant cities beyond the Alps, on the contrary, putting on a pageant like that of the magi to make a political statement remained a matter of mobilizing and reflecting the resources of a plurality of urban power centers. If in the north a royal like Charles V could repeat the activity of his "brother" kings from deep antiquity, the upwardly mobile burghers of southern climes, by playing at kings, could enrich their cities and make the world wonder at their ability to turn burgher tin into royal gold, frankincense, and myrrh. Before all else it was Milan, and then Florence, that would show the world still other faces of the story and the image of the three kings.

Ludovico Muratori first published the Dominican Galvano Fiamma's sensational report of a magi festival in Milan on Kings' Day, 1336, in the early eighteenth century. Unfortunately, students of Milanese history have not subsequently enriched this account with any significant contextual information, so we must describe the event pretty much as we have it in Fiamma.[32] The year 1336 saw the Visconti family nearing the peak of its power in what was nominally a commune composed of many patrician families. Beyond that, only one other important piece of background, admittedly central in character, remains to be put in place. While it is now clear to historians that for long after the relics of the magi were taken from Milan around 1164, the Milanese were unaware of the loss or of the relics' importance. By the end of the thirteenth century, the loss and its meaning are clear in the words of the Milanese patriot Bonvesin de la Riva, writing in 1288, "Oh shame! Oh Pain! . . . The bodies of the three Magi . . . were stolen from the city by the enemies of the church. . . . Ruin upon the citizens of this city who, despoiled of such a treasure, spend their time destroying each other rather than finding a way to cancel such a stain. . . ."[33] Naively but compellingly, Bonvesin equates internal strife with the absence of kings, and thus he introduces us to one potential function of magian theatre in northern Italy, the production of a type of legitimacy in its essentially republican cities.

The *festa dei magi* reported by Fiamma occurred within a half century of Bonvesin's lament. He leaves us in no doubt at the outset that this first Milanese outdoor celebration of the three kings was sponsored or at least supported by the Dominicans, whose crèche was the goal of the magi. Thus the event was an attempt to get people to attend the church of S. Eustorgio (Dominican since 1220), one that had by now itself become part of the magi legend and probably already had a brotherhood that fostered cult to the three kings.[34] However, that attempt reached a level of splendor unknown in previous European plays. With obvious pleasure, the author describes "three crowned kings on large horses, accompanied by pages." They were "dressed differently and with many beasts of burden, and had an enormous retinue."

The magi journey in open air. Following a golden star that went before them, they reached the Roman columns of S. Lorenzo, where they encountered a figural representation of Herod, along with seemingly "real" scribes and wise men.[35] In this case, then, the court of Herod was outside the church, probably in a monumental setting in the public square, where all might bewonder it. Herod's scribes answered the magi's ques-

tion where Christ had been born, upon which the kings were again underway to cover the "five miles" between Jerusalem and Bethlehem. Repeating his admiration for the size of the retinue and the number of load-
bearing animals, Fiamma pictured "these three kings crowned with gold
crowns, grasping the gold vases in their hands" that held the mandatory
magian gifts. Their trumpets sounded, and there came cages in front of
them that contained apes, baboons, and the most various types of animals, followed by an incredible mass of people. Arriving at the church of
S. Eustorgio, they quickly came to the crèche, which stood to the side of
the main altar.

Nor was this all. After the adoration the magi were seen to sleep, while
an angel appeared at their side to tell them "not to return by the neighborhood of S. Lorenzo, but rather by that of the Porta Romana," that is,
in Matthew's words, "to go home by another way." "There was such a
concourse of people, both of knights, ladies, and clerks: Nothing comparable had ever before been seen." For all that, it is not clear if the order
that the festival be repeated annually was ever carried out. Milanese historians have come up with no evidence of another magi spectacle being
performed in Milan.[36]

There can be no doubt that the overwhelming impression this festival
made on Fiamma was its exoticism. What could be more predictable than
that a magi spectacle, which presented wise men from the East, would
offer itself excellently in this regard, especially if it was performed in a
trading center like the Lombard capitol, overflowing with magian "gifts"?
In short, the magi cavalcade, as it began to unfold in Milan, was a type of
triumph that the rising merchant class offered to itself, legitimating itself.
Of necessity, such communes tended to be somber burgher things, where
burghers dressed down to avoid envy, as they do in the following rare
adoration from northern Europe. In a festive magian format they could
play aristocrats, developing quite another self-image. It began by recognizing that the things merchants acquired were equal in their exoticism to
the charisma of the aristocratic social group they emulated.

The logical conclusion of the merchant magi thrust in northern Italy
appeared not in Milan, which indeed was soon ruled by a duke, but rather
in the city of Florence, which could not bring itself to such "ennoble-
ment." From 1390 until about 1470, Florence witnessed a large number
of outdoor magi spectacles that carried the message of Tuscan opulence
throughout Europe. The confraternity responsible for the festival during
much of this time, that "of the magi," called only in half jest *la repubblica
de' magi*, was for the last two-thirds of the fifteenth century under the
control of the Medici family, the de facto rulers of the city, and indeed in
some still obscure fashion functioned as a substitute government. In
Florence, magian fancy became reality. As I have detailed elsewhere, the

17. *Adoration of the Magi*

city's established political geography came to be subverted, its neighborhoods instead divided up into magian "kingdoms" that were one type of
power base for Medicean family interests. Because this confraternity has
been admirably studied by Rab Hatfield, we may limit ourselves here to
those of its activities that are particularly illustrative of the magi's function
as a legitimating icon.[37]

The production costs of Florentine magi festivals were, almost from
the beginning, borne by the public for God, "the fame of the city, and for
the consolation and joy of all citizens."[38] These public festivals varied in
the form they took, however, since they were organized by the Confraternity of the Magi, which was partly private in nature. Every report we have

indicates that the court of Herod, which (unlike the churchy adoration) is uniformly in open air, has been moved from one location to another, so the relative importance of this king in relation to the adoration can be markedly different. In at least one report, Herod's troops ruthlessly mow down the innocents, played by "imaginary children," but other reports make no mention of the slaughter, which was one of the dramatic highlights of Herod's role. In the midst of this variability there was one constant. What was important to the chroniclers of these *feste* was in most cases the cavalcades and the sheer magnificence of the equestrian panoply. Thus on Epiphany, 1428, came "about seven hundred costumed men on horseback, among whom were the three magi and their retinue, honorably dressed."[39] And again on the city's great patriotic feast of San Giovanni, 1454, the magi took their part in a complete telling of the Bible "with a cavalcade of more than two hundred horses decked out with great magnificence."[40]

In time the magi festivals in Florence actualized the story that the magi had come together from disparate kingdoms, relating these kingdoms to the city's own political and social geography. Most interesting in this regard is Giovanni Caroli's description of a 1468 magi spectacle in which the festive city, just like the political city, was divided into four parts, three of which housed the tents of the magi, the fourth, the palace of Herod. "It is incredible," Caroli writes, "to tell how each contended in the elaboration of its king, lest one part should outdo another in richness and magnificence."[41]

This note of intraurban competition had a long history in central and northern Italy. In a description of a magi festival held in Parma in 1414, for example, one magus with his retinue "came from San Sepolcro, another from San Uderigo, and the third from San Gervasio," each king wearing his proper coat of arms.[42] Much before then, however, it had been customary in these towns to have regular parochial battles on Sundays and feast days between the feast of the kings and the first Sunday in Lent.[43] The competition that Caroli praises may have been the product of the growing political centralization characteristic of the fifteenth century, not of the civil pluralism of the late Middle Ages. The masters of ceremonies, or *festaioli*, of these celebrations and the audiences saw magi pluralism as a gloss on the city's own pluralism. The magi festival mirrored the successful construction of a polity out of its several different parts, just as the magi, coming from different cultures, nonetheless managed to make themselves understood to each other and, united, to make their adoration in a comprehensive fashion before the infant.

From a fanciful letter written in 1471 and published by Hatfield, it is clear that the Company of the Magi effectively controlled spectacles in the city. For instance, it supervised a joust that the confraternity of S. Bartolommeo was about to perform in the Piazza Santa Croce. Further, it is evident that a large number of neighborhood festive companies, with evocative names like "Armenia," the two "Indias," the "Red City," etc., in short with geographical names from the East, were under the control of the brotherhood of the magi. The city's neighborhoods had taken on the identity of such distant realms, if only for the purposes of festive planning.[44]

Another characteristic of the Florentine magi spectacles was that the government was involved in the play. As early as 1429, the law required it to make an offering at the church of S. Marco on the Epiphany, and it carried out this duty by actually accompanying Mary and the infant to San Marco as the latter prepared to receive the magi.[45] In the process, many of the leading citizens of Florence joined in, playing different parts, and in the middle third of the century, that included the de facto lord of Florence, Cosimo de' Medici.[46] Thus the government of Florence, like the confraternity itself, played the magi journeying to and adoring the infant.

This "counterfeiting" of the real city in the festive recreation of the Epiphany reached its pinnacle in the spectacle of 1468. First, we learn that in that *festa*, the young members of the Confraternity of the Magi had created such convincing masks of their fathers and had learned the latters' gestures so perfectly that, in launching the parade to the palace of Herod (the journey), they actually seemed to be their fathers joining the parade.[47] Second, the play so departed from normal convention that its real focus was not the kings but their legates or youthful messengers. In a profound sense, this spectacle was about adolescents learning how to behave in the public sphere, where many of them would indeed perform in actual embassy. Once again, this single heraldic iconograph in the Christian tradition proved its merit for a Christian society.

THE EXOTIC MAGUS

We have completed a survey of the main employments of the magi at the high political level of late medieval public representations. I have omitted mention of many of the important Epiphany and magi celebrations of this time, since from the beginning my aim has been to drive home the obvious political lesson of legitimation. The royals of Europe, and their bourgeois emulators, had cast themselves as magi—or as one particular magus. They seemed to derive their authority by reenacting the biblical event that featured those they emulated. They participated in great outdoor cavalcades in the guise of the journey of the magi to that legitimating end. In the process they positioned themselves as outdoor authorities over and against the clergy who, jealously guarding the execution of the adoration inside churches, were their natural competitors.

It is clear that the political classes were not the only ones to learn to use the magi for festive and representational ends, nor was public space the only space in which that development took place. Not only were the banquets of 5 and 6 January ever more substantial in the late Middle Ages, the election of temporary kings—and at time queens—was ever more popular. Extortions and beggings to the end of raising the wherewithall for these celebrations were quite as exuberant in this time. Finally, new customs appeared.

In chapter 5, we shall examine such customs more closely. For now, however, it is more important to address a fundamental question about high and late medieval magian imagery that has not yet been confronted, What exactly did this age see as it watched the magi? Did people see merely the one, indistinguishable image of the magi, just one more legitimating image drawn from the grab bag of Christian history? Of course not. We have already seen clerical boys playing secular monarchs in liturgical dramas, and we have demonstrated that secular monarchs picked not just any magus to imitate, but played the third king, or even a fourth. Clearly, those who watched the magi in parade and adoration saw not just one image, but a plural number of monarchs reflecting in some guise the plurality of their own existence. What then does a study of the picture archive of the magi in this age reveal about the figures who came together to worship the child?

We may arrive at a better understanding of the problem by immediately problematizing these several magian images, as we did earlier, for example, in discovering a fourth magus. It must appear puzzling to all but the incurable patriarch that while the story of the magi has always been advanced as a statement of all humankind's devotion to the Christian God and church, the image and cult of the magi has always been purely masculine in character, so that it is men alone who legitimate the infant, not women. Our normal understanding of the magi is one of mature, solemn, and reverent (not to say dull) men hoary with wisdom. Indeed, in the Middle Ages that particular gentilic piety assumed a dramatic form that was played out against the character of the violent and irreverent, curiously subversive Herod. Yet who actually performed these magian roles in the liturgical dramas? None other than young adolescents, the least reverent and sexually mature of possible male actors, who could only solve these disabilities by donning fake beards.

There seems, in short, to be a significant hole at the center of the cult of the magi. Though the magi formed an assertedly ecumenical image, no part of the female majority of the population, and no part of the male youth in that population, seems at first blush to have contributed to the legitimation of the infant in the image of the magi. These two groups formed the majoritarian outsiders in any polity, yet who could imagine that only the minoritarian adult male population represented the totality of the infant's worshipers? Especially since the very outside status of the magi had made their legitimation of Jesus so important! The magi thus risked becoming a tired image of solemnity somehow legitimating a spanking bright God.

However, a close examination of the art works showing the magi in the high and late Middle Ages, directed precisely at recognizing these quanta of gender and age in the image, will show how much more interesting the magi are among themselves than the solemn, tired men we might expect. Certainly the preachers of this age would have us see the magi as one body: exemplary orants at constant prayer for us in paintings. Yet I will show that the actual figures of the magi are often in uneasy, certainly unexpected, relations to each other.

Recall that in the early centuries, in the period when the three magi were not yet kings, they all looked like legates of one king. Christians who could afford it had themselves represented on their sarcophaguses in the same spaces, when not immediately behind, the three identical magi. Almost from the beginning of Christian art, this "fourth magus" shows that there was a dualism at work in the theme of magi art. In the case of the Hohenstaufen, for instance, we found Nicholaus of Bari imagining Frederick II as the living magus, the latter's father and grandfather as dead maguses. This literary image of the living versus the dead magi was not without visual echoes. Long before Bari, the tenth-century Codex Egberti presents the three kings in heaven looking down on three earthly kings at adoration.[48] An early sixteenth-century Cracow gravestone shows an adoration of three princes, without gifts, in which the third figure is a skeleton.[49] Finally, and most directly to the point of Bari's etiquette, an engraving from a 1652 royal almanac shows the French monarch Louis XIV preparing himself for his coronation. In a cloud above him, one sees Louis IX, Henry IV, and Louis XIII, grouped like the three magi, associating themselves to the charismatic young ruler.[50]

One might wryly suggest that this contrast between living and dead magi in itself explains one of the most easily observable facts about the magi in art, which is that the first two kings often seem no more than uninteresting stock figures, whereas the third king repeatedly sparkles with life. Yet this will not do as an explanation of such dualism. In the following pages, I will focus attention more carefully first on age—the polarization between old and young age that was almost the rule in West-

ern magi art—and secondly on gender—the polarization the careful
viewer will find between masculinity and effeminacy, or even femininity,
in high and late medieval magi art. Often, even though three kings are
always represented in medieval art, we are meant to see, to recall, and to
experience only two persons or groups. And one of the two is not always
just male.

The Young Magus

The emergence of magi images that show a dichotomy between life and
death can be seen as one expression of a larger bifurcation between inside
and outside, or the conventional and the exotic. The essence of the magi
story was that they came from the outside, exotic East to legitimate the
Western king, Jesus. Matthew recognized that without such magian
strangeness, Jesus himself would have no clout.

Yet an essence of any *cult* is that its offerants are domesticated. That is,
no matter that the charismatics come from far away: If the culture into
which they enter is to control its own fate, they must be seen to worship
designated divinities at certain times and in specific places with recognizable and unchanging gestures.[51] To be effective, outside charismatics
must over time come to speak the language of the inside.

Like any saints, the magi offerants became insiders—Imitate the Magi!
said Ambrose—and yet a certain outside character had to be maintained.
This was done by subdividing the three magi between such opposite de-
siderata, using age, color, and gender to represent this polarity. In each of
these areas, as well as through certain formal qualities, the third king becomes an exotic figure in some way unrepresentative of the establishment
that is offering to the child, while the two previous kings represent the
established inside authority.

We have seen that in the established canon, a "fourth magus" might
stand apart from the evangelical magi in early Christian art and even in
the art of the later twelfth century. But in the growing articulation among
the three kings themselves that proceeded apace in the central Middle
Ages, a definite if by no means universal polarity grew up. That is, the
identical three magi of early Christian art were replaced not by three distinct and recognizable physical types, but only by a polarity of two. The
adoration in the Echternach Gospel (fig. 18) about 1050 illustrates the
polarity, showing two identical older kings and one young one. In scores
of other paintings of the high and late Middle Ages, the picture may not
be quite so stark. An artist introduces a beard on the first king that is
longer than the beard on the second king; perhaps the hat of the oldest
king is different from that of the middle king, and the like. But more

18. *Adoration of the Magi*

generally, the rule is that only two physiognomies are shown in many paintings. There are in effect two, not three, magi types in scores of magi paintings and sculptures.[52]

We sometimes remark this separation between the "two magi" through the simple distancing of one magus type from the other. In the rare case, the second and third kings combine together at a distance from the prostrate first king; indeed, as in a Visconti adoration (fig. 19), they may share a common age and physiognomy.[53] But more commonly, the first two kings stand or kneel close together; the third stands apart from the other two, indeed at times as if he is observing a ritual that only the first and second perform. A good example of this spacing is the illumination (fig. 20) in which the third king—Charles V of France, no less— looks over the shoulders of the first two kings to catch the action.[54] This dualism of magian figures might be thought to spring from simple artistic lethargy, but more often it is the result of an artist's or patron's determination to emphasize the person of only one king, usually the third one. In the high and late Middle Ages and Renaissance, in scores of paintings and

19. *Adoration of the Magi* (Visconti Hours)

in sculpture, it is this youthful and alert prince who is made to stand apart, and he becomes the true visual crown of the work to the neglect of the other two. The sculpted third king on the tympanon of the Liebfrauen church in Frankfurt am Main (fig. 21) could not more clearly manifest this phenomenon.

What can explain such prominence? According to Matthew and his commentators, of course, this third king at best represents just one-third of the cosmos before the infant, while the other two monarchs, whom we locate at Frankfurt after somewhat more effort, represent the other two-thirds. Obviously, this does not get us far because this sculptor clearly meant to establish a forceful contrast between the brilliant, unbearded young king in the center and the two bearded kings to the side, the latter sharing a common physiognomy and differing from each other only in the length of their facial hair. The picture is much the same across Europe, including Italy. There the youthful third king is commonly blond, though blond hair is and was rare in Italy; that of the other two kings is usually somber in tone. The third king often wears rakishly short or tight

21. *Adoration of the Magi*

20. *Adoration of the Magi*

22. Gentile da Fabriano, *Adoration of the Magi*

clothes, the first and second kings usually wear knee- or ankle-length cloaks. He wears Asiatic or other exotic clothing; they do not, and so forth. The exotic young king is, indeed, nowhere more prominent than in fifteenth-century Italian painting. One thinks of the sterling prince in the Strozzi altarpiece of Gentile da Fabriano, but the examples could be multiplied at will, both in Italy and in the rest of Europe. With all due room for exceptions, one may assert that the third king was exploding into prominence in the arts, ever more brilliant over and against the often lifeless features of the first and second kings. Thus the primary phenomenon I draw attention to is the unmistakable tendency to polarize the representation of the magi into two. The secondary phenomenon is the way the age of youth was increasingly used to mark that polarity as apart from the mature or old age of the other kings.

Where, we may ask, was this unmistakable visual impulse coming from? My most precise answer is that a little-attended detail about the age of the kings, contained in certain liturgical dramas from the first half of the fifteenth century, almost certainly helped inspire, or at least historically accompanied, this visual polarization of the evangelical royals. First, some background. In a tradition of Armenian infancy texts that reaches back to the eighth century, each of the magi is said to have seen Jesus in a form appropriate to his individual gift. In Marco Polo's late thirteenth-century report, each magus' vision of Jesus depended specifically on his age.[55] In short, the principal of varied generational experience had long been established. The three magi saw the God that matched their own identities.

Second, the reader should know that in a number of liturgical dramas, and in plays in the living languages, there came a moment just before the adoration when the three royals discussed who should go first. This belongs to the pedagogic element in these plays that I have emphasized so much, the youthful audience being instructed in this way that because of his youth, their king was to go last. And so he did.[56]

However, in the German play from Erlau (near Passau) dated to the first half of the fifteenth century, an important innovation was made, which King has excellently studied. In this play, performed as always by young clerks, the young king first expresses the wish to have the privilege of adoring first, and then follows this up by simply asking the oldest king for his age. The young king wants to be first, but he wants to look the part of the eldest. The older king goes along. He removes his beard and puts it on the third king, who then goes first, while the erstwhile oldest king, now the youngest because devoid of his mask, goes last. As King notes, this is not just a gag. Something serious is happening, as attested by the fact that variants of the story pop up in several other places. Thus in a coeval German kings story from Bressanone (Tyrol), the young king is so anxious to be first that God brings it about that he in fact goes first; there is no mention of transvestism or transformation.[57] In another fifteenth-century play, this one from Eger near Budapest, the young king acknowledges that he must go last because of his age, but wishes earnestly "that I was old" so that it could be otherwise.[58] Finally, King discovered that in Cologne itself in the early sixteenth century, the young king burned with such zeal to be first that the infant Jesus again made this king too into a bearded senior.[59]

While King successfully demonstrates that this motif had a large regional extension, he did not realize just how far. It extended into northern Italy, where it became firmly rooted in the general imagination. Here, the theme emerged first in a vision which the Milanese Veronica di Binasco (fl. 1490s) had of the three kings in the midst of their adoration; as previously indicated, it was common for visionaries to expand the general knowledge about the magi through such experiences. To grasp the import of this vision fully, note that in the whole of the previous Erlau tradition, an implicit dualism rather than triadic thought was at work. While the authors all assume that there were three kings, not one of them conceives of more than two ages, that of the old king and that of the young one. Writing in the early sixteenth century (not long after the German texts), Veronica's spiritual director marvelously refashioned the Erlau story in such a way as to conceive not three, but two kings!

According to what Veronica envisioned, on approaching the infant the three magi began to argue over who would adore the child first. In the end, she says, the youngest of the three approached and kissed the infant's feet first; "the others," the text continues, "did the same," though she does not say in what order.[60] Veronica then notes "that the youngest king, who had done his adoration first, was seen, amazingly,"—and here note the wording—"to have turned older and to have become of one age with the other two."[61] A moment's reflection reveals that in this formulation (a mental slip?), the writer at best conceived of the two older kings as of identical ages, a notion with no canonical weight whatsoever. From the author's point of view, the axis of the whole story was the polar difference between "age" and "youth."[62]

This bit of biographical information about the three kings was not limited to dramaturges, but had spread among the general populace, according to the mid-sixteenth century Italian art critic Gilio. He urged painters to paint things as they really were. They should not make someone old who is young, nor one who is young old, "as the common people say of the first King-Magus. He went to offer gold, myrrh, and incense to our lord. Being young, he did not want to give way to an elder who was to offer ahead of him, and so he became miraculously old, and the elder young."[63]

There can be no doubt that this tradition of written evidence strikingly confirms our visual observation that many magi groups in art are dualistic in character, not triadic. Many contemporaries were operatively conscious of young and of old magi, but not of more human types. What are we to make of this dramatic and visual tradition? In my view, no reading of this visual and conscious phenomenon can ignore the fact that in normal social life, male generations did indeed compete with each other in this age. Hoary and hellish males came apart in matters of mutual reverence. And so do they reflect comparable tensions in drama and art. The two groups of magi do indeed come apart at the moment of adoration. As in normal social life where generations of males concerned about authority and inheritance competed with each other in this age, so did they in drama and art reflect a comparable tension.[64]

Such a competition can easily be imagined among the clergy who wrote these stories and the young townsmen and clerks who acted them out. Let us recognize that the adolescent and youth groups who ruled towns and villages for many a holiday, and who must often have played Herod and his court in that king's face-off against the magi and infant God, sometimes manifested an antagonism to their fathers' established order, which they mocked in Yuletide.[65] The situation cannot have been much different for the clerks who played in the court of the magi, for they too, we have suggested, came from the same social group of those wanting some education without full commitment to the clerical estate. Those who acted the kings were commonly young. Such youth might indeed resist the constant paternalistic hammering away at the duty of the young to be submissive. Were the Twelve Nights not essentially a time of inversion in which the young might indeed "miraculously rule" the old? At this point it is worth repeating that the subversion lay at the root of the story. Jesus no more legitimated kings than kings legitimated the church.

The Black Magus

The most obvious of the dichotomies in late medieval and early modern magi representations involved color. Blacks began to appear among the magi in the late Middle Ages. From the mid-thirteenth century, an occasional black servant can be found in a journey or adoration, ministering to a white king. But not until the 1360s, and then in earnest only from about 1440 onward, does the black king become common in European art.[66] The German-speaking areas of Europe led the way in this innovation. Stated programatically, it was in central Europe that color first began to replace or at least overlay age as the exotic characteristic that set the third king off from the first two.[67]

Significantly, Italy—the land of blond third kings—was the most conservative area in this regard. Though its artists painted magi with strong Asian characteristics from the early fifteenth century onward, they clearly resisted accepting the new northern custom of black kings for most of the fifteenth century.[68] In the unusual case that they did portray a black king, they were chary to surrender their exotic third white king, with the result that in those few cases they tended to place a black king alongside a young white king as a couplet of a type, thus confirming the primacy of exoticism for artists and patrons while indeed showing three distinct persons.

The presence of a black among the three kings remains a standard iconologic type to this day. So explosive was the new style that, as Kaplan has shown, perhaps in a dozen cases, painters went back and retouched one white king after another to be sure that one of the trio was black, often leaving the legs or hands of the same kings a telltale white.[69] What could have been the cause of this mania? One possible explanation can be ruled out from the beginning. It had nothing to do with biblical exegesis. For centuries theologians had been saying that one of the kings was black, without bringing about any change in iconography.[70] An inherently more probable explanation is the increasing exposure of Europeans to blacks. Around 1440, when black kings were becoming de rigeur in German art, was precisely when the first African slaves could be bought

23. Cosimo Tura, *Adoration of the Magi*

on the market in Lisbon. For the first time, a hint of ecumenicalism in the
representation of world royalty was being introduced in the visual, not
just in the literary, arts.

This is not the place to discuss the reasons for this transformation, and
yet the story of Prester John must be mentioned in this context. From the
time of his first appearance in the mid-twelfth century, Prester or Priest
John was said to be a descendant of the three kings. In the course of the
early fourteenth century, the putative homeland of the Prester slowly mi-
grated from the East to the upper Nile or Ethiopia, and he became
black.[71] This is roughly the point when black kings began to appear in
Western art. That is not to say that the black king was a figure of Prester
John. To the contrary, after 1360, when so many European royals had
themselves represented as magi, one will look in vain for an actual black
ruler, including the famous Mansa Musa of Mali, who figures as one of
the three kings.[72] Indeed, the black king may appear in art without a
crown or its equivalent to a disproportionate degree.

What Prester John did provide was the all-important principal that
monarchs could be black, an assumption that facilitated the representation of blacks as kings. The fictive monarch Prester John himself only
possessed a limited representative character. He appeared on a few maps

and manuscript illuminations and that is all. But everyone knew of him. More important, especially in the fifteenth century, his presence was felt in the Ethiopian embassies that began to appear in the Mediterranean; these ambassadors were happy to use the notion that their monarch was called "Prester John." All this accustomed Europeans to the notion of black monarchical sovereignty.

The stark contrast between this third king and the two often prosaic white kings was inevitable, for the first and second kings—let it be clearly said—always remain white, even when one of the two is outfitted with a turban to identify him as a Near Easterner, allowance even being made for those rare cases in which the middle king was black. Are we to conclude from this that color, still more fundamentally than youth, transmitted the sense of exoticism, of the outside, that is so evidently the goal of many artists?

With some important exceptions, I doubt it. The first and most obvious exception is earrings, the one particular object of clothing that was exclusive to the black kings, and to their black servants.[73] The Western prejudice against men who wore earrings was ancient. At least as far back as the Satyricon, Romans associated pierced ears with the "Arabians," and in the Middle Ages, one may find mosaics of men wearing earrings burning in the Christian hell.[74] It is not surprising that despite an extensive search, I could not find a single white king or magi servant sporting earrings, not even in the seventeenth century, when earrings were occasionally worn by white males in other pictorial settings.[75] But their exclusive presence on black kings in most magi representations does definitely confirm my thesis. Earrings may be said to show that their bearer came from outside Europe, but that carries us only so far. More fundamentally, in these paintings the third king is often the exotic pole of a *dualistic* representation of a nominal *trilogy* of magi.

As part of a total sumptuary assertion, the earrings make a brilliant statement for their wearer, distinguishing him from his fellows. This brings us to a second possible distinguishing feature of black kings— dress. In general, I believe that the astonishing opulence of their dress unites black and white third kings. Indeed we can often blink and substitute a black for a white youth, or vice versa, each of comparable opulence,[76] and students of dress usually focus on the third magus, whether he be white or a person of color, for the information they seek regarding festive dress.[77]

It is my impression that an occasional black king does outdo himself in this respect. Certainly many a first and second king is elaborately dressed, and I am not suggesting that the black figure is the commanding one in all cases where he is present. I only submit that of the three, he is more likely to be exotically gotten up—"gaudy" is Kaplan's word—and on oc-

24. *Adoration of the Antichrist*

casion even wearing clothes no white magus ever wore. As we shall see, the black king can also behave in a striking fashion.[78]

The third area in which possible distinctions are to be made is the actions of that third, black, magus. Let us accept that the rakishness that is common to the fine young white man and the black king is of primary importance, but also then notice the narcissistic assertiveness that is somewhat more pronounced among black than among white third kings. This narcissism is hardly a quality we would expect from a king about to adore the maker of the world. There is some reason to suspect that in some cases the artists present us not with a devotee at all, but with a "darker" force altogether.

In one tradition dating back to ancient Syria, the magi were thought of as magicians whose fealty to Jesus amounted to a recognition that magic had been conquered by religion.[79] But in the Middle Ages, as the church

25. *Adoration of the Magi*, detail

was forced to deal with "heretics" who for all the world looked like orthodox Christians at prayer, more ambiguous "adorations" came to the
fore. One early fifteenth-century tapestry, for instance, shows three wild
men and moors adoring a wild woman and child in the best magi fashion.[80] Another features what appear to be magi worshiping not God, but
the Antichrist.

With such examples at hand, we should think twice about the inherent
well-meaningfulness of each of the kings. The adoration of the magi was
at times imagined as the civilized opposite to a state of nature, in which
wild men and animals worshiped disorder. Why should that same bifurcation between solemnity and raucousness, between piety and narcissism,
not be found *among* the magi themselves? Perhaps it can be.

So marked is the opulence and sensuality of these third kings that one
is tempted at times to imagine that there is cultural criticism here: of
lecherous youth, and of their devilish temptations! It seems to me that
at times the third king represents not the conversion of the young or of
the black to goodness, but the abiding evil of being young or black. Take
the magnificent black king in the so-called Bob Jones University adoration (fig. 25). Here is a totally self-sufficient third king who mounts his
own separate stand to advertise himself. The other kings—all clones the
one of the other—want to draw the attention of the devotees to the child,
but this third king, conscious that all eyes are upon him, looks off into the
distance rather than upon the infant, as if totally absorbed by his own
beauty. This adoration, one of the most remarkable adorations of the
Antwerp mannerists of the mid-sixteenth century, brings to the edge
of the stage, so to speak, all those qualities that we have been emphasizing. Commonly, it is the third king who invites the audience into his
charmed circle, and yet, at times, his very liveliness and earthiness can
stun the viewer's senses. James Snyder characterizes a white third king of
this type in a similar fashion, saying that he "sways foppishly like some
carnival barker unveiling his show to an audience."[81] While such seductive figures can be most appealing for moderns, they, and others of the
same stamp, may be a type of denunciation that artists made of these
magi's damnable excess.[82]

The Feminine Magus

Beyond the polarities of life and death, youth and age, white and black,
we come finally to gender. It has been on the margins of much that has
already been said. "In fashion," says Roland Barthes, "both sexes tend to
become uniform under a single sign . . . , that of youth."[83] The purpose
of the following pages is to suggest that, with all due allowance made for
the difficulty of evaluating an age's gender construction, on a gender line

among biological males running from those who would have been identified as "very male" by contemporaries, to those who would have been
defined as "effeminate" by those same contemporaries, some third kings
lean strongly toward effeminacy.

This is not to argue that those third kings were women; with one possible exception, they always remain men. That some third kings were
characterized as being "like a woman" (effeminate) is interesting because,
as has already been noted, the story and image of the magi seem on the
surface to be the exclusively parthenogenetic sacred story par excellence,
in which men, and men alone, give birth to and legitimate the Christian
community before God, or rather, legitimate the infant himself. The existence of this gender line, therefore, can refine this seeming anomaly.

We are steering into the wind of historiographic indifference, to be
sure. For almost the whole two thousand years of Christianity, for instance, no one gave careful attention to the question of whether the magi
were married. In the fourteenth century in his influential *liber trium
regum*, Johannes of Hildesheim proclaimed that these monarchs, whom
he wants us to believe were virgins, indeed never married.[84] True, the
so-called German Passional printed in 1471 says that the third king was
married, in fact that his wife gave birth at the same time as did Mary.[85] In
the twentieth century the German visionary Theres Neumann saw that
wife in a vision.[86] But in general, it is still the case that few have showed
interest in magian sexuality.

More modern notions of gender in the study of devotion put much of
this ancient obfuscation in doubt. Thus Jean Wirth has shown that in
several paintings of the holy family, Anne, the mother of Mary, is a witch-
like woman, the type of woman who challenges male access to supernatural powers.[87] For her part, Caroline Bynum demonstrates that medieval
peoples at times conceived of the crucified Jesus, and of medieval monks,
as women.[88] Perhaps most significant in its implications for our work,
Wendy Doniger has shown that at least in certain Hindu mythologies and
practices, praying to the gods required a heterosexual asymmetry between the object and subject of prayer, with "women" always praying to
a "man," and vice versa, even if that required one of them to change
sex.[89] Clearly, in the light of such recent work, a careful look at the magi
is called for.

Let us examine what role women actually do play in artistic adorations,
beginning, obviously, with Mary. As is intimated by Leo Steinberg, Mary
plays no substantial narrative role in painted adorations of the magi, except as a type of sacred canopy.[90] Her pictorial role is much more sub-
dued than her role in dramas, where we have seen her accept the gifts
for her son, or in the Eastern tradition, actually give the magi gifts in
return. Steinberg finds the kings concerned with inspecting the genitalia

of Jesus to satisfy themselves that he is "human." But the kings are obviously looking to be sure Jesus is a male, an inspection that Mary sometimes furthers by making those genitalia more visible.[91] Still today, parents around the globe celebrate the birth of a male child after just such examinations.

If Mary plays no significant story role in these paintings, there is one group of paintings in which other women are interesting. These are ones in which the male magi are symetrically balanced by a group of females. Perhaps the most striking representation of this general type is an early sculpture at Oberpleis that shows opposite the magi three quite feminine-appearing . . . angels.[92] Yet in an occasional painting after all, as in the adoration in the *Très Riches Heures* of Jean de Berri, one finds Mary and the infant joined with midwives in such a way as to suggest that the female world greets the male world of the magi.[93]

There is a second small group of magi-like paintings, similar to those of the *Heilige Sippe*, or extended holy family, that feature what we may think of as female magi. They were probably made most often for nunneries. The most noteworthy painting of this type is in the Ortenberg Triptych produced for a nunnery. In its right wing is an adoration of the magi; in its left, a nativity scene. In the large middle panel a number of women saints, among whom three crowned queens, gather around, or worship, Mary and child. There can be little doubt that the artist and patron meant to say that the adoration of the magi showed males submitting to Jesus, but that women also did so in their own way.[94]

Where then did such inspirations for female magi come from? To the extent that biblical exegesis has anything to do with explaining such matters, the answer might point to the historical visit of the queen of Sheba to Solomon, which we have seen to be an Old Testamental type or prefiguration of the visit of the magi to Jesus. But André Chastel cut closer to the truth. Recognizing that this image did, after all, show a woman doing obeisance to a man, he demonstrated that the Solomon/Sheba image was meant indeed to contrast maleness with femaleness, reason with passion, nurture with nature, etc., to the extent that in some traditions the queen in Solomon's presence is shown with animal-like characteristics like hairy hooves.[95] My contribution to that insight is to show that the story of the magi as well was meant to project such binary, not triadic, oppositions, this time from within the seeming unity of three kings.

I would take that argument one step further. It is certainly true that in the long list of fundamental human polarities the story of the magi does speak to—poverty against riches, power against powerlessness, age against infancy (all polarities between the kings and infant), as well as youth against senility and white against dark (both internal polarities)—the gender dichotomy male/female did play a limited direct role. Look-

26. *The Ortenberg Altar*

ing more closely, we may perceive *in some of the qualities of the third king* traits that contemporaries identified with effeminacy or femininity. So marked are these qualities that, in working on this subject, I came to expect, sooner or later, to encounter an actual woman as third "king."

By "female" or "effeminate qualities" I mean nothing more than what contemporaries labeled as such. It did not necessarily imply homosexual behavior, as such terms do today. "Effeminacy" referred to a body of fluid gestures, as well as ones that were rapid or gauche or exotic in any way, or particularly delicate or dancelike. In the medieval view, "effeminacy," commonly associated with male adolescents rather than with mature adults, included enthusiasm of any kind.[96] And "effeminacy" began then, as it does today, with the male wearing what are identified as female accoutrements.

Thus we have discovered that, differing from their fellow monarchs, black kings commonly wore earrings. This made them "like women" in the contemporary view. Diane Owen Hughes has written a learned article on earrings in European art, limited entirely to those worn by women. She found that contemporary artists used earrings as identifying tags for female prostitutes, Jewish, and upper-class Christian *women*. Not a word about earrings as objects of male apparel, suggesting that they belonged to women alone.[97] If she had considered the innumerable black magi with earrings in her discussion, she would have seen that a factor she did not mention—exoticism—was quite as fundamental a signifier as any other, and she could have linked foreignness or outsider status to femininity or effeminacy.

The range of "effeminate" dress among third white kings could be extended by stressing, as did contemporary moralists, the number of young royals who wore formfitting tights.[98] But let us move instead to the world of gesture and bearing. As we have seen, the Bob Jones adoration features a king who, far from preparing to adore Jesus, is actually "strutting his stuff" for spectators, a type of behavioral narcissism (male) contemporaries identified with youth and with women. Both characterological and physical bearings of females are often encountered, as in an almost dancing magus-knight by Vasco Fernandes (fig. 27).

Whereas I am confident of the above categories, there is reason to be more circumspect in identifying maguses who, like so many Sir Women, appear all but female in their physiognomy. I am thinking of the third king sporting braided hair in an adoration of Filippo Lippi, who is backed up by a series of feminine figures as well; of the delicate third king who hangs back in an adoration of Lorenzo di Monaco, wearing a bodice that is bound up beneath his breasts;[99] and of the effeminate black third king in an adoration by Joos van Ghent, who faces toward the viewer to take his gift from his servant. Finally I have in mind the marvelous third king

27. Vasco Fernandes, *Adoration of the Magi*

28. Filippo Lippi, *Adoration of the Magi* (the "Cook Tondo")

of Sodoma, whose face seems to quote a female figure of Leonardo da Vinci. The reason for my caution in this regard is due to the tendency of the lords of style themselves to move their images of young men in time back and forth on this gender scale, itself a political activity. This is another way of saying that in their dress and representations, young males have historically been shown as more, then less, dependent on the society of their fathers, the absolute and unchanging pole of that dependence being represented by women. In early modern Europe, the trend was toward a greater manifestation of such dependence. Thus the presence of so many effeminate third kings is particularly important because such young men were being slowly weaned by proto-absolutistic kings of their ancient conviction that violence was the sum and summation of their status. In this "civilizing" crusade, picturing the young man as a powdery effeminate was one chosen method to acculturate him.

Such thoughts had long been on my mind. I had the visual documentation of the magi before me, and I was aware both of the sexual delicacy of the so-called international style around 1400, and of the starkly feminine body conventions that for instance, the Nancy artist Jacques Bellanges (d. ca. 1617) gave to his drawings of the apostles.[100] There can be no doubt that in the fifteenth and sixteenth century, there is a profound turn toward showing male subjects or dependents "like women." So there was a larger stylistic context for my search as well, and for some time I had expected to find an actual female magus somewhere in the visual archive of third maguses. That expectation has been approached, at least, through the alertness of two colleagues.

In the Westphalian town of Soest, the Germanist Kurt Wölfel found the following anonymous adoration of the magi and brought it to my attention, recognizing its significance for my theme. It is the left panel of an altar retable showing the dormition of the virgin on the right, and the crucifixion in the main panel (fig. 31). Dated to about 1420, this painting's claim to our interest is not the first two almost identical kings who, kneel before the infant, the one kissing the latter's foot, the other his hand. Rather, we are drawn to the person of the third king, who stands to Mary's left and puts forward a gift with his right hand. The king wears tights, visible up to the crotch, and a blouse reaching down to his hips of the same golden color as the mantels worn by the two older kings. Over this blouse he wears a cape open at the sides. He is clearly a male.

The king's attire above the neckline is, however, unusual indeed. First, for unknown reasons his face appears smudged—almost like those of some white kings whose skins were later painted brown. Second, and most striking, this king is wearing a veil that covers his hair. Finally, the king's crown rests firmly on his head. It is possible that his left hand is being raised to remove it, but more probably that hand is merely pointing

29. Joos van Ghent, *Adoration of the Magi*

30. Sodoma, *Adoration of the Magi*

or extended in greeting to the child (as is the hand of Joseph, opposite). It is as if the veil and the crown are firmly in place in obedience to Paul's dictum that a woman's hair should not be uncovered in the temple.

Does this figure represent a man with the accoutrements of a woman? Given the pictorial evidence, I cannot respond negatively. The third king's crown presents no problem. It is of the same structure as those of the other two kings. Rather, it is the veil that is striking. In marriage ceremonies in medieval Germany as elsewhere, it was customary for the bride to wear a veil as a sign of her virginity. But with the rare exception of such a veil or stole being placed on the heads of both partners in so-called same-sex male marriages, I cannot find males wearing veils in

31. *Adoration of the Magi*

32. *Adoration of the Magi*

church or sacrifice.[101] Whatever the final reading on this essentially un-studied painting will be, it must be admitted that the figure strikes one immediately as made up to be effeminate, one complementary to the fig-ure of Mary to the third king's right. We have found a king who is for-mally gendered female.

Once a truly female magus is glimpsed, the inexorable trend toward effeminate third kings will be apparent to all. I was elated, but not shocked, when Christiane Klapisch-Zuber identified a black monarch wearing earrings, who seems very much a woman. She is the third king in an adoration of an anonymous Antwerp mannerist, which is housed in Palermo (fig. 32). Alone on the left wing of an altar retable that she shares with Joseph on the right wing, and with Mary, the child, and the older two kings in the center field, this young monarch wears Roman military clothing complete with a sword and a dagger. Similar to the virgin's, her face is soft and her breast is full. She is certainly a strikingly youthful opposite to the aged Joseph on the other side of the scene. Just as evidently, we may see in her or in him the fertile opposite of a Joseph who clearly could not have fathered Jesus.

The early modern trend toward effeminate third kings had indeed been important. How else, one may ask, would our painter have come upon his idea of a quasi-female magus if not from a context of third kings who had so many of the characteristics contemporaries assigned to women? No matter how rare this painting remains, it was the predictable outcome of a long process of rendering exotic and seductive this subversive opposite to the solemn, aged fathers of patriarchal society.

Despite the feminine or effeminate qualities of some of the third maguses, to find a woman magus or a sensual young male king in any particular painting has had merely anecdotal value for me. My reading of the corpus of magi paintings and sculptures has rather a structural character. I have sought to describe a propensity on the part of some artists to have us remember their magi as singles or as a duet, though they may appear as a trio.

The Game

In describing the binary perception of the magi, I have until now not considered what is perhaps the most obvious polarity of all, the tension between play and reality, the simple recognition that all impersonations of the magi, whether in dramas or in representational art, are consciously imaginary. Looking beyond the walls of churches, whose enclosed dramas we have already examined, we found our first direct evidence of such consciousness in the imagination of Nicholas of Bari, to the effect that real Hohenstaufen kings were "like" the magi.[102] And from approximately mid-fourteenth century, when Emperor Charles IV, and then King Charles V of France had themselves pictured as magi, until about 1520, scores of rulers too numerous to list allowed themselves to be shown as maguses, for reasons that obviously had to do with their legitimation via their appearance among these "brother kings" or princes.[103] Most commonly, they appeared as the third king, but sometimes, they took their place as the first or second king.[104] The convention peaked in the usage of the Habsburg family, which in one case had two of its members shown as kings in the same painting.[105] This was followed by a rapid decline in the later years of Emperor Charles V, but not before most European rulers of the age had played the magus in one way or the other, not to mention the dozens of leading citizens who played such roles in paintings of the magi coming from Florence and other European cities.[106] The magi had become a beloved "game" of late medieval lay society.

33. Peter Bruegel, *Adoration of the Magi*

A second play area where contemporaries entered into the seemingly dated historical field of the magi was in the practice of patrons having themselves recommended to Mary and child while playing a magus or a client of a magus. Besides being a general means of representing the patronage of most saints, this practice also owed something to the ancient habit of showing clients as fourth kings in early and medieval Christian art. A carved adoration in Florence is typical of the genre. It shows King Balthazar, gift in hand, recommending to the divine pair his protegée Baldassare degli Ubriachi, the Florentine who introduced the cult of the magi to Florence at the end of the fourteenth century.[107]

A third play area is of much greater social import, and one that we shall return to in a later chapter of this book. I refer to the practice of simple laity making themselves into kings and queens at Yuletide, and in that

34. Domenico Ghirlandaio, *Adoration of the Shepherds*

guise at times playing the magi. In some village scenes, the representation of exotica was the more vivid because of the simplicity of the players. In his London adoration, Peter Bruegel has left a masterful painting that shows three kings, all of whom wear modest clothing, two looking for all the world like village fools. They worship a child who obviously comes from a family with no pretensions.

This artist could only have intended to represent the elders of a small Dutch village playing the magi on the feast of the epiphany, an activity we see in all its dignity in a contemporary etching of just such a festival.[108] In similar ways did some of the silent masses of Europe in these centuries carry through the "kings' game" on that feast.

These three disjunctions of time, space, and society, which make up much of the sense of play in magian performances, must be supplemented by a fourth game, which I shall call historistic. It is well known that in the fifteenth and early sixteenth centuries, Italy especially was gripped by a fascination with its Roman past and by a desire to retrieve its glories, especially those aspects that had public faces, like festivals and spectacles. Games, or *giuochi*, ensued, in which whole courts and cities re-created famous triumphal moments in the Roman past. Such Roman triumphs,

35. *Adoration of the Magi*

like those of Aemilius Paulus and Julius Caesar came to be painted and carved by the leading artists of the time. Until recently, classical representations of this type used to be taken as evidence of the declining Christianity of the "pagan Renaissance."[109]

But we know that to the contrary, the Christian theme of the magi was having its own apogee in this same latter Quattrocento. Italian intellectuals showed much interest in the star and in the intellectual caste of the magi that had watched the heavens,[110] and the magi's pictorial popularity was immense. A type of fusion between Roman antiquity and Christian magi was to be expected, perhaps predictably in that very area of Roman behavior that the magi had indeed brought into the Christian lexicon and for which they had always spoken: the Roman triumph.

The magi art of these years returns to its roots in Roman triumph, confirming the profound meaning that the icon of the magi always retained in the Christian centuries. One might imagine that no representation could make this point more forcefully than Domenico Ghirlandaio's *Adoration of the Shepherds* (fig. 34), a painting that at one and the same time commemorates the triumph of Pompey and celebrates the birth of the infant Jesus. To the left of the painting, the magi proceed with the cortège along the road toward Bethlehem. And triumphantly so, for we see them passing beneath a triumphal arch whose inscription perpetuates the glory of this great Roman general![111]

Another contemporary work is quite as forceful in conveying the message that in the new dispensation, the three kings announce Christian triumph. It is an anonymous woodcut from about 1500 (fig. 35). The setting is Rome. Between Hadrian's tomb on the left and a Christian temple on the right, both the ancient and medieval faces of the city are referenced. The same holds true in the adoration of the magi that takes up the foreground of the print. Moving from the left toward the Christian right side are the three kings, at least one of whom is dressed in the armor of an ancient Roman warrior. An adoration in the very setting of the Eternal City, as well as the presence of this ancient warrior costume, produces a palpable sense of a mixed religious-secular triumph. The antiquities of Rome salute each other in this triumphant, if fanciful, scene.

Where was the line that separated play and reality? Did it lie in the reality of princely power, distinct from the chimera of dead magi kings (who had never existed), or in the reality of princely power, as distinct from those players who in this time became kings for a day? The answer is devilishly difficult, precisely because power is impossible without culture, that is, without images from the past. In the coming pages, we shall encounter real princes who beg, and real beggars who rule as princes.[112] As always, "gifts" will be unmasked as the "tributes" that were the foundation of states and estates of the time.[113] Everywhere, two worlds (not three) really, will be in play, each mediating between the one and the other.

Thus no need to rush to describe the magi as a trinity in the way the Christian God is said to be a trinity. Triadism is indeed a male preserve, while dualism or quadripartition leave room for all those forces that also must concede legitimacy to any political order—the young, the female, and other outsiders. Let us dwell on the female, or effeminate, youthful and rakish side of this dualistic universe. In these paintings it is the androgynous rake who stands for the biological reproduction of the races, and not the impotent first and second kings, who merely want to maintain, or culturally reproduce, the existing patriarchy of their societies through a stale and authoritarian ceremonialism.

In the iconography of the magi there is conflict, not consensus, around the crèche. I have not shown that one needs the presence of women, or of magicians, to pray successfully, but rather that negation, the conflict of denied women and youth with their lords, is life. Males like Matthew reach into space and fetch outside magi to prove their Lord is king and God, thus reaching into the future of time. Yet with the power from outside, forecasting the future, there comes the danger of youth, the threat of woman.

Chapter 4

EL DORADO

IN THE years after 1406, when the ports of Pisa and Livorno fell to the previously land-locked city of Florence, diarists recorded a steady stream of details regarding the arrival of the first Florentine galleys and their bundles of new and often exotic materials. It was a new world, and the Arno city reveled in it. Among other reports, one by Paolo Pietrobuoni of 1423 is particularly interesting. He reports that among other valuables incense and myrrh had arrived on the galley from Alexandria.[1] There was no mention of the magi, probably none intended, and yet that offhand observation has to ring a bell for observers of a city by now almost obsessed with magi festivals. It was as if the new maritime power had accessed two of the lands from which the fabled wealth of the magi had come. Only the land of gold itself remained to be found.

This chapter describes the role that the magi played in making sense of the world as discovered by Europeans in the late fifteenth and sixteenth centuries. In the century before 1480, the search for the homelands of the magi was a matter of religion and curiosity, less so of economics. With the discovery of the extra-European world in the following century, the search for the magian homeland was motivated by "sacred geography," as cartographers sought to apply the geographical information in the Bible to the worlds they were registering for the first time. Economic motivations were also present, as some explorers became convinced that to discover the homelands of the magi was to capture for oneself inestimable wealth in spices and in precious metals. To an extent little imagined by previous historians, the search for El Dorado, for the seven cities of Cibola, and indeed later for Shangri-la, is part of a search for the magi.

EARLY INFORMATION

The history of the late medieval search for the magi is associated with a series of lay travelers and missionaries, beginning in the first third of the fourteenth century. These eyewitness accounts started with the report of Marco Polo, which was written after his return from the East at the end of the thirteenth century, continued with the description of his homeland and Tartary by the Armenian prince Hayton in 1307, and a short report by the Franciscan Odorico da Pordonone about 1330. The last account came from Giovanni de' Marignolli in or around 1334.[2]

These reports have certain things in common. First, they all claim to have located the cities or kingdoms of the magi in Persia or to the east, some saying that they had indeed seen one or the other of their burial sites. Second, their common tendency is a conviction that at least in the kingdoms of the magi's successors, Christian communities continued to exist, groups that had been evangelized, if not by the magi themselves, then by Thomas, apostle of the Indies, who was erroneously equated with the doubting apostle Thomas. Finally, such reports share a common motivation. Any Christian communities that could be located behind the Islamic lines, so to speak, might help turn a Christian flank against the world of Islam and bring the latter to ruin. Under the impression that the Mongols might be brought to turn against the Muslims, Marco Polo claims that one King George, a descendant of Prester John in the sixth generation, had entered an alliance with these "Tartars" in the hope both might attack Islam.[3]

Some clarification will help the reader keep track of the following discussion. First, at this time the term "India" often meant not only the subcontinent but also east Africa; thus, the litoral of the whole Arabian Sea could be designated by the term "India." Second, while writers of the late Middle Ages began by assuming that "Thomas" and especially "Prester John" were living individuals, as time went by and these individuals did not surface, contemporaries began to claim that the descendants of the original "Thomas" or Prester John assumed the names of these ancestors as a condition of office. Marco Polo, for example, already knew that Prester John was dead, but later writers clung to that name to designate the contemporary legendary eastern ruler because they viewed the name as an official, hereditary title. Next, it seemed certain that, Prester John being from "India," so were the magi and their descendants, if there were any.[4] In keeping with Otto of Freising's statement that the families of Prester John and of the kings were related, the magi's location would also be associated with the so much more alive and seemingly useful Prester. Finally, these accounts have one common omission—any developed notion that there might be profit in exploiting the material wealth—most especially the magian gold, frankincense, and myrrh—in the lands of any of these principals.

Much the same can be said about two important overviews penned about 1360 by persons who had in fact never been to the East, John of Mandeville—probably a Frenchman named Jean de Bourgogne—and John of Hildesheim, the all-important Carmelite friar whose *liber de gestis et translacionibus trium regum* became the main resource for information on the magi in the late Middle Ages, being regularly consulted by the dramaturges and artists of the age.[5] These works of romance, more than of science, had something new about them, however. While still said to be from "India," Prester John can be seen, on closer examination, to be black and to rule in east Africa—part of "India," as we have seen. As a result, at least one of the magi soon followed the Prester into Africa. Before long, Prester John and his family were thought of as the rulers of Ethiopia, and it is from this location and with this status that they appear in European historical sources in the early fifteenth century.[6]

The first years of the fifteenth century gradually brought an end to this more or less relaxed search for the Prester and for the magi. An important emblem of the sea change about to take place is, indeed, already found in John of Hildesheim. Identifying King Caspar as the ruler of Tharsis, where the body of Thomas lies buried, the writer adds, with a new academic consciousness, "Where myrrh is grown more than in any other place."[7] A century later, the Franciscan Francesco Suriano spoke of Nile waters being so pure "because in leaving the Terrestrial Paradise, it passes through Ethiopia upon a bed of pure gold."[8] Henceforth, we shall not be surprised to find explorers searching out connections between the magian gifts and the material goals of their expeditions.

The precipitants of this new and more earnest search for the easterners were three. The first, beginning in 1402, was a steady stream of African embassies that appeared in Europe, many for the first time since Antiquity. The second was the impending fall of Constantinople to the Ottoman Turks, threatening traditional European access routes to the East. The third was Mediterranean Europe's recognition, dating from the 1420s, that Portugal was becoming a major world power purely by expanding outside Europe. Mostly by sea, the house of Avis was proving a new crusading champion to be sure, but also a medium for strong profits in slaves and gold along the west coast of Africa, and foreign investors were courted by that dynasty. Ideologically, this Portuguese undertaking was cast as a search for Prester John, who by now was almost exclusively viewed as an African monarch. Just as surely, the Spaniards, when their time came, would cast their explorations as a search for the three kings.

Magian Embassies

The stunning run of legations that crisscrossed Europe in the fifteenth century, coming from strange and unusual places and challenging nothing so much as the Europeans' credulity, have been described in detail by many writers, and these pages will make no effort to repeat that detail. Our purpose is merely to sketch the outlines of a curious dissonance between literature and visual media in representing events of this type. At the verbal level, the Europeans identified almost any eastern embassy as coming from Prester John, that is, from the ruler of Ethiopia; for much of this century, the magi themselves receive scant mention in relation to the explorations and discoveries. Yet in the visual arena, there simply is no significant record of Prester John, whereas this is the unrivaled age of the magi. Thus any visual record we have of these visitors is doubtless magian in character.[9]

The embassies I label "magian" visited Europe in the first three quarters of the fifteenth century. They began without any apparent ecclesiastical sponsorship, but reached their peak and began to decline under the aegis of the postschismatic, newly reunified Renaissance papacy. Perhaps at the outset, the most powerful influence on the contemporary image of Prester John came not from a work of history, but from late medieval romances like the Florentine Andrea da Barberino's novel *Guerino il Meschino* (1409), which has an incredible description not only of the Prester himself—so old his eyes had seen the deeds of Alexander and Caesar—but also of the Prester's throne room. "At the top of the stairway was a marvelous room sixty yards long and forty wide, and in its middle two colums of solid gold. The walls were of alabaster . . . , in the middle of each window a crystal column . . . , a chair all of gold, [and] the seven steps . . . all of pure gold. . . ."[10]

Obviously, readers of such literature were predisposed to be positively impressed by any visitors from this region. Thus in mid-1402, Francesco Novello da Carrara, lord of Padua, finally claimed success in his determination to view the "strange things," that the "ambassador of Prester John," brought to Venice by a Florentine merchant, had gifted to the latter city's government: the skin of a wild man and that of a zebra.[11] In 1406 another group of three Ethiopians visited Rome. They evoked the warm admiration of a Friulian clerk, who wrote home about them in two respects. First, he was obviously moved by their persons. "Believe me, dear sir," he wrote, "it is a great solace for me to be with them, to hear of the ways and customs of the orientals. . . ." He also paid close attention to their behavior and speech, comparing his impressions in this area to what he had read in a borrowed book and expressing astonishment at how accurate the book was. As Kaplan has shown, that book could only have been John of Hildesheim's work on the magi. Evidently, this standard work on the magi was also being used as a source of information about the East. Finally, our reporter concludes by stating that the visitors "all obey Prester John; [and] in spiritual things they support the patriarch Thomas as we venerate the supreme Roman pontiff as the pope."[12]

It did not disturb this writer that the Ethiopians were dressed, as he said, like the Franciscans, famous for their simple, not to say disheveled, appearance. There is a simple explanation for this dress. In the fifteenth century, most Ethiopians who appeared in Europe were monks who were attached to the Ethiopian monastery in Jerusalem, not lay personnages of

the stamp required by, say, a magi portrait. Not until well into the sixteenth century, in fact, did Europeans—and then the Portuguese rather
than Rome—establish regular contact with the court of Ethiopia itself.

During the Council of Ferrara/Florence (1435–41), the papacy played
a central role in attracting exotic easterners to Italy. Already in Ferrara,
Pope Eugenius IV received an epochal travel report that was made to him
personally by the Castilian traveler Pero Tafur. Its most sensational elements were based on a report Tafur had received by chance in the Sinai
desert from the Venetian Nicolò de' Conti, a traveler who had been in the
East since 1416. According to Tafur, Conti claimed not only to have seen
Prester John "in India," but to have been married by him. That was
clearly enough for the pope. Within days, he wrote to the Prester, "illustrious king and emperor of Ethiopia," informing him of the pending arrival in Ferrara of Greeks from Constantinople and urging him to send an
ambassador to the council.[13]

Eugenius did not let the matter rest. A year later the council had
moved to Florence and there, on 7 July 1439, the day after the announcement of the Latins' union with the Greeks, the pope vaunted that
achievement in one letter to Coptic Christians and in another to their
patriarch in Cairo. These letters introduced to their recipients the Franciscan fra Alberto da Sarteano, who was to deliver the former as apostolic
delegate. In the following month, on 28 August 1439, the pope wrote
two identical letters, one addressed to "Emperor Thomas of the Indians"
and the other to "Emperor Prester John of the Ethiopians."[14] Eugenius'
intention was clear: Sarteano would round up as many Eastern Christians
as possible and bring them back to the council to keep the unification
bandwagon rolling.

Things did not work out for Sarteano as well as he had hoped, but on
26 August 1441, he returned to the council with Ethiopians and Copts,
and perhaps even with the famous Nicolò de' Conti.[15] By now, Florence
was full of unusual faces and costumes from Armenia, different parts of
Greece, Russia, and varied parts of north and east Africa, most purport-
edly there to enter into union with the Roman Church, but in any case,
all marching about in the city in costumes that impressed the locals.[16]
Contemporaries could not know that the unions achieved would all prove
illusory. They were convinced that the pomp and ceremony of this ecumenical gathering was history in the making. Our best recollection of this
gathering in all its exoticism is in the Journey of the Magi frescoes done
in 1459 by Benozzo Gozzoli in the Medici palace in Florence, but there
is only one black figure scattered among the three frescoes, and he is a
servant. This absence of imposing black figures may, as Kaplan has suggested, reflect the gap between the imagined opulence that might have
been expected of these Ethiopians and the actual poverty of Ethiopians

who really were just monks. "They were black men and dry and very awkward in their bearing," one Florentine wrote. "Really, to see them they appeared to be very weak men."[17] Was this the best that Prester John could offer?

The truth was that even at this early point, an air of irreality had settled around this legendary figure. Increasingly, contemporaries meant no more than the (existing) ruler of Ethiopia when they referred to "Prester John." Yet even this linkage was proving hard to maintain. In a speech to the pope in 1533, the Portuguese ambassador would do what intellectuals have forever done in such circumstances, namely, label Prester John a lower-class superstition. Though it was clerks who had come up with Prester John fully four hundred years earlier, now their spokesman claimed that the ruler of Ethiopia was only called Prester John "by the masses," while the editor of this speech adds that "he is not called by them Prester John, as the masses falsely believe. . . ."[18] Prester John began to be spoken of as a type of past historical figure, for instance, who had once upon a time sent a magnificent embassy to the emperor Frederick.[19] The circle of fantasy was closed.

Even before Prester John hit this low point in the sixteenth century, his star had fallen so far in the later fifteenth century that charlatans thought nothing of making him up on the spot, if that served them. This was what the Franciscan Ludovico of Bologna did in 1461. Fra Ludovico specialized in bringing to the West various eastern "ambassadors" in the hope that through their exotic self-presentation at courts, he might raise a Christian army to join with the imaginary Christian armies in the East that these ambassadors spoke of. In large part, Ludovico's activity with his band of easterners was a hoax, and this started to become all too clear in early 1461. In the words of the gang's historian, "the part began to resemble a circus. . . . To the French and the Burgundians, the show must have seemed like the tales of Mandeville come alive."[20] Indeed, by the time he arrived in Paris, the friar had produced out of nowhere a person he identified as the representative of Prester John himself. At this juncture Lodovico was on the verge of being discovered, yet before going under he gave a speech with a helpful, if fraudulent, reference to the magi! Meeting the duke of Burgundy at a chapter of the Golden Fleece on 23 May 1461, Ludovico all but sang out to his majesty, "Here are the Magi come from the East toward the star they have seen in the West, that is to say, toward you, whose puissance shines today so brightly, as far as the shores of the Orient, illuminating their prince and nations and guiding them toward the true image of God."[21]

Fortunately for humanity, Philip of Burgundy never did take the cross, as the friar wished. Yet the latter's fraudulent words do reestablish for us the bynow ancient image of men of the East come to the West being replicas of the very magi. They still follow the blazing star, this time in the person not of a Byzantine or Ottonian emperor, but of the duke of Burgundy, whose light pierces deep to the East, as had Jesus'. Thus in the celebratory world of pomp and parade in these crucial years, while almost all the world seemed to talk of where in the East the Prester and the patriarch Thomas might be found, we find Eurasia still expressed in magian terms.[22]

THE PORTUGUESE SEARCH

Portugal's entry into the African continent at the beginning of the fif-teenth century is certainly one of that century's dominant geopolitical facts. Early in its effort to enrich the crown by reaching the Indies, the house of Avon married into that of Burgundy so as to procure it the Eu-ropean recognition it needed, while at the same time it solicited especially the Florentine and Genoese merchant capital necessary to its African and Indian aims. In pursuit of both ends—sustaining Portuguese activities in Europe and in Africa—King John I (1385–1433) made a substantial in-vestment in the Florentine public debt.[23]

The Portuguese dynasty invested as well in the European pictorial stock available for expressing their new successes. Perhaps especially be-cause of European humanism's interest in Roman antiquity, the history of the magi in these new worlds would preserve the message of triumph with which the trio had been associated since the time of Constantine, even if that history was now inextricably mixed with a pronounced inter-est in the "king of gold." In a painting by the Portuguese Master of Sar-doal, dated about 1535 (fig. 36), one generation after Vasco da Gama reached India by ship, we see the infant raise up the gold coin with cross from the chalice. It is the triumph of the cross, as if to say that Portugal had inherited the triumphal pretensions of the Romans. Indeed, we shall find the Constantinian celestial message *In hoc signo vinces* implicit in this image. Whenever they do emerge in this Iberian tale, the magi are about conquest.

Precisely because of their distance from the European core, the claim of the Portuguese to the European cultural heritage and their efforts in the realm of public relations draw our special attention. The most impor-tant harbinger of this development was the long visit that Dom Pedro, the son of King John and the brother of Prince Henry the Navigator, made to Germany and Italy between 1425 and 1428. This came at a time just before the Portuguese crown began its annual caravel trips along the west coast of Africa, excursions that inexorably led to the rounding of Africa in 1487. For some time, Dom Pedro served the Holy Roman Em-peror Sigismund. In early 1428 Pedro came to Florence, entering the city

36. Master of Sardoal, *Adoration of the Magi*

on 21 April. One eye-witness spoke of "the biggest reception [he] had ever seen."[24] Four days later, a pompous joust was held in the Piazza Santa Croce in Pedro's honor, at which the Portuguese comported themselves impressively.[25] The type of impression Portuguese jousters made in these events is further manifest during a visit to Florence by the Marquis of Valença of Portugal on 15 May 1452. A mature Florentine chronicler not given to enthusiasm blurted out spontaneously, "These Portuguese are marvelously dressed."[26] At this moment of history, the Florentines clearly had little to teach the Iberians about fine clothing.

Toward the middle of this century, the Portuguese developed the oration that was part of the obedience their embassies rendered each new pope into a report on their discoveries.[27] It is quite possible that contemporaries thought of the embassy to Rome to honor the new pope as a magian embassy to be commemorated in an apposite adoration of the kings; at least, a later poet would compare his pilgrimage to pay homage to the new pope to that of the magi who went to pay homage to the infant.[28]

These Portuguese reports became the second form of self-presentation that the Portuguese developed to foster their political goals. The fiction in this rite was that all of Portugal's new possessions rendered the pontiff obedience, requiring the orator to spell out in some detail just what his landsmen had discovered in the years since the previous obedience. For instance, the first printed obedience oration, addressed by the emissary Vasco Fernandes de Lucena to Innocent VIII on 9 December 1485 in consistory, detailed Portuguese activities in the Gulf of Guinea, promising the pope that soon Portuguese ships would appear in east Africa, as they indeed did. Speaking of the approximately forty-five hundred miles of discovery and exploration the Portuguese had under their belts, the ambassador addressed the pontiff as follows: "I seem to be able to perceive how many and how large accumulations of fortunes and honors and glory will befall not only all of Christendom but also, and chiefly, you, Most Blessed Father, and your successors, and this most sacred see of Peter."[29]

The oration held in similar circumstances before Alexander VI in summer, 1493, though given well after Dias had rounded the Cape of Good Hope, had little new to offer except the assurance that through his agents, King John had planted the Christian red cross on white (that is, the sign under which Christians conquered), "and insisted and taught that it be adored and worshipped by the very savage barbarians who spurned it."[30]

The next such oration was delivered in 1505, after Vasco da Gama had discovered India, led there by an Arab seaman. Diogo Pacheco was elated that the fleet had found Christians along the west coast of the subcontinent, and the sensational character of the news, along with Pacheco's cocky self-congratulatory tone, led it to be circulated throughout Europe, bringing the good news, so to speak. A high point in this series of obedience orations was reached on 20 March 1514, when the same Diogo Pacheco addressed the new pope, Leo X. After reviewing some of the Portuguese explorations, Pacheco dramatically turned to Psalm 72, which had already been used in the address to Innocent VIII, to conjure up, in Roger's words, a vision of union between East and West under the pope.[31] The by now familiar magian theme of triumph rings out:

> Thou shalt rule indeed. . . . The kings of the Arabians and of Saba shall bring gifts, and all princes shall adore thee and all nations shall serve thee . . . , so that, with the Indus and the Ganges, the Tagus and the Tiber, brought together into the same bed, as it were, and at the same time flowing in harmony under thy auspices, there may be one fold and one shepherd.[32]

Evocations of Isaiah 60 as well as Psalm 72 run through this flattery. The very same combination of biblical dream texts, which had for centuries been used to locate the magi, now inspired Christian rulers to set off for foreign lands in their search for loot and salvation.

A fitting climax to this complex of magian legations before the newly crowned popes—whom we see here identified as so many infant Jesuses—is provided by one last submission, this time by an ambassador of the ruler of Ethiopia himself to the Roman pope, in the presence of the Emperor Charles V. It occurred on 29 January 1533 in Bologna, where these princes were meeting. Ethiopia threw itself at the feet of the pope, Africa before Europe, in the church of San Petronio.[33] This is the very church that, in the Bolognini chapel, houses the important magi cycle painted a century before, to which we earlier drew attention. That cycle, we recall, had indeed succeeded in representing not just blacks, but Asians on their way to see the infant.

What is of interest in these Portuguese reports to the popes, as in other propaganda of the period, is the European language of conquest and triumph. The Portuguese usually acted as if everyone they encountered in their travels was a "pagan" (whether they were Christian or not) and treated them accordingly. The task was to subordinate, if not enslave, everyone they met. In the process, allusions to the magi, as well as to Prester John, play a modest role. King Manuel the Fortunate (1495–1521), for instance, might write to the Zamorin of Calicut on the west coast of India in 1500, soon after Vasco da Gama's arrival, noting that both the apostle Thomas and Saint Bartholomew had preached "in your part of India."[34] And in the following year there is a report, otherwise unsubstantiated, that the Cabral expedition had found the body of Thomas and had it brought back to Lisbon![35] But in fact, not until 1523 did the crown's servants make an "authoritative" discovery of the tomb.[36] It had taken almost a quarter century to get around to finding Thomas.

Although the role played by the magi in the ideological underpinnings of these conquests was modest, at times it was the decisive modality chosen to express the brutal facts of the subordination of foreign peoples. On the return of Vasco da Gama from India, Manuel the Fortunate had taken the grandiloquent title "lord of the conquest, navigation, and commerce of India, Ethiopia, Arabia, and Persia." In the January illumination of his book of hours, begun in 1517, Manuel, but for his death in 1521, might have seen his title on one among several coins "wrapped around" the adoration of the magi illustrating that month. What makes this illumination a particularly revealing example of the relation between triumph and magi in the age of discovery is not just that the painting is dominated by an Indian servant in the foreground, but perhaps especially because of

37. Gregorio Lopes (attrib.), *Adoration of the Magi*

another coin sprinkled across its bottom half. On one side of this coin is inscribed the name of John III (1521–57). On the reverse is the cross, circumscribed with the words, in hoc signo vinces. Thus the artist has the son of the "lord of the conquest, naviation, and commerce of India, Ethiopia, Arabia, and Persia" hearken back to the world ruler Constantine, and he does it, as we see, in the magian format before us.[37]

Portuguese missionaries also made use of the magi theme in their Indian evangelization efforts, an effort they characterized as a triumph of the cross. A Flemish tapestry of about 1550 (fig. 38) shows that having found their way to India by sea, they would use the magi to teach potential converts how to pray, just as European clergy had long used the kings to that same end. Suddenly, the traditionally black magus becomes an Indian prince, demonstrating a missionary flexibility that we shall encounter in the Americas as well.

We know how one Mogul reacted to the reception of such adorations. In 1608, the pope sent an adoration of the magi to the Mogul Jahangir as a gift. So taken was this ruler with the painting's beauty (certainly with the way that Christians copied the homage of the magi in their own obeisance as well) that he instructed his artists to paint onto the top of the frame of the adoration his own royal countenance, evidently so that when the small flock of converts fell on their faces before the painting that taught them how to worship, they would simultaneously be worshiping his royal visage.[38] Transferring worship in this fashion was so simple; the rulers of the West had learned it centuries before!

A subsequent chapter will bring us back to consider the modern search for the magi in the East. During the explorations the search for the magi was not as important for the Portuguese as was the search for the apostle Thomas and for Prester John. To think that was the end of it, however, would be to underestimate the search for Christian origins at the time. None other than Christopher Columbus and the Spaniards had long since taken up the search for the magi in the Indies and studded the record with just such associations. While the Portuguese had concentrated on Prester John, the Spaniards ignored him, instead searching out the apostles Thomas and Bartholomew, and the three kings.

THE SPANISH SEARCH

The Venetian chroniclers Priuli, Pietro da Ca' da Pesaro, and Marin Sanudo immediately grasped the baleful significance for Venice of the Portuguese discovery of the sea route to India. They knew it meant a great challenge for Venetian command of Eastern trade. "God [has] made [the Portuguese king] the King of Gold," they remarked, their

38. *Adoration of the Magi*

39. Master of Viseu (attrib.),
Adoration of the Magi

words evoking the magus who controlled gold and had offered it to the infant.[39] Yet by that time Columbus had established to *his* satisfaction that he had found the land of the same magus, and perhaps of another as well, and that he had located the site of Ophir, the fabled Old Testament land of gold whence some said the magus of gold had gotten his gift for the infant. Students of the search for gold and great wealth in the Americas have ignored the magi, who in fact furnished the New Testament inspiration for precisely that exploration.[40] On his way from Sinaloa to the Seven Cities of Cibola in 1540, Coronado can be seen still searching for the homeland of the magi.

That Columbus was interested in the magian element of sacred geography even before he sailed west is clear in certain marginalia he entered into his books. For example, with clear reference to the magus from Tarshish who had visited the infant, he wrote, "Note that the king of Tarshish came to the Lord at Jerusalem, and spent a year and thirteen days en route, as the blessed Jerome has it."[41] In December 1492, on the first of his four trips, natives told the explorer that a land teeming with gold was nearby, and that it was called Cybao. Columbus soon put this into a magian, or at least Thomistic, context. In his memoir, Marco Polo had described Japan—Cipango, he called it—as full of gold. So Columbus, sure that this was the land of the magus who had brought gold to Bethlehem, decided that the natives had simply got the name wrong. "Cipango, which they called Cybao," he said, was just over the horizon.[42] The search was on! When later in that same first voyage the explorer touched on this island—actually Cibao in central Hispaniola—and found a bit of gold, he named the fort he established there "St. Thomas, unconquerable by those Indians."[43]

But it was the second voyage that proceeded notoriously under the star of the magi. In October 1495, Michele di Cuneo described the admiral's anticipation as his ship approached what was actually the island of Cuba. He announced to his crew, "Gentlemen, I wish to bring us to a place whence departed one of the three magi who came to adore Christ, the which place is called Sheba."[44] Michele di Cuneo continues his account. "When once we made that place and asked its name, it was answered that it was called Sobo. Then the lord admiral said that it was the same word [Saba or Sheba], but that [the natives] could not pronounce it correctly."[45] Yet the search went forward. Evidently, what the Spaniards had found was a far cry from the decorous kings whose great horse and camel trains Columbus had seen gracing the frescoes and oils on the walls and altars of Europe. Another source for this second voyage, Syllacio, says that the Europeans now pushed into the interior of this land of the Sabeans:

[T]o King Saba, a monarch of great wealth. . . . It is believed these are the
Sabaeans from whom frankincense is obtained and who are mentioned by
our histories and foreign chronicles. For according to the well-known text,
kings shall come from Saba bearing gold and incense.[46]

Thus there can be no doubt that in his role as a sacred geographer,
Columbus structured his expectations in this part of the world, inter alia,
around the presumed homelands of the three kings. He did so specifically
because he assumed that finding their homes meant finding where the
precious metals and spices he so desired had been "born." In addition to
direct references to the magi, the admiral expressed confidence that he
had found the fabled city or land of Ophir, a great source of gold in the
ancient world and thus often associated with the first of the three kings.
At first, Columbus claimed that Hispaniola was Ophir; in the following
century the geographer Ortelius guessed that just Haiti had that honor.
Later, however, Columbus changed course radically, being convinced
that the gold mines of Veragua (on the Panamanian coast of Darien) were
those of Ophir.[47] With this, the search was well underway among the ep-
igones. Some found Ophir in Peru, others in Mexico or New Spain, and
still others thought the name covered both areas.[48]

Needless to say, Columbus' claims along this line were part of his
larger assertion that he had indeed discovered India. But before the commentators had time to lay out the ground rules for the coming debate
over Columbus' claims, the Portuguese produced a painting (ca. 1505)
that could not have helped shape that debate, since it suddenly and
bluntly portrayed one of the magi as a native American cacique!

This important painting (fig. 39) resulted from the Portuguese
Cabral's (accidental) discovery of Brazil in 1500 while on his way to the
Indian subcontinent. Usually dated to about 1505, the painting is today
kept in Viseu, a modest Portuguese town over which Henry the Navigator had once ruled as duke. Was it intended as Portuguese propaganda,
appearing just after Columbus, on his third voyage (1498), had discovered and explored the continent of South America? Perhaps. But why
then would the painter not also have added a black to the same painting
to heighten the Portuguese claim to fame? Another explanation for this
painting proves no less attractive. Perhaps the painting claims that a native American had actually worshiped the infant at Bethlehem. Or perhaps rather than reflecting such a belief, the painting actually helped produce the subsequent notion.

According to the Augustinian Antonio de la Calancha (d. 1645), fray
Bernardo de Armencia wrote to Dr. Juan Bernal Díaz de Lugo on 1 May
1538 with evidence that the apostle Thomas had been in Brazil; he was
called Payçume, or Pay Thome, Calancha adding that the word "Pay"

meant powerful and wise.[49] Then in 1549, Manuel de Nóbrega, a Jesuit working in Brazil, wrote home to his provincial that without doubt, the apostle Thomas had preached in Brazil. An imprint of a large foot had been found that surely belonged to the saint (doubtless like the one that had been found in Mylapore, India); the Brazilians, according to Nóbrega, referred to this big foot by the name Zome, or Sanctum Sumè.[50] Then Bartolomé de Las Casas (d. 1566) incorporated the contents of this letter into his influential *Historia de las Indias*, and, in no time at all, the notion that Thomas had preached in the eastern part of South America, and the apostle Bartholomew in the western part, had taken hold among some influential persons.[51]

Magellan's circumnavigation of the globe (1521–23) was now a generation past, yet it was at this juncture that a large number of European scholars began to weigh in with their views regarding American sacred geography. This took place in an ongoing atmosphere of gold fever, especially marked by the legend that some societies, perhaps in the mountains of present-day Colombia, periodically covered their ruler (el Dorado) in gold dust. Obviously, only mountains of precious metals could produce such profigacy. Not surprisingly, the location of biblical Ophir was perhaps most earnestly anticipated in these lands of El Dorado.[52]

The most common approach to the sixteenth-century history of Ophir was linguistic in character. Beginning with François Vatable (d. 1547), a professor of Hebrew in Paris, many scholars took note of the identity that was asserted between biblical names in Hebrew and the names of American, predominantly South American, locations. Far and away the most important such site was Peru, whose name was "identical" to certain Hebrew words.[53]

A second approach was crude enough, but no less persuasive for believers. The fact that Peru not only had gold mines, but certain types of wood for which Ophir had also been known, meant that the environments, and thus the places, were identical.[54] Anywhere mines of precious metals appeared was liable to be labeled Ophir.

A third claim had nothing to stand in its way but good sense. Under the assumption that each presumed immediate descendant of Noah had been consigned part of the planet, some scholars determined that in their dispersion Noah's son Shem and his descendants had occupied different parts of the Americas, as could be seen from name affinities.[55]

There were sound reasons for rejecting all of these hypotheses. The linguistic arguments and the argument from Noah fell of their own weight; others pointed out that no Old Testament source indicated that a great body of water, such as the Atlantic Ocean, separated Israel from an American Ophir. Still others noted that though there might be gold mines in America, many other things, like elephants, said to have been in ancient Ophir, were not found in America.[56] But well into the eighteenth century, there were those who still sought magi, apostles, Ophir, and the variously spelled Tarsis in the Americas.

One of the main spurs to such belief was the general impression, widely shared by early missionaries and by some native Americans and lay mestizos, that several cultures, (most notoriously the Maya with their crosses) showed "obvious" links to Christianity, which could only be explained by previous evangelization. Early on, the great Las Casas, who was himself not certain that Thomas had preached in Brazil, but was persuaded that the apostle Bartholomew had worked at conversion "nearby," pointed to the Yucatec crosses as clear evidence of pre-Conquest evangelization.[57] Toward the end of the century, the Jesuit Acosta was ready to believe that Tarsis might be in the Americas.[58]

But just as important in this debate was the indigenous and mestizo contribution. The view of the mestizo Garcilaso de la Vega (d. 1616) on the relative merits of European and Andean civilizations is well known. Put bluntly, the Spaniards had behaved so bestially that if they exemplified good-mannered Christianity, then the native peoples, and especially the Inca, must have been Christianized before the Spaniards ever arrived. The figure of Guaman Poma de Ayala (d. ca. 1615) is less well known, but this native American, who in 1609 finished his now-famous *Nueva Coronica*, shared the view of Garcilaso, and then some. Not only had the apostle Bartholomew (whom the Andean peoples called "Tunupa"), missionized in the Andes long before the Spaniards arrived. One of the Incas, or at least some native American ruler, was actually one of the three kings who had gone to Bethlehem!

> In the time of Sinchi Roca Inca the child Jesus was born in Bethlehem from the parturient ever-holy virgin. He was adored there by the Three Kings of the Three Races that God had put into the world: the king-magus Melchior an Indian, Balthazar a Spaniard [!], and Gaspar a black.[59]

Thus the idea of an Andean magus was in the air at the time, even if it met with caution. Writing soon after Guaman Poma, for example, the influential Augustinian Calancha went on record with his belief that Thomas had indeed taught in the eastern part of Peru, and so had the magi been there, for according to tradition they had accompanied Thomas in his missionizing. Yet Calancha denied the natives an indigenous magus. None of the three had been born in these parts.[60]

For all that, an original creative moment had occurred in the ever evolving story of the magi, one whose power can still be seen today in the Andean crèche, where one of the kings, if not Mary and Joseph as well, is still shown as a native American. Faced now with the new orthodoxy that there were four continents, not three, contemporary commentators on the biblical tradition of the magi had two options. They could think of the magi as representing the three races of mankind, not continents. This solution, proposed by Guaman Poma, became the new orthodoxy.[61] Alternately, one could in effect deny the existence of four continents by viewing America as a former part of Asia, so that in olden times an American sovereign—a descendant of Noah, be it recalled—might in fact have represented Asia at Bethlehem.

This was almost exactly the point of view assumed by Jacques d'Auzoles Lapeyre in two works of 1629 and 1638.[62] Surely one of the more imaginative theorists to emerge from this sodality of holy geographers, d'Auzoles, as we shall see, could bring himself to argue that the magi were in fact none other than the prophets Melchizedek, Elijah, and Enoch and that these wise and powerful magi were still alive and well. Hence the bags of bones in Cologne were fakes.[63] Still, d'Auzoles's claim that there had been or was a landbridge between what came to be called Siberia and Alaska proved correct, and was not at loggerheads with the geographical thought of the time.[64] Such an argument tended to legitimate the already elaborated view of Guaman Poma, and certainly others who remain to be identified, that a native American *curaca*, or Inca, had indeed represented the Americans at Bethlehem.

We earlier suggested that the visual tradition, as represented by early paintings showing native American maguses, could have inspired a spoken tradition of American magi and apostles, rather than vice versa. Still, the reader may conclude, as do I, that it is unnecessary to take a position on this matter in the American context, in which such biblical figures were being sought all over the Indies, both "East" and "West." Nor is it necessary to assert the probable (but unprovable) notion that missionaries were behind this flattering notion of an indigenous magus so as to attract converts. What is important at this juncture is that a movement was afoot, embodied in Guaman Poma de Ayala, to fit these indigenous peoples into the social-organizational universe around the infant Jesus.

Guaman Poma meant that an Inca had gone to Bethlehem. Shortly after Guaman Poma made his claim regarding the native American magus, two paintings appeared that visualized Guaman's verbal image. Unlike the adoration of the Master of Viseu, these paintings were displayed on the walls of Peruvian churches not in Europe.[65] Take this adoration by the mid-seventeenth century Jesuit artist, Diego de la Puente (d. 1663), showing the three races, which the Bolivian ethnographers Gisbert and Mesa found on the wall of the church of Juli on Lake Titicaca.[66] The ruler that you see on the left is probably meant to represent an Inca, that is, the ruler of the Inca, or *orejones*. Or look at a slightly later painting by an anonymous hand, also discovered by Gisbert, this time in the nearby town of Ilabe (fig. 41). It too probably shows a legendary

40. Diego de la Puente, *Adoration of the Magi*

41. *Adoration of the Magi*

Inca, perhaps the Sinchi Roca mentioned by Guaman Poma as one of the three kings, swinging a censor before the infant to the right of representatives of the other two races. All in all, these vestiges of a magi cult on Lake Titicaca provide a powerful visual documentation of what in Guaman Poma was a purely literary association, i.e., America was that land from which had come the king bearing gold to Jesus.

As ever, Christians—in this case violated and exploited Christians—used the story of the magi to imagine their place at the crib of the hero-god. As ever, it is the structural or organizational facet of this past history that impresses the student of this image of travel and adoration. We are torn in our appreciation of native self-assertion. As I have shown elsewhere, at one level the emergence of ethnographic self-consciousness among native Americans was to some extent the result of Spanish effort, which was imposed on the indigenous cultures. But watching an Epiphany play or a crèche in a Latin American center today, especially in Peru, persuades one that this contortion of an ancient ecumenical image to make room for one's own American culture has been of some benefit for the latter because in the process, something of pre-Christian memory has been preserved.[67] The question we turn to now is how the image of the magi functioned to help organize America for the Spaniards.

ORGANIZING AMERICA

Some things never change. Even before most Spaniards had any understanding of the real social processes their conquests had unleashed, those events were made to fit into a biblical, and specifically magian ideology, to make sense of Cortés's arrival in America. The Franciscan missionary Juan de Torquemada (d. 1624) tells the well-known story of how the Toltec ruler Quetzalcoatl had been banished by his people to the east, but was expected to return after he did penance. When the Spanish fleet appeared off the Mexican coast in 1519, some native people readily accepted Cortés, thinking he was Quetzalcoatl. It was just like the birth of Jesus, said Torquemada. The natives watched the heavens for signs of Quetzalcoatl much as the magi had once watched from Mount Victory for the star. Then Montezuma was notified by messengers that Cortés had arrived off the coast. Torquemada continued, "And just like when the magi entered Jerusalem asking about the newly born king, Herod had gotten angry . . . thus these Indians of the royal Council [were] perturbed and confused as was [Montezuma]."[68]

The conquerors and their missionaries found many other biblical stories that were applicable to the conditions they found in America. What proved peculiar about the magi evocations was that the Spaniards activated that particular story as an important part of their strategy for colonizing these peoples. They would seek to represent through the magi an image of people coming toward the Spaniards, in good order, and submitting. Thus one missionary play, the "Four Last Kings of Tlaxcala," contains an obvious conceit that pictures the defeated rulers of Tlaxcala near Mexico City coming and submitting themselves to Cortés just as *los tres rreyes benerables* had come before Jesus and prostrated themselves.[69]

A second characteristic of the Spanish missionary strategy was that alongside the magi, the missionaries also exploited the dramatic potential of Luke's story of the shepherds and their adoration. We know their reasoning in this regard from the Jesuit Pérez de Ribas, who was a missionary in rural Sinaloa and Sonora in the mid-seventeenth century. The people he served were obviously socially closer to shepherds than to urbane kings. Confident that Luke's shepherds, and not the magi, were the "firstfruits" of the gospel, he wrote:

> The first in the world to receive the fruit of preaching and the good news of the gospel were not scribes and intellectuals, but instead shepherds raised to watch sheep, people who knew how rustic they were and that they belonged in the fields, like our Indians. . . . And there was another circumstance that added to preaching the gospel to this poor and rude people, which made them more celebrated than that which was effected with the magi kings and wise men. For it was enough for God to teach [the latter] by means of a star . . . but to teach these poor and simple shepherds, he dispatched an army of wise and great angels from his court. . . .[70]

Let us not miss the forest for Pérez's self-serving and defamatory trees. Here, two very different biblical stories were employed as seemed best to the missionaries for bringing these native populations under their control. The following pages show how both stories functioned in the organization of social life in sixteenth-century America.

We have seen that such imaginings were ways in which men and women conceptually organized the geographical world. But they were also means of representing the world of *their* social beings and contracts, *their* competitions, treaties, and wars. The imagery of the magi, and now also the shepherds, proved so useful because they were legitimizing social-organizational icons. Tracing the histories of such representations, especially those of the magi, is no mere commemoration of human fancy, but a study of human plasticity in adapting narrative ideal types to the organization of an expanding world. If I am right, further research will find not only that the magi also marched in east and south Asia and Africa, but that once the conquerors began to reorganize these other worlds around Christian altars—as indicated by the following variegated images—they did, as had rulers in Europe, insert their taxations, their enslavements, their new political orders, and their diplomatic insti-

42. Left: *Adoration of the Magi*. Right:
Edmond van Genechten, *Adoration of
the Magi*

tutions into a magian context. The three kings could convert the kings of
the missionary world into supplicants before the hero-child Jesus. We
shall concentrate on the magi at their organizational work in Mexico, or
New Spain.

I have never found a Mexican ruler shown as a magus, nor any notion
that an Aztec magus had visited the infant in Bethlehem. In this, the
Mexican tradition differs from the Andean. In the matter of the apostle
Thomas, however, the linkage between north and south appears superfi-
cially close because in Mexico, a later savant or two claimed that Quetzalcoatl, the Plumed Serpent, had been none other than Thomas.[71] As so
often in the Americas and in Europe, clerks tended to be more interested
in their own apostolic predecessors, like Thomas or Bartholomew, than
in the magi, who were not priests and had never been canonized. In 1586
the Franciscan prelate Alonso Ponce entered the small town of Coapa
to the south of Mexico City, where he found a picture of the apostle
Thomas with a royal crown on his head, a representation Ponce found
incomprehensible.[72] We have less difficulty, knowing as we do that
Thomas and the magi were tight in legend. But while further pictorial
and literary traces of the magi in Mexico remain to be ferreted out, and
while clearly the magi never became as important a part of native religion

as they were for the Hispanic population, the important evangelical use to which the missionaries put that great image of the magi can already be described.

The first function of any adoration iconography is to instruct and induce people to adore certain sacred figures. The first such figures propagandized in Mexico were the missionaries themselves, and then through them the infant. When the so-called Franciscan Twelve Apostles arrived in Mexico City in 1524, Hernan Cortés ostentatiously descended from his horse and threw himself at their shoeless feet, much as the first magus did before the infant. It was *not* customary for Spanish grandees to behave in this manner before the Minorites, and Cortés did this for a purpose. He wanted to instruct all the Aztec caciques who witnessed the scene how to behave in the presence of friars, an instruction he fostered by assuring that this scene was reproduced in hundreds of paintings that adorned all churches in the valley of Mexico—an almost unparalleled propagandistic ploy to reach the mass of natives in New Spain.[73] The second step in adoration iconography was festive, and it also stemmed from Cortés. According to his mandate, whenever a friar on mission approached a village, the residents were to welcome that friar just as Cortés had welcomed the Twelve.[74] In short, a friar's visit was to be a diplomatic entrée, just as Cortés had turned the entry of the Twelve into a diplomatic act.

Thus Cortés's reception of the Twelve Apostles to Mexico City was the primary mental image of adoration transmitted to the aboriginals in early Spanish America, an image, it should be kept in mind, that had to compete with a marvelously sophisticated entry ritual proper to the Aztecs themselves. This secular historical record was soon intertwined with the magi theme, which was, after all, the primary Christian mode of representing triumphal entries. The fundamental taxpaying or gift-exchanging message of that image was obviously an important element in teaching the "good news" of the gospel. Perhaps we can already hear magian echoes at Christmastime, 1526, when the Franciscan lay brother Peter of Ghent attracted so many natives to the patio of the capital's church of San Francisco that, in his words, "They did not fit in the patio. . . . And each province had made its tent where the principals collected themselves."[75]

By the year 1540, Ghent's mere hint of magian assemblies of the provinces is replaced by the certainty that the feast of the magi had developed some roots, and that its tributary character was of elemental importance. Writing from the nearby city of Tlaxcala, one of the Twelve Apostles, Motolinía, makes clear that a drama of the magi, complete with a star pulled along "from far away" was part of that abuilding tradition. He states that the Tlaxcalans considered the magi particularly their own, for just as the magi had been the "first gentilic fruit" of the gospels in Europe, so among native Americans the Tlaxcalans had been the first to convert to Christianity. Motolinía goes on to describe the many gifts the Indians brought as their offerings to the child on this feast, consisting mostly of game.[76] We can in fact visually reconstruct the scene from his words: the great triumphal arches that gave access to the immense patio around the Franciscan church, through which these and hundreds of other processions of natives would pass in the coming centuries (the link between these triumphal arches and the worship by the magi was well established); the portal of the church itself, which was called Bethlehem (that is, a crèche); the painting of the infant on that portal, worshiped by the pope on one side, and by emperor Charles V on the other.[77]

These early references demonstrate that the friars were using the theme of the magi to flatter the native American lords as latter-day wise men, and that, more significantly, the native social and political units were factually presenting themselves to the child, and thus to the flanking pope and emperor, in (three?) visually distinct political units. The feast of the magi was soon established in the so-called new world, since it facilitated exchanging the salvation of the Americans for the wealth of the Indies. It brought native peoples before the one altar of the child, and it allowed the dramatic union of the different indigenous social configurations, from the calpullis, or neighborhoods, up to the various tribes. That was precisely what the Spaniards needed, for even if they would tolerate ethnic diversity at the representational level, they were concerned to show the union of all the American tribes at the feet of the infant, that is at the feet of the Spanish crown and the European clergy.

The fullest middle-American documentation of this tangible processionalization of the magi story is the extensive 1587 description of a magi festival at Tlaxomulco near Guadalajara by Antonio de Ciudad Real, amanuensis of the Franciscan general Alonso Ponce, a festival he says had been performed annually since at least 1550.[78] Coming from over the mountains around this city, the three native magi, mounted on horses and preceded by banners, made their way toward the patio of the friary, which functioned as both Jerusalem and Bethlehem.

Even as they marched toward town, the patio was full of "shepherds" performing their own adoration of the child and entertaining some five thousand spectators with dances, mock bullfights, and the like. From a somewhat later period, we get some faint echo of such a celebration of the adoration of the shepherds. In mid-seventeenth century, Pérez de Ribas describes how the Tepeguana tribe, in its adoration, appeared in church dressed as shepherds, that is, outfitted in theatrical fashion. Some elders took part as well, "which they do not do often for the entertainment of the boys." All gave gifts to the child, Pérez continues, and those who had nothing else gave their souls.[79]

But the festival just described was a pale imitation, it would seem, of the celebration of the shepherds in Tlaxomulco in 1587. These "shepherds" were preceded by angels singing the "good news." Other native dances were performed in the native language. The shepherds then appeared, made their offering to the child—their reverence so great, it was said, that they moved observers to devotion—and then entered into gaming competitions with each other. Included in this was a form of mock bull fight.[80] These games were reminiscent of the ones that became a part of the entertainment provided for "decent people" by the "commons" in sixteenth-century Europe.

Now the kings arrived on the scene. They were distinguished by their bearing, if the instruction to "ride like lords" in other plays of the time may be credited. First Herod received them diplomatically in one ornate and richly retinued part of the patio; then they proceeded to the crèche to yield their gifts. Here, as earlier in Tlaxcala, these gifts included native frankincense (copal), and of course gold and silver.

Ciudad Real gives no details regarding the large cortège which followed, but one must assume that the natives were coerced in one form or the other to march beneath their king's flag, just as they were forced to march to other divine services. The Franciscan Mendieta describes what must have been typical:

> The day before the festival, each centinary or ventinary informed the people of the *barrio* for which he was responsible that the day was approaching when they had to sing and appear with flowers at the temple and in the house of God, in order to acquit themselves of the duty they owed him. . . . The centinaries cried out to the whole area that the people should prepare themselves to assemble at a chosen place in their neighborhood, in such a way that one could verify that each person was in attendance. . . . From there one got underway toward the church, in good order just as in a procession. The men formed one line and the women another, guided by an Indian who marched in front and carried the flag or banner of the neighborhood, which was made of colored taffeta. With the image of the *barrio*'s patron saint, they moved forward while singing. . . . When they arrived at the patio, they said a prayer to the blessed sacrament. There, one checked them off from the lists with their names on it, and those who were not present when their name was called out were singled out so as to receive a penance consisting of a half dozen whip lashes on the shoulders.[81]

A truly remarkable description of the moral underpinnings of the so-cial-organizational use to which the magi image was put is available in Guatemala, at a slightly later date. In 1648, the respected English clerical traveler Thomas Gage penned a report about a crèche in the city now called Antigua Guatemala. According to Gage, this "Bethlehem" included statues of the three wise men with their gifts, and of the shepherds off to one side with their gifts in kind. Gage describes how, obviously imitating the images they saw before them, every Indian came in procession to see the crèche with some offering in kind or money. He continues:

Nay the policy of the priests hath been such that (to stir up the Indians with their saints' example) they have taught them to bring their saints [that is, the statues kept in churches which they carry outside on litters on the saints' days] upon all the holy days until Twelfth Day in procession unto this Bethlehem to offer their gifts. According to the number of the saints that stand in the[ir] church, some days there come five, some days eight, some days ten, dividing them into such order that by Twelfth Day all may have come and offered, some money, some one thing, some another. The owner of the saint cometh before the saint with his friends and kindred (if there be no sodality or company belonging unto that saint) and being very well apparelled for that purpose, he bows himself and kneels to the crib. Then rising, [he] takes from the saint what he bringeth and leaveth it there, and so departs.

But if there be a sodality [or confraternity] belonging to the saint, then the *mayordomos* or chief officers of that company come before the saint, and do homage, and offer, as before hath been said. But upon Twelfth Day [Epiphany], the *alcades*, mayors, judges, and other officers of justice must offer after the example of the saints and the three wise men of the East (whom the Church of Rome teacheth to have been kings), because they represent the [Spanish] King's power and authority. And all these days they have about the town and in the church a dance of shepherds, who on Christmas Eve at midnight begin before this Bethlehem, and then they must offer a sheep amongst them. Others dance clothed like angels and with wings, and all to draw the people more to see sights in the church than to worship God in spirit and in truth.[82]

From no other image in the Christian lexicon could such a pattern of devotional behavior have been consequentially developed. Gage describes first a clientele around the owner of a saint's statue acting in unison to have its image follow the magi's tribute. Then he describes situations in which confraternities or their councils, or *cabildos*, which exist to protect such a statue, themselves accompany that saint to his or her offering. And finally, on the Epiphany itself the representatives of the whole community, and of the crown, make their offerings, all "after the example . . . of the wise men" whom they see before them. We would not be mistaken to speak of a type of Christian republic, for purposes of tribute, organized beneath the infant's star.

In the same years as the great feast at Tlaxomulco can be dated the earliest of three extant magi plays meant to be performed on a stage rather than across open spaces. All had been written down in Nahuatl by 1607, but all certainly used dramatic materials of earlier date. That material offers us our first detailed insight into what the emerging Hispanic-American culture in New Spain was making of the story of the magi itself, and also will provide us with a foretaste of what we shall encounter in the magian culture of early modern Europe.[83] What is immediately striking about these plays is that the kings are poor not rich. This increasing poverty of the kings over the decades is such that the magi seem in fact not much different from shepherds. They were monarchs of wastelands, so to speak. In the early years Motolinía boasted of the masses of goods that the natives around Tlaxcala left for his friary on Epiphany, but by the end of the century the talk is of poor kings who have little to offer. And in turn, the striking poverty the kings describe themselves as suffering provides the linchpin for relating their gifts to the infant to their chances of salvation.

On this score as well as others, the three Mexican plays, presumably performed on a stage set up in a patio, obey certain conventions that were peculiar to the Spanish tradition of the three kings. Most important for our purposes is the strong sense of exchange between the kings and the infant. The kings give the infant gifts on the condition that he will one day sacrifice himself for them. In short, the kings "restitute" to the infant the *tribute* that the latter, in turn, owes God the father. As in Europe, the gifts of the magi are viewed as payback or as tribute.[84]

This background of payment and restitution, so central to Christian theology, sets the stage for a remarkable characteristic of these plays: the presence, especially in the *Comedia de los reyes magos*, of a prophetic payback by Mary to the kings for their gifts. As always, these plays were used to organize groups, to inculcate principles of correct decorum (how to kneel, how to address, etc.) all so as to stimulate the gifts or tribute that flowed to the church. But the *Comedia* of 1607 goes further, revealing that one strand of the magi tradition associated the three kings with different social classes. In short, Mary decides that the kings deserve something in repayment for their gifts, and what the kings want in exchange is knowledge of their future.

To Caspar, a noble who, as a fine person, cannot tolerate manual labor, Mary promises heaven because he had given her precious metals. Balthazar's gift of unguent and myrrh was poor, but his exertion for her son was decent, and so Mary promises him that his prayers will be answered. Melchior, however, with his "bit of incense and myrrh," could hope for little recompense, and Mary tells him gloomily that he and his sons will remain dirt-poor and tied to the land without hope of betterment.[85] Thus in that wonderful (if here sinister) plasticity of the magi theme, the organization into the provinces of New Spain that had been a hallmark of the application of magian pluralism, now yields at the end of the sixteenth century to an inculcation of class ideology by means of the magi story for the newly emergent colonial society.

The more one gave, the better one's chance to be saved. The kings of these plays protested to the Virgin that they had "given all" they had, but it had not proven enough. The Tlaxomulco play ends with an eighty-year old man, who for no less than thirty years had collected contributions from onlookers to this magi spectacle, stepping forward as he always had. So well established was this festival! Placing his empty collection basket on the ground before him, he addressed the infant in Nahuatl, saying that he had nothing to give besides the basket and the fatigue he had had in carrying it. "But he offered him that."[86]

Almost a century after the Tlaxomulco spectacle, and in the very different cultural setting of a five-hundred-member Jesuit mission among the Hurons of North America, the processional imitation of the magi was still being employed by missionaries and being engaged in by natives who thought thereby to be incorporated into another colonial power's procession. Though it is beyond our immediate sphere of interest, the decisive similarity of a French Jesuit Epiphany among the woodland Hurons of the far north in 1679 to that of the Jaliscans of central Mexico a century earlier is so relevant to the social history of the magi as to require its inclusion here. As ever, a missionary presents the native Americans as zealous emulators of European practices. Wanting to carry through their village the ceramic Jesus that was in the crèche (*grotto*), which they incessantly visited, the Hurons decided first to

imitate what in other ages had been done by the three great foreign captains, who came to confess and adore Jesus Christ in the manger, and afterward went to preach about him in their own country. All the Hurons, Christians and non-Christians alike, divided themselves into three companies, *according to the different nations that constitute their village; and, after choosing their chiefs*, one for each nation, they furnished them with porcelain, which [the chiefs] were to offer to the infant Jesus. Everyone adorned himself as handsomely as he could. The three captains each had a scepter in his hand, to which was fastened the offering; each wore a gaudy head-dress to imitate a crown. Each company took up a different position. The signal for marching having been given them by the sound of the trumpet, they heeded the sound as that of a voice inviting them to go to see and adore an infant God new-born. Just as the first company took up their march—conducted by a star fastened to a large standard of the color of sky-blue, and having at the head their captain, before whom was carried his banner—the second company, seeing the first marching, demanded of them the object of their journey. And on learning it, they joined themselves to them, having in like manner their chief at their head with his banner. The third company, more advanced on the road, did as the second and, one after another, they continued their march, and entered our church, the star remaining at the entrance. The three chiefs, having first prostrated themselves, and laid their crowns and scepters at the feet of the infant Jesus in the cradle, offered their congratulations and presents to their savior. As they did so, they made a public protestation of the submission and obedience that they desired to render him; solicited faith for those who possessed it not, and protection for all their nation and for all that land; and, in conclusion, entreated him to approve that they should bring him into their village, of which they desired he should be their master. I was engaged in carrying the little statue of the divine infant; I took it from the grotto, and from its cradle, and carried it on a fine linen cloth. Everyone seemed touched, and pressed forward in the crowd, to get a nearer view of the holy child. Our Hurons left the church in the same order in which they had come. . . . They marched, then, in that order toward the village, chanting the litanies of the virgin, and went into a cabin of our Hurons, where they had prepared a lodging for Jesus. . . . There they offered thanksgivings and prayers, in accordance with their devotion, and the divine child was conducted back to the church and replaced in the grotto. The Christian Algonquins were afterward invited by the Christian Hurons to a banquet. . . ."[87]

This procession agreed in every respect not just with the one done earlier in Mexico, but precisely with what one might have expected in Europe at the time, right down to a major dance done by the Huron women, which closed out the festivities. Cognoscenti will even recognize the surviving Iberian and Ibero-American custom of having church saints visit homes once a year. We shall encounter such little Jesuses on the roadways of seventeenth-century southern Germany as well.[88] But what is of decisive import for our story is the repeated association these Jesuits recognized between the magi story and the principles of social organization and behavior the missionaries were sworn to enforce. It is a lesson those "captains" (not monarchs in this account!) would teach into the present century.

REBELLION

We might conclude this chapter merely by demonstrating just how successfully magi plays have survived and revived the centuries, continuing to offer the creole, mestizo, and indigenous cultures of Latin American both diversion and a sense of solidarity. Until recently, there was the important magi play performed at Mitla in central Mexico. From Popayán in Colombia to the Pueblo cultures of New Mexico, 6 January still brings with

43. *Adoration of the Magi* (with a statue of a secular priest representing Jesus)

it celebrations of the magi.[89] And in the parish of San Blas in Cuzco, Peru, a new twentieth-century magi play continues to grow in popularity (fig. 43). The list of such plays and spectacles is long.

Yet chronicling is not what this book is about. To conclude this chapter, I want to open up another vision of the magi as it is revealed in Latin America sources, so that, in the following chapter, I may carry that vision back to the European world. To date, my inquiry has taken two different tacks in assessing the moral quotient underlying the dramatic and pictorial image of the magi. First, the story has been understood to be ecumenical in character, a plurality of peoples becoming one for purposes of common reverence and thus social order. On the other hand, a strong case has been made that the seeming unity of the three kings actually conceals a series of competitions and conflicts pitting social groups against each other. Indeed, in these present pages I have shown that that conflictual model in the Americas could take on an open class character. The magi became poor and found that different rewards awaited them in the afterlife, depending on the size of their gifts to Jesus, that is, to the church. What I wish to show now is that for all the seemingly solemn law-and-order nature of this iconograph, the dramatized story of the magi induced some devotees to rebellion.

The Hispanic-American institution that was the seedbed of subversiveness was the cabildo, which entered the Americas from Spain with the earliest settlers. In its simplest, archaic, peninsular form, a cabildo was the governing council of a confraternity or brotherhood. In Spain, the monarchs had traditionally required males to join such confraternities, which linked them institutionally to the crown. That link was particularly important for men who were not otherwise bound to the crown through other political institutions, like blacks or Italians. The system was firmly in place in Seville, whence it came to the Americas.[90] With the arrival of the Spaniards in the Americas came a system of cabildos that over time brought native American "foreigners," as well as incoming black slaves, under the administrative authority of the Spanish crown. They were led by "mayors," or "kings," who represented members before and were responsible for their behavior to the crown.[91]

Often enough, these cabildos had the task of organizing community festivals, and commonly enough, those confraternities with secular (as distinct from ecclesiastical) duties were named after the magi. Even today among the Mayos of northwestern Mexico, in the town of Banarí, a cabildo called Bahi Reyesím (group of the kings) is responsible for heraldic festivities, whereas its opposite, the Bahi Mariam, is responsible for events in churches.[92] One must imagine that, among other things, groups like the Bahi Reyesím in centuries past had factual control over the magi plays, and thus over the paraphernalia used in the magi plays, such as the chalices and other ecclesiastical silver that so commonly held the gifts owed the infant.

In 1769, the archbishop of Mexico took steps to prohibit—again—the biblical dramas for precisely this reason:

> [The plays] have [always] been dissonant, and they violate . . . a general repeated prohibition two and a half centuries old because of the grave sins, imponderable consequences, ridicule, vain observances, irreverences, superstitions, and other things . . . which motivate them. We [also] declare . . . prohibited . . . the representations of the Pastors and the [Three Magi] Kings, because of the irreverences and profanations of vestments and sacred ornaments that accompany them.[93]

In Europe, one has no trouble finding episcopal inventories that contain lists of such things as crowns that were worn by play kings on Epiphany; they were obviously to be returned to the sees after being used for any particular festival.[94] In Mexico, the plays had been outlawed for over two centuries because the Americans, after taking over these cloaks and vessels, had obviously been using them in secular enjoyments, for example, to booze and banquet on the eve and day of Epiphany, as must also have happened in Europe. Doubtless, the native cabildos, both those in charge of secular matters and those supervising the churches, helped make such objects accessible to the locals. In the conquered and subordinated world of the Indies, one imagines that the Epiphany could serve as a means for such units to turn the world upside down through playing kings.

That is especially so given the importation into the Americas of the European custom of begging on and around Epiphany, a custom to which we shall give closer attention in chapter 5. We have already seen the tip payed beggars, called in late medieval French the *aguilaneuf* and in Spanish the *aguinaldo*, in play at Tlaxomulco, where the Epiphany play was followed by a collection that should be viewed as a type of tip.

The social group that participated in this begging and giving was often a patronal network of a type, including but not limited to groups producing a common product. Ortiz, for instance, believes that in Cuba, such begging may have begun among the king's slaves, who on Epiphany honored the prince or viceroy with a performance of some type and were in turn rewarded by "payment" of the *aguinaldo*. As Ortiz sees it, that early practice grew to the point that finally, all the blacks of Havana joined in what was indeed a carneval to amuse the ruler and thus earn the *aguinaldo*.[95] In this reading, one moved from communitarian to social networking on Epiphany. The "magi's" search for the *aguinaldo*, on Epiphany, was the one and only link that this begging had to the ecclesiastical story of the magi.

Just as with the utilization of the chalices, so the "magian" right to demand gifts that would then be passed on to the child—an impressive example of representational tribute—opened up the possibility of social unrest as the "kingdoms" of the magi organized themselves and saw the power of their numbers. At a minimum, the evidence we shall present forces us to recognize that the colonial rulers of the Americas watched apprehensively each year as the wretched of the earth exercised their right to dress up, conceal their identities, and then demand some greater or lesser redistribution of wealth during the feast of the kings. We see that De Bopp was indeed right when she claimed that the three poor kings of the dramas we have described had already come "to identify themselves with the conquered."[96] But could power be redistributed by the collections of the magi?

The period that began in the late 1530s was one of considerable unrest throughout New Spain, and it will come as little surprise to find that the figure of the magi was part of the cultural backdrop to these uprisings. Thus in October 1537, the viceroy wrote to the emperor that on the previous 24 September, a date having no connection to the magi, the blacks had elected a king and had sworn among themselves to kill all the Spaniards and to lead an uprising in which the natives had agreed to take part.[97] Nothing seems to have come of this, for in the following year, black kings and queens took part in a great celebration in Mexico City. The everlasting to and fro between the danger and the necessity of festive presentations here comes to the fore.[98] Again in 1540 and 1541 there were disorders that may have involved such festive monarchs. Then in 1609 another commotion occurred in Mexico City:

> A rumor circulated regarding a rising of the blacks. It was said that on the previous 5 January, the night of the Kings, many blacks had joined together and elected a king, and others with titles like dukes and counts, and other princes found in any government. And even though this rumor spread through the city, in the first place it troubled the spirits of the viceroy and the other lords of the Audiencia. Looking into the matter, it was found that it was limited to the blacks.[99]

A few whippings, and the whole thing seems to have come to nothing.

The danger associated with Epiphany extended to Lima, Peru. The rumor there in early 1667 was that more than three thousand natives had come together outside town in preparation for an uprising on the eve of Epiphany. The Spanish force that went out to find these people returned with the leaders of the uprising, who were punished on the following 21 January.[100] With this modest evidence of blacks already using their right to organize and celebrate on the feast of epiphany, we conclude this powerful manipulation of the magi image in the Americas both as a means of stimulating the Spaniards to explore for gold, and as a means to reorganize the indigenous peoples according to a "Christian" model. Native Americans as well as settlers have responded. In many towns of present-day Latin America, the three kings dress up and parade through the streets on Epiphany, if mostly in simple ceremonies.[101]

On the other hand, the modern festival of the kings is the occasion for gifting only among the Hispanic, not the native, population. Native resistance to the adoption of European cults is a positive, not a negative, matter, perhaps especially in the case of the Epiphany, which was historically used by the Spaniards to tax their native subjects. Still, along with the Corpus Domini (which has a monarchical rather than a "republican" structure), the image of the magi provided the most important restructuring image for Spanish attempts to convert the natives. In the sense that the native magian kingdoms might find a place within the plural political universe of the American viceroyalties, or find a place that subverted the praising of the God-child, the results of our inquiry are both worthwhile and significant.

Meantime, back in Europe the rage to find first Prester John and the land of Ophir, and then the lands from which the magi came had subsided as geographical knowledge, as well as the very real conquest of gold mines, consumed men's interests by the mid-seventeenth century. True, Protestant protests against the magi tales also took their toll, but only very slowly and then mainly in northern Europe. But the terrestrial search for the magi fell of its own weight, especially after one last spectacular claim proved a chimera.

In 1610, a Dominican named Luis de Urreta made what he considered an astounding discovery when an Ethiopian named Joan Balthezar visited him in Valencia. Joan claimed that he himself descended from the family of the magus-king Balthazar. Indeed, he went on to insist that the descendants of all three magi were alive and well and living in Ethiopia. King Caspar had been a native, while the descendants of Balthazar and Melchior had long since moved to Ethiopia from their former homes in Arabia and Persia to escape persecution by non-Christians. Still more amazing, Urreta learned, rule over Ethiopia rotated from one magian family to another, the ruler himself being called Prester John. It seemed to Urreta that the millenial puzzle of the whereabouts of the magi had been solved at last.[102]

Urreta's claim had almost no half-life. By 1622, an outstanding kenner of Ethiopian history, the Jesuit Pedro Paez, had composed his own multi-volume history of the land, a centerpiece of which was a corrosive dismissal of everything Urreta had said. Paez had taken each of the major planks of the latter's argument and presented them to the ruler of Ethiopia, who assured him that neither Urreta nor his source knew anything about Ethiopian history or institutions.[103] Still more indicative of conservative European Catholic thought on the magi at this time is a remark by Manuel de Almeida in 1628 in still another assault on Urreta. It had been a baseless fabrication to say that there were descendants of the magian kings in Ethiopia, Almeida charged. "The oldest and best informed men," he decisively asserted with unintended wit, "aver that they know nothing about the Magian kings except what is written in St. Matthew's gospel."[104]

Chapter 5

THE ANCIEN RÉGIME OF THE MAGI

MARTIN LUTHER was having none of it, that eve of Epiphany 1531. Into his second decade of rebellion against Roman Catholicism, Luther in a sermon that day exhorted his listeners to forget the three kings, and instead honor the baptism of Jesus, which as we know was also commemorated on 6 January.[1] That occasion had been truly historic, the preacher said, whereas the memory of the so-called three kings was insignificant and could be dumped. Their cult had been created in the first place to make money (*pecuniae causa*), and but for the credulity of Christians, it might as easily be consigned to the dustbin of history. Luther would have seconded Nikolaus von Dinkelsbühl's fifteenth-century protest against the many adorations that showed the infant greedily grasping at the gold coins and pieces offered him by the first king. That was not what Jesus' epiphany was about.[2]

The whole blessed tale of the magi relics was a lie, Luther repeatedly insisted. How were these Arabian kings supposed to have gotten to Germany in the first place, he wanted his listeners to ask. And to whom did those bodies in Cologne belong, after all? He himself had seen them, and, in his view, they could just as easily have belonged to peasants as to kings.[3] Luther made his listeners feel as if they had been duped into kneeling at the feet of pagans, if not peasants. Sounding much like a typ-ical medieval preacher at this juncture, he then urged his listeners not to make the pilgrimage to Cologne to see the relics. It was all a lie and a shame.

Luther's condemnation of the cult of the magi was itself not decisive in shaping attitudes toward the magi in early modern Europe. Who could take the Saxon that seriously in this matter? Besides other exaggerations, his statements that the Roman Church considered magian kingship a matter of doctrine and their burial site certain were pure hogwash, as his critics pointed out soon enough.[4] Calvin's criticism of the magi were taken more seriously by contemporaries than were Luther's, but the Reformers' condemnations only very slowly affected the geography of central European celebrations of the Epiphany in subsequent centuries. In general, the rites associated with Kings' Day that were celebrated in Catholic Europe after the reformation can be documented in Protestant Europe as well.[5]

The reason for leading off this chapter with Luther is to draw attention, through his person, to some important early modern shifts in the way the magi were, or were not, emulated in European life. These shifts are the subject of the present chapter, and they may be summarized as follows. First, kings stopped having themselves represented as magi, demonstrating a change in the way royalty or powerful men related to the image of the magi. Second, the spatial and moral focus of Epiphany celebrations shifted from altars to crèches and from kings giving to kings begging. Third, children's plays emerged as pedagogic instruments. This chapter witnesses the arrival of the magi levying taxes.

In the nineteenth and twentieth centuries, the gifts of the magi—gold, frankincense, and myrrh—have become important marketing images for a secular society. Thus the magi still worship at the crèche to the ancient cry "Oh, admirable commerce"! In chapter 6, we shall follow the kings back to their origins through modern visions and imaginings of the nature of reverence and exchange. But first, we turn to the journey of the magi in the early modern period.

BOURGEOIS BANQUETS

The area stretching from Besançon in Franche-Comté eastward to the canton of Fribourg in Switzerland was removed from the main trade arteries of this age, and its resulting cultural conservatism proves to be useful in studying magian cultural forms. The celebrations in this area furnish us with some important details regarding public commemoration of the magi, and also allow us to follow the growth of the Epiphany as a domestic celebration throughout Europe. This area offers us the best evidence for observing the early modern shift in Epiphany celebrations from the civic to the domestic hearth.

The data from Besançon propel us back to the thirteenth century, where we can observe the beginnings of civic Epiphany celebrations in the liturgical dramas of three of that city's major churches. Succinctly, the procedure in Besançon's collegiate churches was as follows. Sometime before the Epiphany, the canons of each church elected a king for that festivity.[6] He would have two central duties. First, he was to be the main celebrant of mass, and in that role, while sitting in a thronelike chair at the offertory of the mass, he would accept gifts from three other canons dressed like the three kings. Thus, the canon elected king by his fellows played Jesus to other canons playing the magi. The second task of this king-celebrant on Epiphany was to sponsor and pay for a banquet for all members of the collegiate. We best understand the whole process when we think of the collegiate as the corporation it was, and so comparable to lay corporations that elected kings in these days. Like them, the canons chose a king to officiate and pay for a banquet they all enjoyed.

The most imposing of Besançon's corporations was, of course, that of the citizenry itself. Some time before 1365, they decided to throw an elaborate annual banquet on Epiphany, preceded by a cavalcade. The "ruler" of that banquet would be known not as a king but as emperor because Besançon was part of the Holy Roman Empire. The emperor for the Epiphany a year hence would be chosen during this banquet, at which point the assembled citizens would cry out a salute to the emperor-elect. Doubtless glasses were raised as part of this toast, with those present almost certainly employing the classic cry, "The King drinks!" ("Le roi boît!")[7] That cry basically legitimated the results of the election or coronation which had just taken place.

The authority on these matters in Besançon, André Castan, found detailed information regarding the civic banquet only for the years 1465 to 1469. During that period, participation was substantial indeed, some 268 persons being wined and dined, including some very important persons from the kingdom of France. After 1469, the banquet was a much smaller affair, with only the members of the city government participating. Still later, it appears that the public celebrations were increasingly taken over by the young people.[8] But the important thing to notice is the feature common to both the ecclesiastic bodies and the civic one. To hold a banquet, both corporations elected a prince. Note that at this point, there is no evidence of the civic and the ecclesiastical kings interfacing. We may observe the civic cavalcade making its way to the banquet, but no documents allow us to claim that the riders headed for the church to worship the infant, as one might suspect. The ecclesiastical and civic bodies appear to have acted relatively independently of each other.

This basic layout of civic banquets being held outdoors alongside church celebrations of the Epiphany in church, is found over a longer period of time in a broad band of towns in the canton and to the south of the bilingual city of Fribourg, a complex whose Epiphany celebrations have been thoroughly studied by Schärmeli.[9] Her story begins around 1425, with the first evidence in Fribourg of a three kings' play. According to a document of this date, the pastor of the church of St. Nikolaus had to pay the three clerks who played the kings twelve pence apiece,[10] a play that by all accounts took place within the same church, or at most included the kings' short "journey" outside and around the nearby church of the Virgin.[11] Clearly, in European terms, this liturgical drama had come late to the canton.

Whether a civic banquet existed at this date is uncertain. Not until 1578 are the famous *Königsreiche* or *royaumes* mentioned in the Fribourg sources. These were short-term festive corporations that at Fribourg were three in number, two of particular guilds and the third representing one of Fribourg's important families. Together they formed the retinue or constituency of each of the three kings. Each of the three kings had his *Königsreich*. Since the end of the sixteenth century large military units had joined the cortege of each king; these were large units indeed. Each of the three *Königsreiche*, that is, the sponsoring guilds and family, bankrolled a banquet for its members.[12]

The uncertain, complicated history of the Fribourg festive organization yields to easier comprehension in Schärmeli's study of Epiphany celebrations in several towns to the south and west of Fribourg itself. First, a *Königsreich* existed in town after town . This civic cavalcade and banquet was led and partly paid for by a king, whom the town councils usually elected; he was variously called the *roi de bourgeoisie*, the *roi de la ville*, and the like. Schärmeli did discover that the king in the town of Greyerz indeed doubled as the first of the three magi-kings encountered in church services, but more generally, the two structures—city king and magi—were quite distinct for about two centuries, the former a layman and the latter clerks.[13] This is so from about 1468, when information on the *Königsreiche* begins, until around mid-seventeenth century, when the *Königsreiche* disappear everywhere but in Fribourg itself.

The most significant fact about these *Königsreiche* from our point of view is that on the feast of the epiphany the "kings" of neighboring towns made what one may call official state visits to each other. Thus between 1468 and 1512 the kings of Albeuve, Bulle, Vaulruz, and Marsens, as well as the queens of Pringy, were received into Greyerz;[14] Estavayer-le-Lac played host to the monarchs of Payerne, Grandcour, Cuby, St. Aubin, and Murist between 1494 and 1540;[15] Fribourg welcomed the king of Giffers in 1497;[16] and the king of neighboring Remaufens was received in Châtel-St.-Denis between 1595 and 1621.[17] Often these visitors were from towns under the authority of the towns they visited, so that a type of tribute-duty was almost certainly involved. Still, the message was one of amity, the visiting monarchs being guests of the host city at the civic banquet. For a period of about a century and a half the feast of the three kings—in one tradition legates themselves—was the context for an exchange between different towns in the canton, microlevel diplomacy modeled on the macrodiplomacy of the great powers.

At some point in the later sixteenth and early seventeenth centuries, most of these towns began to hold three kings plays, apparently for the first time; the exception was Fribourg itself, which had a long-established play. The late dates for this introduction hint at an almost archaic undertaking, for this was at the very time when elsewhere in Catholic Europe, such three kings plays were on their last legs. Just as important, Schärmeli found that when the plays began in these towns, the *Königsreiche* ended, again except in Fribourg. Her conclusion is that towns south of Fribourg were moving away from secular celebrations of the Epiphany and toward ecclesiastical ones.[18]

Before accepting this conclusion, however, we must refine Schärmeli's surprising findings. What for her was a move from the profane to the sacred was apparently more of a shift in style, away from a nonnarrative banquet or *Königsreich* in which the bourgeoisie acted like a court, toward a narrative, quasi-sacred drama, called a Herod play, that was still run by the laity in a lay space or theater outside the church. In several towns citizens auditioned for parts in such plays, with the exception of the three kings, who were still played by clerks except for the anomaly of Greyerz noted earlier. These clerical magi were, indeed, engulfed within large military cavalcades that left little doubt about their lay inspiration.[19]

In the town of Romont, a local church took steps to capture some of the popularity of the Herod plays for itself. In late 1674 it successfully appealed to the town council to permit the building in the church of a *théâtre de l'adoration*, (a crèche), which would redound to the greater glory of God.[20] In other words, the pastor of this church wanted the part of the Herod play that dealt with the adoration to take place within the church at cribside, not outside on Herod's stage. Yet subsequent events showed that even here the towns retained the initiative. A few years later, in 1678, complaints arose against clerks who did not know their lines in the (adoration) play, and by 1685 the town announced that it would continue to allow the (adoration) theatre in the church, that is, the actors would only come into the church to do that part of the whole story, if the clergy fulfilled its responsibilities.[21] What the town gave it could take away.

Thus it is not surprising that the general thrust of churchmen was to attempt to suppress the Herod play altogether, a task they succeeded in at Greyerz in 1755.[22] This was part of a large-scale European suppression of public festivals that had been underway for some time in other parts of Europe, to which not just the church but also the political authorities contributed.[23] Perhaps Castan was right that in Besançon the fear of public gatherings and the determination to suppress them went back to Philip II of Spain, prince of Franche-Comté, and his fear of Protestantism. In any case, again following Castan, when we look outward from the protected cocoon of conservative Fribourg, we see the domestic celebration seemingly everywhere supplanting the ancient public celebration of the three kings.[24] Royalty itself was an important part of this movement.

Magian Royals

By any standard, the disappearance of royals from European paintings in which they had commonly had themselves pictured as maguses adoring Jesus was little short of spectacular.[25] Both the apogee of this practice, as well as the evidence of its decline, is apparent in representations of members of the Habsburg family. Maximilian (d. 1519) appears in many paintings, and his grandson Charles V (abdicated 1556) is shown in several, but I have not found a single painting in which either of Charles V's successors—Philip II of Spain or the Emperor Ferdinand—are to be found in magian rags.[26]

What makes this even more surprising is that the grandest explosion of adoration paintings in the European tradition was just beginning at this time. While the second third of the sixteenth century witnessed a marked decline in magi art in Italy, among the so-called Antwerp Mannerists, adorations were churned out at a stupendous pace.[27] Nevertheless, very few adorations in this corpus have been suspected of representing historical individuals, and the well-known monarchs of that age seem to be completely absent.

Of course, throughout the early modern period one can find the occasional conceit linking a reigning monarch to the adoration. Flattery of this type was not about to disappear. On Epiphany 1550, a spectacle was held in honor of a visit by the future Philip II of Spain to Milan. After a necromancer had augured Philip well, three sons of Ferdinando Gonzaga, Philip's governor of Milan, appeared armed before the prince, followed by black pages, and announced to Philip that just as the magi had offered gold, frankincense, and myrrh to Jesus, so their father would offer his own blood while consecrating himself to the Spaniard's service.[28]

Just as surely, the occasional reemergence of the magi in their traditional iconography of triumph is not to be denied. An engraving we have already encountered shows the young Louis XIV of France being wished well by three past kings of France, ensconced like so many magi, in a cloud.[29] A century later, the adoration of the magi stood for the church triumphant in the great pediment of the royally patronized church of the Carmelite nuns in St. Denis, near Paris, sculpted on the very eve of the French Revolution (fig. 44). Thus monarchs did not totally reject the magi as their ancient "brothers," and the emblem of the magi as the Christian triumphal icon par excellence was still employed. But the pickings are indeed now few and far between. The time when secular rulers had legitimated themselves by playing kings was largely past.

The reasons for this decline seem evident enough. The printing press brought a revolution in the variety of means by which royal legitimation

44. Joseph Deschamps, *Adoration of the Magi*

could be asserted, so there was less necessity to remain with the magi, whose royal status was now open to serious question among Protestants and some Catholics. Just as important was the slow growth in the bureaucratization of the crowns, whose power could be verified in princely decrees enforced by court servants, both civil and military. The press and bureaucracy thus came to provide a living image of royal authority and power, so that the very type of sacred images patrons would pay for had changed.

Certainly geographical discoveries decreased the power of the magi, for they showed that there were four continents, not three. That realization alone made the magi less relevant as an ecumenical symbol for that majority of Europeans, who could not imagine the three races of mankind—blacks and Asians outweighing whites—as a veritable representation of world order. A particular festivity in Todi, Italy, in 1563 is suggestive in this respect. Wishing to raise money for the Monte di Pietà or official pawn shops, the authorities on the first Sunday after Easter sponsored a *rappresentazione*. "Four kings, representing the four parts of the world," appeared in procession, fabulously dressed and followed by their pages. One of these kings, each of whom wore a crown of great value, was white, another red, a third black, and the fourth olive brown. After the procession arrived at its goal and the preacher had praised the Monte, the four kings stood up and went forward to kneel at the high altar, "which represented paradise."

They then testified that Christ was the king of the whole universe, and because of this they should give him all their reigns, crowns, and scepters. This they did, raising the crowns from their heads, the necklaces from their necks, and the scepters from their hands, and offering them all to paradise, where there were some members of the company of the Monte di Pietà [to receive them].[30]

Then each subsequent part of the procession followed the four kings, and made its alms.

Quite apart from the fact that this festivity did not include a representation of the local political authority, as magi festivities commonly did, it can be seen how little room there was for real royals in such a scene, which attempted to represent four races for the four parts of the world. Thus this festival was not magian, though the magi inspired it in all but name and number, right down to the collection of gifts on the altar. Nor did the Todi festival retain any reference to actual political powers. Royal power had moved outside the space of the adoration of the magi and had chosen other means to drive home its legitimacy.

Even as the magi ceased to be an important vehicle for describing princely power and sacrality publicly, a newly documented type of "private" princely feast appears on the European stage. What is striking about the early modern magi festival is that the princely court steps to the fore as a stage for "private" performances, and that these courts play at the magi with a grammar very similar to that in use among the general public at this time. I refer to the well-known habit of early modern courts celebrating domestically, as did a certain range of their subjects, but then broadcasting the details of that domestic celebration to a voyeuristic public, which would ideally emulate them. We shall come to the bourgeois celebrations of the age in due course. For now, we ask how the princes of Europe celebrate the Epiphany in this period. My answer will reveal a dynamic slowly moving these princes away from the public and urban celebrations we have previously chronicled.

The earliest description of a court celebration of the feast of the kings that I have found is a 1462 account of events in the home of the Constable of Castile, Miguel Lucas de Iranzo, in Jaen. The chronicler of this princely house tells how, after dinner on 6 January, a lady with child and a man entered the hall on an ass, obviously playing the role of virgin, child, and Joseph:

And with great devotion, the said constable received her and led her up to his seat, placing her between the said countess [his wife], doña Juana his sister, doña Guiomar Carrillo [his wife's] mother, and the other ladies and maidens present. And the constable withdrew to a room at the other end of the hall. And a short time later he came out of the said room with his pages,

[all] very well dressed, with masks and with crowns on their heads in the manner of the three wise men and each with a goblet in his hands with his present. And thus he advanced through the hall very slowly in a most dignified manner, looking at the star which guided them and which was attached to a cord which was there in the said hall. And thus he reached the far end where the virgin was seated with her son and offered his presents amidst a tremendous din of trumpets, drums, and other instruments. And after this had been done . . . he dressed differently . . . and he began to dance with the said countess. . . . The same constable kept and solemnized this feast every year, it is said, out of devotion, and also because it was the birthday of our lord the king [Henry IV], to whose service he was devoted.[31]

To all appearances, this fiesta reproduced at home an Epiphany drama of the type traditionally performed in a church, with the constable assuming the role of a priest and of the clerics who usually played the magi, and, importantly, the infant becoming none other than the king of Castile. The real star of this domestic drama—loyally recorded by a chronicler presumably to console his subjects—was the constable himself, who in effect adored his king in the guise of honoring the magi. The constable's chair, whence he usually conducted solemn business, was now the triumphant chair of virgin and child. He it was who solemnized the proceedings with his magian role, gait, and orchestra, and it was the constable, finally, who led the dance. A description in the same chronicle of Kings' Day, 1464, is still more elaborate, giving the details of the banquet that was then followed by the performance "of the History of when the kings came to adore and give their presents to our lord Jesus Christ."[32]

Written evidence of this type in turn throws much light on some of the most important Epiphany paintings of the fifteenth century, which in turn prefigure some important written Epiphany texts of the early modern period. In a famous painting by Jean Fouquet (fig. 45), we see that Charles VII of France is definitely a magus who, like the constable of Castile, steals the show from the other magi. He obviously celebrates the Epiphany at his own court, again like the constable, as seen in the mock battle going on in the background of the same painting, in a play castle that has been added on to an actual building. This image of a mock battle reminds one of the mock battle that Francis I of France staged on Epiphany 1521. At Romorentin, the French court saw the count of Saint-Pol have the luck of the draw, which meant he was crowned King of the Bean.[33] To demonstrate his soldierly prowess, this king then began to defend his castle—as in our painting—by hurling apples, eggs, and snowballs at the besiegers, among whom was Francis I.[34]

In addition to the adoration itself, and to the battles that seem to have been common means of celebrating Kings' Days in this age, the banquets

45. Jean Fouquet, *Adortion of Charles VII*

themselves deserve mention. Perhaps the most impressive princely banquet in the visual realm is that illustrated under January in the *Très riches
heures* of Jean, duke of Berri. In the background tapestry, four squadrons
of knights square off in battle for a castle, apparently referring to the
battles of that day; in the center, a group of burghers push forward to
participate in the banquet, while up front, an all-male aristocratic/clerical
society gorges itself on the rich epiphanic table laid out by the duke.[35]
    This famous banqueting scene is illuminated by some well-docu-
mented banquets of the type that were given by the prince-bishop of
Mainz and his chancery, from the early seventeenth century to the eve of
the French Revolution.[36] Here again, the corporation that held the banquet was called a *Königsreich* or kingdom, and its membership was chosen by lot by the same chancery. The banquet itself was called a *Wirt-*

schaft. Banquet, dance, joust, and sometimes even a magi play were to be found at many courts across Europe in these early modern centuries, and with care can be found complementarily described in both art and literature. As we shall see, each of these events then can be found in the bourgeois celebration of the feast during the same time periods.

The courtly forms that we have described were all celebrations at home in the court rather than in church; indeed, the fiesta of the constable of Castile actually contained a sacred play performed in this lord's living room. There is some indication at the end of the Middle Ages and in the early modern period that in addition to this innovation, other new courtly forms were emerging that actually reached out from the court to the community at large, with just as little involvement of the church.

One new form of the prince magus is found in the region of northern France that we have been studying. According to his biographer, Louis II, the so-called "good duke" of Bourbon (d. 1410), celebrated the feast of the kings each year through a particular charity or devotion that seems not to have involved the church.[37] Before the feast, the court sought out the poorest eight-year-old boy in the city of Moulins—in effect, an infant Jesus figure—and brought him to court, where he was dressed regally and treated like a king by the court. Then on Epiphany eve, the boy-king was placed in the seat of honor at banquet table for the meal.

At this point, the maître d'hôtel set about formally begging "for the poor king" from all those in attendance. Each knight at court had to contribute one franc each, each page a half franc. The duke himself customarily gave £40. The purpose of this begging (*quête*) was to raise money for the boy's education. On the particular occasion described by his biographer, some one hundred francs were gathered by the official, and that sum was turned over to the father or mother of the boy to spend on his schooling. Jean d'Orronville concludes his account by stating that Duke Louis followed this custom all the years of his reign.

An Italian ruler came up with a second "new" courtly form. Accompanied by his court, Ercole d'Este, the new ruler of Ferrara, surprised the citizens of his town on 5 January 1473 by traversing the streets on this and the following night collecting anything that his subjects would place outside their doors; he repeated the exercise—called "an adventure" (*ventura*), or test of one's luck, the following, Epiphany evening, this time on horseback. The idea from the beginning was "to do [the duke] honor." The custom grew, lasting till the beginning of the sixteenth century.[38]

The Ferrarese chroniclers of these events want their readers to believe that all this was done freely by the duke's subjects. In the early days, it is said that the duke would knock on the doors to get goods; by 1501, however, he gathered them "without knocking on the doors, because the gentlemen and citizens came outside [to greet him]."[39] Still, a note of apology creeps in when the same chronicler states that this was done "with good heart, by those who could afford it."[40] And most important, the chronicler Zambotti does not conceal the fact that year after year, in the wake of this epiphanic gathering, the duke appointed the civic officials for the year.[41] Thus the citizens were in fact constrained to give. The collection was a type of tribute, as was clear in 1502 when the goods worth a thousand florins that Alfonso d'Este gathered in his *ventura* were used to defray the expenses of his wedding to Lucrezia Borgia.[42]

In narrating what he took to be a "new" custom, Werner Gundersheimer did not realize the significance of this rite's being performed on Epiphany, and this took a toll. He did not know that the custom of collecting gifts outside doors was ancient, nor did he recognize the tributary character of the Ferrarese gifting when he wrote his recent book.[43] Indeed, Gundersheimer says that the Duke of Ferrara turned over what he collected to the poor, a notion that is not in the sources and is instead, as we saw above, contradicted by them. Yet Gundersheimer did sense what readers of this book will find important, which is that Este enhanced his dignity and power "by institutionalizing a form of humility."[44]

What is central in the activity of both Louis of Bourbon and Ercole d'Este is that they both introduced the notion of the poor, rather than the rich, magus, the begging rather than the simply giving prince. These two princes both went about actualizing the ancient magian principal of taxation or tribute by acting like a beggar, not liberally, as behooved a rich prince. It appears that already in the fifteenth century, princes were rethinking the nature of the prince as a fiscal and a monetary creature. No longer the purely liberal giver, he was now a collector, and the resulting gift became a proof of the prince's legitimacy as a representative of his people.[45]

One powerful traditional image of the ideal ruler was that he commanded an inexhaustible wealth—like the magus who brought gold to Jesus. A ruler this wealthy, of course, had no need to tax his subjects, and indeed the contract between these ideal types often involved swearing off taxation. Yet the reverse of that utopian coin is not just that such tax-free states have never existed in fact. More important, a gift given by such a hypothetical nontaxing ruler to another ruler would perforce lack sincerity and conviction. By its very nature, a gift, especially a diplomatic one, has no moral value to its recipient if it does not implicitly contain within itself the subjects' contribution to that gift. Only a gift that is the people's seals a contract between giver and receiver. The significance of gifts between rulers depends on those gifts representing the subjects of the bestower—their work and their contribution.[46] Like any princes, the magi, if they were to speak for the gentilic world, had to be representational, but also representative figures.

State theorists rarely take into account medieval persons' realism regarding the actual moral content of gifts. But the magi were presumed by their subjects to give the wealth of nations, which had been harvested, or mined, by those very subjects. In fact, that gold had been in someone else's hands before the king sequestered it, to eventually give it to Jesus. What is then so striking about the Bourbon and Este maguses whose behavior we have detailed is that, though rulers, they festively begged from their constituencies so as to command the latters' wealth, a goal that was obvious even when they represented that wealth as going to the poor. And they did so at a time when, among the nonelites of Europe, begging by the three kings was on its way to becoming the classical early modern representation of these monarchs.

Beans, Beggars, and Blackface

The ethnographer Hans Moser has usefully formulated a stark distinction between the medieval and modern days of the kings. In the old days, he says, the magi were pictured as rich men who gave endlessly to the poor. In early modern Europe, on the contrary, those who played the magi were poor and begged from the rich.[47] As we already have seen in the actions of the Bourbon and Este princes, the formulation has something in its favor. But now we must turn to a general overview of epiphanic celebrations below the princely level if the more general contours of this phenomenal change are to be understood.

Because customs are so specific to time and place, it is difficult to achieve an overview of epiphanic celebrations in early modern Europe. For example, the canton of Fribourg witnessed none of the star singing and begging that in the following pages will seem ubiquitous.[48] Yet generalize I shall because a limited number of fundamental festive structures or vocabularies were in use across Europe in this age. However, we must be careful to avoid arriving at a false sense of European unity.

First, many of the customs that I shall describe do not apply only to 5 and 6 January. The social exchanges I shall describe are usually represented as greetings or as threats carried out on the first day of the year. That might be the Epiphany, but it might also be Christmas or, most commonly, 1 January.[49] The one thing that distinguishes the exchanges I shall concentrate on from the ones on Christmas and New Year is that the celebration of the feast of epiphany had clear associations to the magi.[50]

Second, while it is true that in Iberia Epiphany presents were distributed by adults to children of the possessing classes, these domestic presents are not the gifts I shall describe. The exchanges I will zero in on were asymmetrical, passing from the possessing classes to outsiders who could not celebrate the holidays at home, often because they had none.

Third, the Epiphany customs I shall now review should not be understood as flowing from the aristocracy downward. Rather, the historical evidence suggests a concurrent growth of these customs at different levels of society.[51] Nor should these customs be thought of as necessarily early modern in origin. Most of the specific customs to be passed in review are mentioned for the first time in the fourteenth century in several different political and social contexts.

Finally, the reader will recognize that I use nineteenth-century, mostly rural, evidence from the folklore *Manuel* of Van Gennep, mostly for the purpose of confirming earlier information. I have labeled such "modern" evidence as such, recognizing its limitations for proving the existence of a given custom in premodern times. That having been said, let us review the most important customs, beginning with the public festive vocabulary as we already know it and then passing on to what we know of the domestic celebration of the early modern period.

For centuries, reaching back to the earliest Middle Ages, collectivities of various types elected a temporary prince during Twelve Nights who was charged with leading that community through upcoming festivities. This king or emperor or abbot sometimes associated to himself a queen or other female dignitary, as shown in figure 46. If these kings had any connection with the liturgical drama of the time at all, we noted that they were more liable to play Herod than any of the three kings.[52]

Traditionally, the upcoming festivities centered around a banquet, especially the one on 5 January. This banquet can be thought of in the first place as confirming the election or coronation of the prince, a confirmation that was accomplished by a toast. For example, the electors might cry "the king drinks!" (*Le roi boit!*). This cry, first recorded in the early fourteenth century, became a standard part of such banquets, especially in France. We shall see that anyone who did not join in the toast invited punishment.[53]

But basically, the banquet must be thought of as an occasion for various cohorts to bond with each other, or at least to initiate new members into the group. Much food was eaten and drink flowed freely, all of which the king holding office was responsible for, indeed often paid. The need to pay for the banquet sometimes caused the collectivity to kidnap someone whose ransom would contribute significantly to covering the banquet cost, a custom still in place in the late Middle Ages.[54] But more characteristically, it led members of the group to beg for the money and goods to throw the banquet. In France and in Spain and then in the Americas, from the end of the fourteenth century forward, the object for which one begged was called the *aguilaneuf* or *aguinaldo*.[55]

The social dynamics underlying all these traditions were long established in the public sphere. For centuries, the evening before the Epiph-

46. *Procession of the Queen of the Bean*, the Hours of Adelaide of Savoy

any had also been known as a domestic festival, and it is impossible to decide if the public rite or the domestic one had precedence. One important part of this festive grammar, however, stands a good chance of being domestic in inspiration, so that the domestic celebration of Epiphany can be understood as a discrete unit of cultural activity. This rite concerns the means by which kings were actually elected.

Two means emerge from the sources for the election of kings, both involving chance. The most direct involved the so-called *billets des rois*, or kings' chits. Made mainly in Lille, their use was customary in Flanders in the late Middle Ages and early modern Europe; they were still being printed in the present century. These cards came in sets of sixteen that assigned one's place in the temporary kingdom and court, from king

47. Jan Steen, *Twelfth Night Feast* (1662)

down to a humble servant. Clearly, such a means of electing a king could as well be employed in a public as in a private setting.[56]

The same cannot be said for the by far most often mentioned and widespread means of election, the famous kings' cake, either the *gateau des rois* or *gallette des rois*, documented from the early fourteenth century and still a festive standby in much of Europe and some of North America to this day. A cake or pastry concealing a bean was placed before the domestic group, and the one who got the piece of cake with that bean became the king—and sometimes queen—of the bean for the remainder of the feast. To avoid cheating, a senseless and thus "objective" infant member of the family was the one who actually determined who got what piece of the cake.[57] Originally developed in France, the practice ultimately spread across the Rhine to become part of Germany's Epiphany customs.[58]

On its face, it does appear that this procedure was distinctly domestic, or at most courtly, in character. At least, I am aware of no descriptions of such cakes being used in public fora. But while we are enabled to imagine the domestic banquet as a form in itself, we soon find that public forms were very close to the surface of the domestic feast. In the fifteenth century the habit appeared in the familial sphere of crying out "Le roi boît!" when the chosen monarch imbibed after being elected. We know this

48. Jakob Jordaens, *Le Roi Boît*

scene very well because the Flemish painter Jakob Jordaens (d. 1678) painted it repeatedly, with just this title.[59]

The domestic election of kings across Europe shows a good deal of variety, of course. The person who was crowned king or queen might truly be any member of the household. On the other hand, domestics might be excluded from the draw of the cake.[60] As we see in the available paintings, the person who lucked out might be any male, including a very young child as in the Steen painting shown above (fig. 47). On the other hand, the oldest male member of the family might in fact always become king as a matter of decorum, a procedure that must have guided the families Jordaens shows in his paintings, all of whose kings are paterfamilias.[61]

Thus all the elements of these domestic rites, with the possible exception of the *gatêau des rois*, can be found in a public setting as well as around the domestic hearth. When in early modern Europe the established celebration of Epiphany turned inward, a domestic festival incorporating these elements was thinkable across Europe without any necessary "leakage" of the events or the groups practicing them outside the walls of the household. In general, these domestic banquets do not have a biblical model, nor do they usually involve priests or churches. However, such leakage is indeed perceptible in the early modern period in three activities that need to be addressed.

One of the central questions confronting all students of New Year rites—whether they were performed on Christmas, New Year's Day, or Epiphany—is whether any given practice derived from Christianity, or preceded it. One aspect of this question is whether the election of a king by social groups in late December or early January had any clear relation to the biblical tale of the magi or so-called three kings. In our postfideistic age, to formulate a question in this way is to insure that it will be ignored. Today's students of past customs recognize that the underlying premises of many such customs are transecclesiological, and thus the traditional question is proper more to church historians than to ethnographic historians.

Yet I raise the question at this point because of a piece of seemingly weak, definitely modern, and yet important evidence that suggests a linkage between a domestic practice and a church practice in early modern Europe. Without documentation, the modern Catalan ethnography record compiled by Amades asserts that in the Barcelonan parish of Pi, each family did elect a king for a purpose external to the household as well as for the domestic banquet itself. Because it was impossible for all parishioners to visit the parish crèche or "Betlem" to adore the infant, Amades says, each family used the bean to elect a king whose duty it was to go to the crèche as a family representative and adore the infant.[62] Amades adds that in effect, every person who adored and kissed the (statue of the) infant was eo ipso invested with the dignity of a king.

Although this European evidence is recent and isolated, it cannot be ignored because of the powerful early seventeenth-century document of Thomas Gage. Cited in the previous chapter, the latter describes worship around the crèche in Guatemala at that time, a devotion that doubtless had its roots in the Iberian peninsula. There, a representative from each family or from each confraternity, in Gage's words, adored the infant in the crèche. As the magi had represented their gentiles, so these crowned men effectively represented their social groups. I would not be surprised if future research turned up precisely such a model of adoration by representation in European sources of the Barcelonan type, in which a household king of the bean was at the same time a household ambassador, or magus, before the crèche. Here then is one area in which the lay king of a domestic festival becomes a quasi-sacred monarch celebrating in the public sphere the biblical figures whose very essence, it will be recalled, consisted in making available to devotees both the behavioral and the spatial model for reverence.

A second exception to the rule of nonleakage of the domestic celebration on Epiphany refers to the crèche, which became an important part of early modern devotion. If we are to adequately imagine the spatiality and morality of the early modern effectuation of social reverence, we need to reflect on the character of the early modern crèche. The crèche itself has been the object of many studies, so we are well informed about the emergence of the art form in and of itself.[63] Yet very little attention has been paid to the all-important question of how Christians, like latter-day maguses, comported themselves devotionally around this group of figures, which is precisely what is important for our study. In one form or the other, crèches began to emerge in the late thirteenth or early fourteenth century. They were commonly but not necessarily located in a church chapel, but they might also be found at the entrance to a church, near the town hall or, somewhat later, in people's homes. From early on, they consisted either of a simple nativity scene—with a minimum of three separate figures—or of a more complicated adoration scene, with a minimum of seven figures, including the three kings, but with no maximum number of figures, or of something between these extremes. Pride of place belongs to a sculpted life-sized adoration crèche attributed to Arnolfo di Cambio (1291) rather than to any simpler nativity scene.[64]

The reader can quickly grasp the behavioral innovations implicit in the crèches. First, these were figure complexes that could be constructed and manipulated by the laity or any lay group. They could be large-scale or small, made of fine or modest stuffs that matched the simplicity of the historical event, like natural hair, straw, plaster, wood, etc. Second, the figures in the crèches could be changed by these empowered laypeople or at their direction over the yule season to concur with the calendar. One might begin with a nativity scene around Christmas, move to a scene with shepherds, then peak with a full-scale adoration at the feast of the epiphany. Next, these *homines fabri* could add a bewildering variety of other objects to the scenes, for example, every imaginable object of wealth the magi *might* have brought with them.[65]

Perhaps most fascinating, the structure of the crèche, especially in its early days, encouraged devotees to take their place in it. The most profound expression of this new spatial reality is certainly the New Sacristy of Michelangelo, in which devotees wander in the magian space surrounding them; the most popular, and contemporary to the New Sacristy, the early adoration scenes of the *sacri monti* of northern Italy where, before the counter-Reformation decided otherwise, one could also wander about within the space of the magi and make their journey with them, "identifying with the magi as they approached," in Berliner's words.[66] One modern has gotten the potential of crèche-making precisely right: "To construct a crèche is [equivalent] to reconstitut[ing] the offerings of the shepherds and the Three Kings, and in some way to participate in [the event]."[67]

I am not inclined to ascribe to the crèches a disproportionate social importance; they formed, after all, but a small part of the armory state and church disposed of in molding reverential behavior. But to a certain extent, I am drawn to the argument that such activities made it easier for rulers to exploit Christians, sometimes even as they empowered the actors. Further, many crèche critics have, over the centuries, pointed out that these figures were usually little more than dolls and in the process, they imply, the sacred tales they tell lose their artistic interest and sacral importance. That argument is wrong-headed as well as self-interested.[68] Yet our task is not to pass judgment but to construct an image of the kings at work and play in early modern Europe. We are left with little doubt that through the crèches, the peoples of early modern Europe could not only construct their sacred stories of the birth (and death) of their lord, but, by experiencing how much little Jesus depended on the magi's reverence, they could better understand how their earthly rulers depended on them for their legitimacy. As a result, they themselves could shape the way in which their communities organized themselves for reverence, as well as for insult.

This was accomplished mostly apart from the church. Certainly many churchmen, grasping the attraction of the new form of devotion—which peaked, of course, in the magi making gifts to Jesus, that is, the church—charged an admission fee for the faithful to see the parishional or cathedral crèche, at one with those in civil society who had crèches made and installed them on their own premises for the specific purpose of making money through selling admission. A similar tale could be told about the magi automatons that were so popular in early modern Europe.[69] But such church response to the marketplace is precisely the point. At best, these crèches were merely blessed with holy water; they were sacramental, not sacred in the normal sense of these terms, and thus could largely escape ecclesiological constraints. To attract viewers, contemporary entrepreneurs, churchmen as well as some laypeople, sought out and responded to community input regarding these realistic representations. They made and remade crèches to be popular.

A further feel for the important spatial innovation represented by the early modern crèches can be gained as we now return to the domestic hearth to isolate the third form of leakage from the domestic to the public realm of the magi. The first, we recall, was the family's election of a domestic king who went as its representative to worship the infant at the parishional or communal crèche, the second the crèches that mediated between home and church altars. I refer now to the widespread European custom of giving some portion of the domestic banquet on 5 January to someone outside the hearth, commonly in the context of at least feigned opposition to such liberality.

As usual, the details of how this was done are enormously varied, even if the principal of sharing is consistent. Seen from one angle, the northern French custom was the simplest. In this area, the first piece cut from the *gateau des rois*, or cake of the day of the kings, was set aside as the *part à Dieu*, to be given to "the first poor person who came along," as was commonly said.[70] The ideal was pure luck of the draw, a common mode of charity in traditional Europe. This principle of luck tells us something about the original nature of the *part à Dieu*, which may have escaped the notice of previous researchers. Precisely that term was used in the Middle Ages by canon lawyers to designate a sum owed by parishioners, most notably testators, to God for the maintenance of the fabric of their church, and more generally, for the maintenance of their poor. In certain canonical traditions, one could settle that debt by giving the sum, generically, to "the poor," that is, to a deserving person or persons otherwise unknown to the giver.[71] The famous *part à Dieu* of the French Epiphany is in fact a vestige—now seemingly absent any canonistic flavor—of a debt the rich owed their "genuinely poor" neighbors.

Though the notion of a *part à Dieu* was not well anchored in German-speaking Europe, this area's customs did of course include banquet rituals, as well as the practice of gifting visitors on Epiphany Eve, as the research of Hans Moser and others has shown.[72] Indeed, visits of beggars seeking gifts actually started on the three Thursdays before Christmas (*Klöpfelnächte*), with those who had no home announcing to those who did that Jesus was about to be born, and receiving small gifts in kind and coinage in return.[73] In the fifteenth century one finds evidence in southern Germany and in some areas of France not only of persons knocking on doors and begging for something, but even at times of being welcomed in to participate in the domestic banquets.[74]

Who were these persons who begged on the night of 5 January? The paternalistic tradition might lead one to think that "the poor" just happened by, to accidentally become the recipient of the house father's largesse, but a moment's reflection makes it clear that groups of poor existed who were always prepared to take advantage of the need of the possessing classes to manifest their generosity. In fact, the later fifteenth and early sixteenth centuries in Europe are notorious for having produced a culture of begging that was perhaps unprecedented in this continent's history.[75]

The research of Moser in Germany, and Van Gennep in francophone Europe, will allow us to identify the social status of these groups of beggars and their dates of emergence in the century from 1470 to 1570, but let us first establish that the magi—*poor* magi—did emerge eventually as formal or cultural bearers of the begging message. According to Van Gennep, the oldest evidence of begging *rois mages* comes from Colmar in

49. Johan Conrad Seekatz, *Dreikönigsspiel*

Alsace in 1462, a date that may stand for France as a whole.[76] Moser presents somewhat later first evidences for Germany. On perusing the early modern ethnographers (Boemus, Franck, Kirchmayr, Waldis), all writing before the mid-sixteenth century, Moser found repeated mention of Christmas singing in general, of formal banquets (*Wirtschaften*) and of the election of a *Bohnenkönig*, but no mention of the star or of the kings who in the future will always accompany that star.[77] With unimportant exceptions, all references to the kings as public beggars, singing beneath a spinning star, date from after 1550 (cf. fig. 49). Perhaps a holiday practice had again passed from the West to central Europe. Perhaps princely beggars like the Bourbon and the Este had provided the begging forms for those in the streets.

From sometime in the early sixteenth century, trios of serenading young males, wearing inexpensive crowns and often armed with a sword or scepter or even a bludgeon, were to be found abroad on the night of 5 January begging for sustenance they claimed they had a right to. Their behavior was simplicity itself. First, they sang, announcing at the front doors of the possessing class that they were three kings who had "come from afar."[78] Their songs usually insisted that it was cold outside, so that the inhabitants should decide quickly if they were going to give something to the kings or not.[79] If the latter did gift them, they would then sing a song wishing the inhabitants the best of new years, with good crops and business. If they did not, they were directly or indirectly warned of evil consequences awaiting them. Thus a disappointed beggar might wish a stingy householder besieged by rats.[80]

A minor but important comparative element that emerges from the German evidence must be mentioned here. In several cases, it becomes clear that the poor kings brought with them on their rounds a statue of the infant Jesus, which they presumably offered to their hosts for their pious embrace and kiss.[81] We do not know if the infant Jesus came from the local crèche or was something the magi beggars themselves owned. In the previous chapter we found local magi bringing statues of supernaturals from churches into the homes of Huron devotees at this time, and in that American context I noted that it is today customary in parts of Latin America for neighborhood saints to "visit" the homes of parishioners on feast days. By any measurement, we have here a comparable practice, that in the present context was linked to stimulating alms for the poor magi.

These beggars were the same kings who in the story were on their way to visit Jesus at Bethlehem, and yet now their image was that of poor kings, as Moser noted. Yet like any rulers, these magi got their wealth through tribute rendered by their "subjects," and these modern magi openly manifested their tributary needs through begging. Now the ancient ecclesiastical underpinnings that had constrained earlier magi to pretend to yield up their accumulated wealth to the infant and his church were less constraining. Generally speaking, these new magi were themselves the wretched of the earth, who used this day to make meals for other days.

Let us be clear about who these early modern magi really were. First of all, it is the uniform view of ethnographers that the magi were younger than they once had been. As compared to the Middle Ages, when seniors, youth, or at least adolescents had played the kings, children were now the usual actors and beggars.[82] We shall follow this generalization, with one important qualification, which is that these were not the children of those who could celebrate Epiphany with the traditional domestic festival. There is no evidence of children going begging, and then celebrating the holiday at home, as is customary today. Rather, these children appear to have been either the homeless poor or the poor without adequate support.

Certainly young students were the most common of the latter group. As we have already learned from the tale of Louis II Bourbon, there were many youngsters who, different from more fortunate colleagues, could not continue in school without help from outside, including the begging that they did at opportune times of the year like the feast of the kings. This was not only their claim, but that of the school authorities who at times vouched for these poor students and petitioned communities to allow them to beg with just such logic and to just such ends.[83] Not surprisingly, these sums did not necessarily go into the students' pockets, but occasionally were handed over to the school or church.[84]

It was easy for elders to claim that the children or young people who begged did not need to, that they merely made trouble when they did, and in general that they did not use what they gained wisely. Complaints were common, and the tendency of the authorities to suppress such begging was ever present. One synodal constitution of Angers protested in 1595 that beggars in this season said they were going to buy a great candle for the Virgin, but they ended up dining instead, while another source described kings who had received four shillings and used it to drink *ein halb fas bir*.[85]

Clearly, magian beggars were by no means all children in these early modern centuries, as the registers of the folklorists make abundantly clear. Isolated individual adults can be found receiving permission to beg—like the half-blind widower Hans Walch who was the father of "countless children" and could only survive by begging.[86] Much more significant are the discharged soldiers who appear in the sources. They came crowned but also well armed to the homeowner's door, presenting the more menacing an appearance because they were far from home and had no restraints on them. They were a regular menace to communities, for they had nothing to lose by threatening to burn down the homes of stingy Christians.[87]

In addition to soldiers, there were other groups that did have a geographical focus and pursued the *quête* on Epiphany in their own region. A recent account gives us the flavor of a sentiment that was doubtless much older. Before 1860, the people on the right bank of the Saône, near Autun, complained bitterly that on New Year's Day people from Bresse across the river came over with empty sacks, which they filled for their many children and even for their pigs.[88] It was truly an exploitation of the charitable soul of the people on the right bank, they said.

Though recent and regarding New Year, not Epiphany, this document does point to the fact that from the beginning of *Dreikönigssingen* and begging, the magi did indeed often come "from distant parts." In fact, Moser could show that some journeys, which might appear innocent enough in complaints that people flowed en masse into towns from the countryside on 5 January, indeed sometimes continued for weeks, with small bands from distant villages moving from town to town with their songs and entreaties before turning homeward.[89] To summarize, while a majority of the cases of the begging kings I have found do feature ex-

changes between members of a given community, including those homeless in that community, an important minority of perhaps 40 percent of
the cases in fact concern regional exchanges by beggars far from home.

I now turn my attention to a little-known custom featured among
these kings that was found widely in Europe, where it is still practiced: in
France, the Rhineland, and Catalonia, but probably elsewhere as well. It
puts a new face on the magi as they interacted with audiences in early
modern Europe. I refer to the common presence, among the magi, of
one king made black. The meaning of this practice stays uncertain because the document base is still narrow, but it remains important to comment on it and to take note of some of its obvious implications.

The oldest documentation of this practice I have found is in a letter of
pardon of 1415 from the Ile-de-France. Without further explanation, it
says that in that region, 5 January was called *les rois brousés*, that is, the
day of the blackened kings, or "the day that the [Three] Kings were
blackfaced." Van Gennep, our source for this information, suspects that
that appellation was also the name of a charivari held in Paris at nightfall
on that day.[90] The rites of charivari usually involved a series of inversions,
including (as in this one) a great deal of so-called rough music, made with
"instruments" like pots and pans. Perhaps one element of this charivari
vocabulary involved blackening the faces of certain participants.

With this late medieval evidence in place, we can show that from an
early point in the history of early modern three kings celebrations, blackface was widespread in western and central Europe. In some areas, a
blackfaced king was elected in house, as a type of opposite number to the
domestic king of the bean. We can be confident of this because in some
modern settings, household domestics could not be drawn as king of the
bean, but did enter the lottery for choosing the black king.[91] Thus within
such domestic celebrations, a distinction existed between white kings,
who were related to the homeowner, and black ones, who commonly
came from the domestics (much like black servants often accompany
white magi in adorations). Furthermore, blackfacing was the punishment
in-house as well as at the local pub for those who refused to cry "le roi
boît!" each time the king imbibed, that is, for someone who spoiled the
fun by refusing to recognize the king's coronation, which is to say that he
allowed year-long antagonisms to continue into the holiday season.[92]

The specific practice of blackfacing the magi who appeared in public is
also found from an early point. It is implied that this action, accomplished
with soot or a piece of coal, was a type of punishment, even if in the world
of play.[93] What is most striking about this practice is that with exceptions,
the sources describing this blackfacing of the kings refer to one king alone
and do not indicate that either of the other two kings was represented
distinctly the one from the other.[94]

This is new evidence that the magi had an essentially more dualistic than a triadic nature, as I argued in chapter 3 on the basis of the visual evidence. This new ethnographic evidence also thickens the plot surrounding another curiosity involving magi paintings. As emphasized by Kaplan, there are at least ten paintings across Europe in which the third king, while black in his face, remains white in his hands or legs.[95] Not unreasonably, Kaplan supposed that before the new rage in the fifteenth century for black maguses, these figures had originally been painted white. After popular taste changed, artists returned to the canvases and made at least the face brown or black. But the ethnographic evidence strongly suggests that in the same general time period of the early to mid-fifteenth century, the blackface of the paintings was somehow related to a growing festive habit of blackening the faces (but not the rest) of the last magus. The question of the relationship between paintings and festive representations is a longstanding one in western art history.[96] This case appears to demonstrate the link, if not causality. It can only be speculated that the paintings show the status of festive black kings, rather than vice versa.

Although much of the evidence regarding medieval blackfacing remains to be gathered, it must be related to the distinct role the begging black king assumed in early modern and modern festive representations, with every allowance made for regional variations. In most areas of Europe, the black king is charged with the actual begging. He collects the donations of those who hear the magi's song and plight.[97] In Iberia, the same king is associated with tom-foolery and clowning of a type that amuses children.[98] In Germany, the black king, called Caspar in some traditions, almost certainly provided the inspiration from which sprang the well-known trickster figure of Casperle.[99] It needs scarcely be emphasized that in this new figure of the third magus, everything that Europeans knew about blacks was close to the surface.

No doubt, the European image of the black was on balance negative in these centuries, there even being one modern case in which a blackfaced girl played the role of third "king."[100] Much of the blackened king's public foolishness certainly derives from stereotypes about Africans.[101] Yet it would be foolhardy to make racism responsible for blackface without taking into account other behaviors of blackened kings that offer more mundane explanations for some of these rites. I refer to blackface employed primarily as a way of concealing one's identity. This kind of masking was widely used by those who threatened while begging or forced themselves into homes to insure that they would receive their "gift."[102]

Careful examination of the evidence shows that blackfacing was employed not only in-house, and not only by one of the three kings outside. There were festivals of groups of blackfaced kings, and we have seen one source refer to the "heilige Drei Käspar"![103] We also mentioned one case of 1415 around Paris in which 5 January was called the day of the *rois brousés*, or blackfaced kings.[104] But the period after Epiphany may have been just as important in this regard, with a sense of climax informing the cases I have found in this time frame. In modern Novéant-sur-Moselle on the Octave of Epiphany (13 January) the "little kings" (*peuts rois*), were celebrated. This involved both boys and girls blackening their faces and transvesting, that is, disguising themselves, before marching through the village together.[105] On the Sunday after Epiphany in nineteenth-century Hautvillers (Marne), the epiphanic (white) monarch had to host a meal for all those who had been in his court. In the midst of this festivity, that king, only seeming to resist, was blackened by his former courtiers, presumably putting a term to the holiday season.[106] If the earlier feast of the *rois brousés* may use blackness as disguise, this postepiphanic celebration seems to have been used to put an end to the festive kingdoms, the fate, alas, of all phony kings.

With the little information at our disposal, it is best to wait for more information before trying to grasp the meaning of these practices. Making a person black did indeed have a negative tone. In the Americas, friars blackened themselves on Epiphany to play the black king going to Bethlehem.[107] In Cuba, natives of Africa about to celebrate the Epiphany in mid-nineteenth century were known to darken themselves further if they thought themselves too light.[108] And in modern Puerto Rico, the three kings as a part of their penitential offering all paint themselves black as they pursue their begging.[109]

This completes an overview of the magi's journey in early modern European history. Remarkable transformations have been observed. Even as some of the more conservative areas of Europe first perfected their public banquets and church plays in this time, the princes of Europe were beating a wholesale retreat from their earlier penchant to show themselves as magi-kings in paintings and festivals; other means of legitimation offered themselves to these royals, who seized them and went on to build the modern state.

Yet the sources of the time also show that these same princes had taken to celebrating the magi and the Epiphany in a domestic way, freer from ecclesiastical constraints than their predecessors had been. And in these epiphanic games one first glimpses the "poor magi" of modern times. Thus in the nonelite spheres of European society, the phenomenon of begging kings grew up, and it was such kings who definitively marked the magian festivals of early modern times. Crèches, blackface, and the *part à dieu* were encountered everywhere, as the societies of the old regime, through domestic festive instrumentalities, attempted to deal with the very public poverty of those who knocked on the doors of the bourgeoisie. The crowned poor magi of these centuries constructed their own types of constraint to force upon those who owned. The threat posed by these homeless kings might have been bothersome to contemporaries, yet at a distance, we may remark how far did these little kings, who could at times appear subversive, seem from the assertive three kings of yore!

REVOLUTION AND REACTION

And yet, as the age of revolution dawned in the second half of the eighteenth century, it became clear that the three kings still remained a symbol of some power among contemporaries. The *encyclopédistes* of the French Enlightenment, no friends of the popular festivals of their time, applauded the European rulers who brought about their suppression.[110] Voltaire himself reflected on the festival of 6 January, noting just how much emphasis remained on the royal character of the magi, despite the long period in which the educated had certainly learned how dubious that claim was. "Everywhere," said Voltaire, "the feast of the Kings is celebrated, nowhere that of the Magi. One cries out: '*le roi boît*,' and not: '*le mage boît*.'"[111] Certainly, the philosophe would have agreed with the modern Vicomte Poly that a celebration like that of the kingdom of the bean survived even the French Revolution "because it conforms intimately to the essentially monarchical temperament of our race.[112]

Thus on the outbreak of the French Revolution, the link between the magian three kings and the institution of monarchy was still evident to some social critics of the time. It comes as no surprise that three years into the Revolution, at Bordeaux in 1792, one such critic tried to suppress the pastrymakers' custom of making and selling *gâteaux des rois* to their clients on Epiphany because such cakes were "hardly compatible with the republican spirit." At that moment the city simply sidestepped the counselor's zealotry by having these cakes henceforth named "cakes of liberty" and the day itself "la fête des Sans-culottes."[113] In subsequent years, the custom was interdicted at the national level. On 4 Nivôse of Year III (Christmas Eve 1794), pastrymakers were denounced for still making the cakes, and, the mayor of Paris ordered such men to be arrested, "for these pastrymakers have none but liberticidal intentions." By marketing these cakes, these pastrymakers were in effect supporting the "festival of the said Kings."[114] Nor were these cakes the only victims of such revolutionary alertness. The countless taverns and hostels in the French sphere of influence named after the *Rois-Mages* or *Drei-Könige* had their names changed to something harmless like *Zu den Drei Mohren*.[115]

Early in the twentieth century, Chabot argued that the average French person attached hardly any political importance to the festival, though the festival itself remained as popular as ever.[116] Perhaps the zeal of the honorable revolutionary had been overdone, perhaps not. What is important is that the image of the three kings retained its charisma, not just among monarchists, but even, as remains to be seen, among the triumphant bourgeoisie of nineteenth-century Europe. The romantic reaction against the Revolution would actually lead to a magian revival that would last a good part of the nineteenth and twentieth centuries. Our concluding chapter will chronicle less the last days of the magi than their emergence as modern visionaries of the market.

Chapter 6

RETURN BY ANOTHER WAY

THE POLITICAL importance of the magi came to an end in early modern Europe, but their social significance, transformed for modern needs, has persisted. This transformation has been significant, even as the movement from a traditional to a modern world has been massive. Lay society has increasingly turned the magi into ahistorical ghosts in their recent Epiphanies. An ancient symbol of power and triumph anchored in the notion that they had indeed once visited Jesus, the magi have been transformed by modern cultural pessimists into fetishes producing gifts. The magi embody a peculiarly modern spirit of hope.

In general, the magi are no longer the three kings and again bear the designation of the "wise men from the east." Increasingly in modern times—as in centuries long removed—the magi are thought of as hoary counselors for a troubled world rather than as "brothers" of the monarchs who (used to) rule us. Modern secular society has come to use the very word "magi" to designate wise males, whatever their religion, indeed whether they worship gods or not. The magi we shall examine in this chapter are ever less Christian. Beginning with some latter-day Christian visions that already betray dehistoricization, we shall follow the magi from "behind the mountain" where Spanish children await these gift-bearers each year, by way of modern department stores where the magi's gifts can be purchased by ordinary humans, to the mountain fastnesses of far-off Asia, where these know-it-alls stand ready to rescue us from the Occident's perceived soullessness. Denizens from the West search answers from a world saturated with conflict, and some find it from wisened old Asian males.

How does today's global social order sustain its authority? What are we to make of the international exchange system in which we swim? These and the other central problems of social life that we have previously described still command our intention. The journey, indeed even the adoration of the magi, understood as the cosmic symbol it has always been, still images solutions to these problems.

THE MAGI AS AGELESS PROPHETS

Publishing his *La saincte Geographie* in 1629, Jacques d'Auzoles Lapeyre undertook a serious attempt to locate on the globe the various lands of the descendants of Adam and Eve.[1] In the course of his research, he came upon the Jewish prophets Melchizedek, Enoch, and Elijah, who together with Moses, according to d'Auzoles, had been bodily assumed into paradise and had never died. They thus became what has been called "mediums for the revelation of heavenly secrets to humanity," of the type d'Auzoles himself sought to answer.[2] Seven years earlier d'Auzoles had done a separate monograph on Melchizedek, which in its subtitle announced that this prophet "was still alive, in body and soul, although it had been three thousand, seven hundred years since he blessed Abraham."[3] The *Saincte Geographie* is accompanied by several fascinating historical tables that demonstrate just how seriously the notion of sacred geography could still be taken a century after Columbus.

Nine years later, in 1638, d'Auzoles brought out a new work in Paris entitled *L'Epiphanie, ou Pensées nouvelles à la Gloire de Dieu touchant les trois Mages. . . .* Part three of this work proposed these "new thoughts," which were indeed unprecedented at the time. According to d'Auzoles, the three kings who came to visit the infant at Bethlehem were none other than the live Jewish prophets Melchizedek, Enoch, and Elijah.[4] He admits that when he wrote his *Saincte Geographie* in 1629, he had not yet concluded that this was the case—and there is no substantive mention of the magi in the former work. All the more firmly, however, does he now affirm this to be true. Melchior is none other than Melchizedek, Gaspar, Enoch, and Balthazar, Elijah. These magi did and indeed still do worship the infant Jesus until, d'Auzoles states significantly, "such time as they will return to the Terrestrial Paradise, which is their perpetual country and residence."[5]

It is not difficult to divine some of the implications of this radical and novel notion, that the "magi" (*not* kings) were Jewish prophets. The most wicked of these was certainly that the whole reliquary theatre at Cologne was a fake, since the magi were not buried, but quite alive, as the author forecefully explains in part 4 of the work.[6] D'Auzoles's idea was dismissed as fantastic by the Jesuit author Inchofer, who brought out his own more cautious overview of the three kings story a year after d'Auzoles.[7] And when in 1654 the Jesuit Crombach, based in Cologne, published his monumental work on the magi and their history, he was little short of apoplectic when it came to d'Auzoles, especially regarding the latter's attack on the Cologne relics.[8]

D'Auzoles's imaginative speculation—some uncharitable souls called it lunacy—did not, to be sure, singlehandedly open up a whole new way of looking at the magi. Since the early Christian centuries and into the early modern period, the astrological skills of these "magicians" were taken for granted, and their annual feast days had often been linked to forecasts of the future.[9] Like the Jewish prophets d'Auzoles now held them to be, they had long been conceived as supernaturals able to help the living determine what the heavens had in store for them.

Within that recognizable context, d'Auzoles's speculations did represent something quite new. Not only were the magi even now still alive. They represented not merely a Christian, but a Judeo-Christian cultural tradition and were at home in what can be called a transecclesiastical paradise. Here again the way had been prepared by a series of treatises of the late sixteenth and early seventeenth centuries dealing with the question of the celestial and terrestrial paradise, and with the so-called four rivers of the world that were said to have their source to the East, in Eden.[10]

In d'Auzoles' hands, the magi seemed to speak for an occult world of hoary but hale wise men, whose power resided in their wisdom and no longer in their monarchical sovereignty. Perhaps it was no accident that later ethnographers in southern German-speaking areas might find scribbled on house doors not only the customary good-luck sign "Caspar + Melchior + Balthazar," but also "E + E," that is, "Enoch and Elijah"![11] This new imagination of the magi occurred not only in the wake of early modern hermeticism but also at about the time when the first court-sponsored academies of intellectuals were taking form in western Europe, bodies which later centuries would describe as scientific priesthoods also able to calculate the future.[12] This modern image of the magi in mountain fastnesses also overlapped with the early modern interest in those many distant corners and edges of the globe that the generation of Columbus and Magellan had left to later ages. They were both physically distant and ineffably spiritual. In time, the idea would take hold that rather than being travelers, the magi—not necessarily the evangelical wise men but magi nonetheless—were immobile in lofty fastnesses, awaiting the journeys to them of hopeful laymen disillusioned by life in the flatlands of the West.

This illusion that wisdom was in the East was obviously related to the missionary conviction that such remote locations of fabled non-Christian religions were so many more regions to subordinate, both spiritually and materially. The mountain fastnesses of central Asia proved particularly attractive. In 1627, a Portuguese Jesuit from India named Esteban Cacella reported to his superiors in a high state of excitement that he and a colleague, Juan Cabral, had entered Xigazê (Chigatsé near Llasa), the then capital of the largely unknown land of Tibet. In his communication, Cabral called this "the gateway to all of Tartary and China and other pagan countries,"[13] hoping if not to find colonies of ancient Christians, then to begin the evangelization of new ones. At roughly the same time, the discovery of an important stele in western China confirmed the West's belief that Nestorian Christians had long ago come that way.[14]

But this was not all. Locals told the missionaries about a fabulous kingdom that lay to the north, called Shambhala, and in a flash Cacella determined to try to find this realm so that he could convert it. Shambhala has never been found, of course, but to this day it remains a mysterious region of the East that is far away and yet at the core of one's self. Books describe it, and contemporary films do not lag behind.[15] Whether Shambhala or Shangri-là, such legendary locations have become metaphors for the place where the world's wise men reside, and thus the seat of our souls.

Since the seventeenth century, and on the back of much serious science, South and Central Asia (Turkistan, Nepal, Bhutan, Kashmir, India, etc.) in general and Tibet in particular have become a magnet for many persons seeking passage out of the problems of modern Western urban life. One of the central goals of some of these travelers has been to give themselves over to individual gurus or groups of monks who, they think, can provide them with a direction they have lacked in their previous lives. It has not been surprising to find these Asian savants viewed as magi, roughly although not directly comparable to the magi who stand at the beginning of Western Christianity. More of this story lies ahead. What we have first to confront is how such a new notion of the evangelical, yet immobile, magi could come to pass.

ROMANTIC PUPPETS

Fascination with the East, whence came Matthew's magi, was one of the important features of European romanticism. The determination of many to seize and hold fast to the origins of their own cultures, especially in the wake of the French Revolution and the beginnings of industrialization, created fertile soil for the notion that wise men abode in largely unexplored regions of the earth, and of the soul.

Romantic visions were an important part of this reaction against revolution and often against modernity, and it is within this context that the magian visions of two remarkable Catholic visionaries should be described. Born in 1774, Anna Katarina Emmerich was a Westphalian farmer's daughter who on falling ill became and remained an Augustinian nun in Dülmen, Westphalia, until her death in 1824. She is said to have had many visions between 1818 and 1824, which she allegedly described to the German romantic poet Clemens Brentano, during a conservative, arch-Catholic period of his life—the age of Metternich.[16] Born a century later, in 1898, in the isolated farm town of Konnersreuth near the Czech border, Theres Neumann remained an important figure in the Europe-wide swell of twentieth-century visionaries until her death in 1962.[17] The world of Neumann encompassed the Weimar Republic, Nazism, and the post-World War II period.

Like most western female visionaries, who in the last millenium have done so much to create the traditional picture of the magi, Emmerich and Neumann described their experiences to males who recorded them and were important for their propagandization. So pronounced was Brentano's role in mediating Emmerich's experiences that, in the modern view and even in that of some of Emmerich's contemporaries, any statement about what Emmerich saw or said was really a statement about Brentano's own creative imagination.[18] The same must be said of Neumann, although no writer of Brentano's stature associated himself to her cause.[19] Thus, the visions of these women must be construed as male glosses of a broad, popular, and literary resentment of the modern. A typical vision showed Mary or Jesus complaining to the visionary that modernity's secularized behavior was leading to catastrophe. Interest in this perspective has not flagged, and an important contemporary literature continues to forward the causes of Anna Emmerich and Theres Neumann.[20]

Although these two women were not contemporaries, their visions bear certain similarities. This is not surprising, since they came from similar backgrounds and were treated by authority in similar ways. As was traditional, the visions of both women occurred in conjunction with the ecclesiastical calendar, and those featuring the magi are usually said to have taken place on 6 January, the feast of the magi.[21] This old (and ever-new) religious notion, that each day in some sense belongs to the supernatural commemorated on that day, has as its modern corollary the view that the visionary who activates the saint of that day is herself in possession of a special sacrality. In relation to any such feast, a seer like Emmerich was, in Brentano's phrase, a veritable "sacrometer."

This made of a woman like Emmerich a special commodity "in our age, [marked by] the weakening, yes here and there the total death of a true, deep sense of the sacred."[22] While the rest of the world has lost its sense for what things were holy, women like these in backwoods Europe shone through as something close to the sacred itself, Brentano continued. They were perfect examples of scientific instruments in the service of the sacred, with functions in time and in things. Pragmatically, this meant that Emmerich was immediately sensitive to the presence of a relic when she approached one, and especially one of the kings, and so people brought things into her presence, especially on the days of such supernaturals, to find out if these relics were what they were said to be. Now this authoritative woman sees the magi live, and she/Brentano marvels at them. "These good people do not even yet know the lord, yet they move along in such good order, so peacefully, and so gracefully toward him. Yet we whom he has saved and overloaded with grace: how confused, chaotically, and irreverently we move in our processions!"[23] Such was the language that an urbane intellectual put into the mouth of the inspired farmer's daughter.

The experiences both visionaries had of the magi may be briefly described. Emmerich/Brentano is especially fascinating in describing their
gift-giving activities. On their way to Bethlehem they always have a large
retinue of locals attached to the cortege because these rich kings constantly dig into their bags and gift all comers. The gentle nun (or better
the worldly wise Brentano) understood that gifting creates retinue, and
thus legitimacy, for rulers as they process their power. On leaving for
home by another way after the adoration, the kings give fewer gifts. They
had learned the hard way the insatiability of the common people, it
seems, and thus have fewer followers.[24] Clearly, Emmerich/Brentano was
interested in the magi as agents of exchange. The itineraries of the magi
both to and from Bethlehem were seen in such detailed fashion that moderns reading Emmerich/Brentano have made maps of "the route of the
magi," certainly one of the greatest achievements of biblical detail in the
long history of visions of the magi.[25]

Theres Neumann's visions of the magi as told to her parish priest reveal
some of the distinctive traits of modern visions. To begin with, she often
states the perspective from which she witnessed a certain event. For instance, the angel, obviously "of a higher order," who announced the
birth to the shepherds, was at a distance "of about three meters" up from
the ground—almost as if she were positioning miniatures in a firma-
ment.[26] Neumann's powers of observation then come to the fore. She
carefully narrates the size and content of the accompaniment of each
king—the black king Balthazar, for example, had about seventy servants,
twenty soldiers, eight intellectuals, etc.—with special attention being ac-
corded this king *and his wife*. This is the first substantial reference in the
whole narrative tradition to the wife of an evangelical magus.[27] Balthazar,
who was quite tall and strong, struck Neumann because of his red lips,
white teeth, and brilliant eye whites:

> His head was covered with a blindingly white turban that was encircled by
> a gold band. On the same there was a staff of gold all around with gold
> world-balls, each of which was decorated with a precious stone. Within
> and above this staff a circular white bonnet protruded that was laced with
> gold. He [himself] wore a costume striped with colors that was held in place
> above and below by a colorful belt. The costume fell to somewhat beneath
> the knees, where it had a narrower gold strip than the broad one on the
> long sleeves. . . . He wore soled shoes on his feet, from which gold bands
> extended that went horizontally around the foot and lower thigh. His breast
> had a gown with gold stitching. He wore about five different necklaces dec-
> orated with pearls, on the front of which were different sized gold coins
> that, suitably decorated, hung out one over the other. His coat, which only
> reached to the shoulders and was fastened in front with silver bands and

silver fasteners, showed a white underside with different colored woven flowers. It was fastened with a gold hem. It was richly pleated and trailed in back of him, where it was held aloft by two servants.[28]

The description of this cortege continues, with equal detail being given to Balthazar's wife, who was accompanied by four servants, etc. Indeed, with the exception of the earrings worn by the latter, Neumann's description of the queen is almost identical to that of her husband (including the pearl necklaces), a fact that tends to sustain the argument in chapter 3 that black third kings, like this Balthazar, sometimes wore clothes associated with women. But no need to quote further. Here are descriptions that in all probability were copied directly or indirectly from one or more adoration images, the usual source from which visionaries throughout European history developed the visual vocabulary required for their apparitions. A particular modern medium that would have been easily at hand were colored holy cards, which were just coming into vogue in these years.[29] The vision of this rural woman or her pastor was certainly a modern industrial reprint, mixed with bucolic sentiment. Neumann and her amanuenses assure us that the kings, though "truly ruling princes, very rich," were not too assertive, but "right warm with people."[30]

Readers of these and similar sentiments about the magi in Neumann will wonder whence come these modern miniaturizations of the once mighty Christmas monarchs. If we reach back a century, Emmerich (or rather Brentano) provides key information on that score, for s/he describes the magi as "childish" (the very quality contemporaries praised in Emmerick and in Neumann). The kings were "clean, guiltless, *kindlich*, and loyal" because they and their ancestors had waited for this true God for centuries.[31] "Oh how stirring is the good humor and childish simplicity of these loving kings," s/he continues.[32] What the kings and their retinues said to the infant when they approached him "was most stirring and childish. As if ravished, in a childish prayer drowned in love they recommended themselves, their lands and peoples, their possessions and everything they had on earth to him."[33] At another point s/he described someone's heart as being "like that of the brown king Sair [Balthazar], so mild and malleable and so loyal, truly a Christian heart. . . ."[34] This is a description reeking with modern anti-intellectualism, in which the magi, and by extension Brentano's popular classes, are admirable precisely because they are rubes.

What remains after reading several descriptions of this type is not at all an image of mighty kings, or even of merely pompous ones of the type one finds in countless paintings of the adoration. Rather, small magi dolls in a family or parish crib are suggested, ones that could be moved around and manipulated, thus finding a place in the heart of a child. The image of the brown Nubian king Sair projected by Emmerich is that of the infinitely malleable, loyal, humorous, and childish slave or servant so endeared to Europeans in the long nineteenth century.

Having discovered the emotional roots of this new attitude toward the magi, we are on the brink of locating the social activity behind these emotions. Apparently Emmerich's world of magi visions had as a backdrop the very real crèche that she herself assembled in the convent each year. She tells, for instance, how in 1821, for a whole month during the magian journey, she envisaged the magi even as she put up the cave (*Höhle*) or crib: "I always saw the Kings coming toward Bethlehem, when I put up the crèche in the convent."[35] With this very tangible activity in mind, Emmerich's many references to her visions of the *Höhle* take on a plausible meaning. Anna Emmerich envisioned the very figures that she manipulated and played with in the convent crèche, and perhaps so did Theres Neumann in her family. This is an impressive documentation of the phenomenon of crèche manipulation I described earlier.

As a result of Brentano's effort to create childish Christian stories for the underclasses of nineteenth-century Europe, the magi emerge not as historical figures on the move but as deathless dolls in crèches, as in Emmerich, or as proud paper figures separated from us by sheathed layers of gold and brilliantly colored cloth, as in Neumann. It is as if the tradition of seeing the magi, which in earlier centuries told us new things about these mysterious figures, is no longer. In the eyes of our modern rural visionaries, the magi appear as our very children, whom we would bend and shape, and then freeze in time and memory.

MODERN MAGI

In the two centuries since the French Revolution, hundreds of often moribund customs and festivals have been reinstituted either by patriotic folklorists or by conservative political forces. The term "invention of tradition" neatly sums up the motivations that lie behind such activities.[36] But, the enduring popularity of the magi in modern cities is hardly anachronistic: The magi image serves, as it always has, as a social and cultural organizer, even in the modern city. Indeed its value may be even greater in this context because of the instant communications and passing gratifications that define a center of consumption. In the following pages, I want to sketch some of the ways in which the popularity of the magi image has been manifested in modern times and contexts.

Many classical behaviors and themes are still recognizable in contemporary feasts of the kings. Thus the custom of three child-kings, one of

50.   From *Le Matin* (*Le quotidien romand*)

them blackfaced, going out during the Twelve Nights, either for their own profit or to raise money for charitable purposes, is widespread in Catholic sections of Europe, if not in the United States, where such blackface is considered racist.[37] We may also encounter the three kings riding into various Swiss towns on 5 January, a festival sometimes sponsored by the bakers' professional organization.[38] Finally, the *galette* or *gâteau des rois* is still easy to buy in much of Catholic Europe, even if it now conceals not a bean but a plastic or ceramic miniature statue.

Such customs are not only found in Europe. The festivity around the *gateau des rois*, which has been in slow decline in France itself, is fairly widely celebrated in the French-speaking provinces of Canada, as well as in different areas of the eastern United States. While mourning the absence of documentation for earlier times, Georges Arsenault—from a family that is known for its cultivation of the Epiphany—paints a lively picture of the contemporary fête des rois at several locations on Prince Edward Island near Nova Scotia.[39] Not having undergone the French Revolution, this largely rural area remains, in one person's words, "a marvelous laboratory" for studying the culture of the *ancien régime*.[40] To the south of Prince Edward Island, in upstate New York, one finds the fête des rois celebrated as an after-dinner dance, complete with school contests for the best crowns, in the town of Cohoes, near Albany.[41] Even in some non-French cities, like Washington, D. C., the *fête* is an occasion

51. A Group of Three Kings

for bringing together French diplomats and international businesspersons, where they share a *gatêau* or *galette des rois*, prepared by a genuine French chef.[42]

New York City is the major center of Epiphany celebrations in the United States because it is the traditional entry point for immigrants who bring the celebration with them. In any given year around the feast of the kings, several newspaper accounts describe how different ethnic groups celebrate the feast. The most imposing of these events is certainly the journey of the kings performed in Spanish Harlem by Puerto Rican/ American school children and their elders on Epiphany.[43] Attractions include camels and other animals from local zoos, many groups of crowned magi of grade-school age (fig. 51), as well as the adult three kings proper. There are also three giant plaster-of-paris kings, each bearing an outsized gift box, banners identifying the children's school, and much else. Like the journey of old, the modern ones still present an image of pluralistic social organization.

This is a case where an existing celebratory format—the Epiphany of Puerto Rico—has been imported live to the mainland. It is full of a city's vibrant daily reality, a reality the more vivid for the children because it is on this day, not Christmas, that they receive their gifts.[44] The Museo del Barrio, which is the focus for the celebration, is itself a center of Puerto Rican culture in the United States. In addition to different exhibitions of

art works, the marvelous Epiphany posters that the Puerto Rican com-
monwealth produced for several years are often on display.[45] When the
children have finished their procession, they crowd into a large theatre in
the Museo where the three kings pass out gifts from the stage. All in all,
this celebration is a major piece of folkcraft in the melting pot of New
York. The ecumenical character of the kings takes on a particular flavor in
this center of ethnic diversity, especially through reports in the New York
newspapers.[46] The magian opera of Gian Carlo Menotti, *Amahl and the
Night People*, is always performed in the city in these days.

The Epiphany remains an important feast in many other parts of the
western hemisphere, including those in contemporary Latin America to
which I have already called attention.[47] Here I wish only to draw attention to a particularly widespread practice in the Americas that awaits serious study: Epiphany children's plays that are known to me in the United
States. Many colleagues have told me they played a wise man or a king as
a child, and yet little attention has been given to the intention and effects
of this practice. One such business-sponsored initiative of the 1950s, oc-
curring in the International Business Machine (IBM) homestead of Endicott, New York, is particularly fascinating because Endicott under IBM
became an important industrial center with an international population.
Given its global ambitions, it should not be surprising that IBM sponsored magi plays both in secular and in church settings for clearly ecumenical purposes. The story of the magi was for IBM a tale of different
peoples getting along by worshiping, so to speak, at a common corporate
altar.[48] This ecumenical comprehension of the magi had been a core part
of the magi's meaning for hundreds of years. The subject of such plays
performed to these ends would reward close study.

All the above-named practices have a recognizable past in Christian
tradition, even if most of them are urban in their emphasis. In more modern settings, however, the magi have escaped the web of Christianity that
had always surrounded them to become popular figures in a seemingly
desacralized, highly commercialized world. A smattering of images will
make the point. A brand of Portuguese wine bears the name of the
Magos;[49] a trio of peaks in Bryce Canyon National Park in Utah is named
"The Three Wise Men"; countless postage stamps in Europe and the
Americas bear their image; each year, Italians give the magi and their servants in their crèches the faces of world leaders.[50] The ancient identity of
the magi as travelers and bearers of messages has taken on modern forms.
For sale in Spain, envelopes decorated with pictures of the three kings
have slips of paper inside for sending (Christmas?) messages, marked
"Urgente"; a telephone card worth twelve marks and decorated with
three crowned *Sternsänger* was marketed in 1994 in central Germany;
and of course there are hundreds of inns in Europe and in Latin America

still named after the three kings. The ancient notion of the magi as sooth-sayers is alive and well in a series of *3 Wise Men* annual publications used by numerologists or numbers runners.[51]

The character of the magi as searching individuals has passed into pop-ular imagery. On one greeting card in the author's collection, the star followed by the magi on their journey leads to . . . a pizza parlor.[52] An-other card announces that it would be nice to put on a nativity play "if only we could find three wise men and a virgin."[53] On still another card, three women arrive in Bethlehem on camels and announce to a puzzled Mary and Joseph that "wise men only happen in story books."[54] Reflect-ing contemporary concern with theft and burglary, Ronald Searle in his cartoon "The First Security Check" shows the three magi being frisked and thoroughly searched by the crèche animals, who wear sunglasses, metal detectors, two-way radios, and Kalishnikov rifles, before they can proceed to the adoration.[55] And so it goes, with a newspaper in Livorno headlining the arrest of the magi, caught bearing cocaine instead of myrrh. In comparison to such lay amusements, the fundamentalist bumper sticker that announces Wise Men Still Seek Him is downright unimaginative. The announcement in one newspaper that the orchestral conductor Zubin Mehta is a descendant of the magi seems positively sober and to the point.[56]

Certainly the most important indicator of the seemingly infinite rele-vance of the magi to modern social organization of whatever ideological stamp comes, however, from another direction, that of reciprocal gift giv-ing. Long a rooted part of magian lore, it is definitely at home in the contemporary world. Thus one church-sponsored Christmas card fea-tures the journey of the magi with the message, "As you bring gifts to Christ, may He bring gifts to you, joys and blessings this Christmas."[57]

Far more innovative than this timeless message of reciprocity is the fact that gold, frankincense, and myrrh have themselves become a universally recognized byword for consumption that has taken on several forms in the hands of merchandisers. In large commercial outlets, such as Bloom-ingdale's Department Store in New York City, merchandisers have carved out areas for separate boutiques, one labeled Gold, another Incense, a third Myrrh. These relatively small spaces, where merchandise is roughly concentrated according to the gift in question, are designed to give shop-pers the feeling of being in a crowded "oriental" bazaar, and to this end a scent of perfume hangs in the air while vaguely Eastern music is piped into the rooms.[58]

It has not escaped merchandisers that not only gold but also incense and even myrrh might be attractive to consumers seduced into these western bazaars. Thus an article headlined Muscat (!), Oman and featur-ing a Renaissance engraving of an adoration of the magi tells the success story of the two bin Hamood brothers from Oman. The three kings had brought frankincense to Bethlehem, the article begins, so now, these merchants were taking it to market in Paris.[59] The product in question is Amouage, "the world's most expensive perfume," which contains only Omani products, including the "silver" frankincense which, we are told, grows in the southern province of Dhofar. "Combining Omani frankincense with French perfume expertise and British marketing consultants," our sellers bring in glass perfume bottles from Germany and handcrafted caskets and presentation boxes from England. The appeal is obviously to people with a taste for the exotic seeking historical roots. Amouage, with its frankincense scent, was "one of Oman's hottest new products," and the brothers were hoping for unbounded future wealth. Certainly their success in recent years can only have been helped by the important series of discoveries regarding frankincense and myrrh centers of ancient Yemen, and roads to the West to move them, that have been highlighted in periodicals like the *National Geographic Magazine*.[60]

The ultimate fusion between modern merchandising and a mysterious, quasi-sacral past awaited the Christmas season of 1990. In a slick full-page advertisement in an otherwise forgettable travel magazine, an advertiser pitched its product, "The Majis' Treasure, Gold, Frankincense, and Myrrh." "Whispering and beckoning from the Arabian deserts and wastelands, the ancient mysteries surrounding the Gold, Frankincense, and Myrrh given as the gift of gifts almost 2000 years ago have returned to captivate the most discriminating of givers."

This ad referred to exquisite hardwood cases containing fixed portions of gold, frankincense, and myrrh, which were "*cradled* in special *tabernacles*." Elsewhere in the advertisement, we are assured that gold has been the most desired of all elements since the dawn of time, that frankincense was the fabled fragrance of the Gods—today found only in such remote places as the fabled land of Punt—and that myrrh, also known as the balm of Gilead, was once used to anoint the heads of ancient kings and priests. Accompanied by parchment histories, these Majas, costing $1250 and $625 respectively, could be ordered by phone, MasterCard and Visa accepted. What is most striking about this advertisement, however, is the direct claim that the person who receives a Maja as a gift will be in some way identical or on an equal footing with the infant Jesus, or God:

> The Majis' Treasure, an exclusive offering of the prized gift of ancient regents, will become a coveted family heirloom. Those who possess it will enjoy for generations the precious gift of the King of kings.

In short: You too can get what Jesus got! By mail order![61]

The contemporary magi images that I have described above are not intended to confirm some imagined vulgarity of modern notions of the sacred. From the time the story of the magi emerged in the Bible, it has loaned itself precisely to such a broad range of seriousness and comedy because it told a story of mere mortals intermixing with divine life, and because, at the different levels we have sketched, it pitted polarized views of acquisition and altruism against each other. Think of the many contemporary books that contrast the rich three wise men with the so-called fourth, poor, magus![62] The only difference between the conceptual richness of the magi now and in the Middle Ages is the narrow range of imagination in magi exchanges of earlier times, which was limited to the Christian world. What is new about the magi in parts of the contemporary West is that they have ceased to be the property of a particular religion, becoming rather the toy image of a mysterious, distant world that is for sale.

TIMELESS EXEMPLARS

This distancing and the miniaturizing of the magi, together with the stripping away of their historical features, has taken on two forms that now draw our attention. The first is a discourse according to which the present has ruined the past. In this reverie about the good old days, the seasonal holidays at the end of the year are imagined to have once been noncommercial and, wonder of wonders, the magi are thought to have been the vehicle for their degradation because of their association with gift giving and accumulation. In late 1941 the following anti-Semitic poem was distributed to passers-by in upstate New York by those opposed to the United States going to war with Germany:[63]

CHRISTMAS

Out of the west [!] came three wise men,
Levy, Moses and Uncle Ben.
Chanting "Hark the Herald Angels Sing"
See Cohen and Ginsberg for your diamond ring.
For Christians were born for Christmas Day,
But Levy gives you six months to pay,
Oh Little star of Bethlehem,
For Christmas gifts, see Abraham.
When the herald angels loom,
Order your turkey from Rosenbloom.
Bring your Christmas trees of pine,
But get your balls from Silverstein.
Down the chimney old Santa will come,
With a bag full of toys from old Isaac Blum.
"Ring out the old, ring in the new,"

But your money goes to the foxy old Jew.
After "Peace on earth good will to men"
You can hock your coat with Uncle Ben.
"Silent night, Hold [sic] night"
Damned if I don't think Hitler is right.
    Amen.

How divorced these latter-day magi are from their own history! These magi are Jews, not Gentiles, who come to sell various products, not to adore the Christian God. This is what Christmas has become, says the author of this verse: nothing but an opportunity for these unwelcome guests, these domestic enemies, to make money. For that, the rhyme concludes, the Jews need to be treated in the United States as they were being treated in Germany (in 1941).

What a misapprehension of the fundamental importance of exchange to any social system! Whereas in the Christian tradition the magi had always been considered the very opposite of the Jews because they had recognized Jesus by giving him gifts, which the Jews had not, now an adoration of the child was being imagined in which people did not give. This hateful poem is a valuable witness to a subculture that imagines social discourse without the exchange of values. A very essence of the magi had always been that one gave—to the state, to the church, to each other—so as to recognize and to legitimate. That essence had always recognized the nobility of those who gave, and yet the centrality of the merchants who facilitated that giving. Now the magi are just shills for merchants, and, in this impoverished view of history and human exchange dynamics, the acquisitive lust is thought to reign unobstructed.

A second type of evidence showing how the magi have been distanced and dis-integrated from modern western culture is the willingness of certain jaded moderns to abandon the West, searching for the magi and thus spiritual sustenance in the "uncommercial" East, if not permanently, then at least for the length of a vacation. The "magi" who are sought are no longer, we recall, mere copies of the evangelical magi of Christian yore, but occult wise men as if designed to serve a modern laical age, often dressed up as the former by latter-day Christians. The search for a mysterious wisdom essence in eastern religions is a relatively recent phenomenon in Western history. Not until the mid-and later nineteenth century did the sacred books of Hinduism and Buddhism become available to westerners, and the Theosophical Society, which would do much to spread knowledge about eastern spiritualism, was not founded until 1875. The first World Parliament of Religions, which brought together representatives from most world religions, took place in Chicago in 1893. Groups of magicians cashed in on the excitement, and in 1910, a Brotherhood or Order of the Magi in Manchester, England began to distribute a periodical, *The Magi*, to its members.[64]

Only in the 1960s did travel to the spiritual centers of Tibet, Nepal, Bhutan, or subcontinental India become important to the lifestyle of some of the western avant-garde, and only in the 1970s did that norm spread to the larger society. In a few elegant words, Michel Jan has characterized the particular importance that Tibet, an almost mythical "center out there," has come to have for moderns. "Beliefs or reveries, humans have often enough found in central Asia or in Tibet the limits of the real world. Here more than elsewhere, history and landscapes are unequalled sources of inspiration. The imagination roams free, in complete liberty."[65]

Let us not imagine, however, that these western individuals yearn for a reality that has no social characteristics. The magi who are sought belong to a collectivity of wisdom. Thus in his *Shambhala*, the Theosophist Andrew Tomas describes an ancient society of scientists and philosophers in Tibet, a brotherhood of peacemakers, that even millenia ago was peopled with sublime men. To this day, he says, the mysterious Shambhala is the quintessential "abode of the Wise Men," or "of the magi," the author consciously conflating the image of the Christian with that of today's hidden wise men.[66] These latter will emerge to the light of day only when the world is on the edge of extinction and desperately needs their help. These Eastern lords of wisdom are visited; they do not come to adore. They represent the great power of the spirit, but they have no political power in and of themselves. Tomas does not hesitate to claim that Jesus had visited India in his youth, or that Prester John had connections with this (imaginary) place Shambhala.[67]

The mythical Shambhala has remained the secret of a small group of students of Western esoterics. Through the success of the novelist James Hilton's novel and film *Lost Horizon*, written near the end of the Second World War, the equally imaginary Shangri-la has become a household word for all that is simple, eastern, and salvational. In the novel, a small group led by the Englishman Conway in Tibet discovers the land of Shangri-la and its lamasery. Amazingly, the lamasery turns out to have indoor plumbing and other things from the West that have proved their utility. The lamas, or monks, must be rich, one of the Englishmen says, but money is not something that is talked about much in Shangri-la.[68] Social graces and good behavior, like moderation not dogmatism, are more important, and the some fifty monks in full lamahood are spared "the effort of counterfeit emotion[s]."[69] Clearly, this is a western, not an eastern utopia, as becomes naively evident in Hilton's novel. It transpires that the monastery, its subsequent traditions blending Buddhist and Christian traditions, had been built by a westerner, a learned eighteenth-century Capuchin from Luxemburg.[70] Through this importation of western genius into an eastern social structure, the monks had achieved things that were not possible in the West, foremost among which being the incredibly long life that inhabitants attained.

The social substructure of Hilton's Shangri-la peers through this forest of individualistic middle-class dreams, which the author offers with no irony. The male society of Shangri-la has only one visible woman; eroticism plays no part in the work.[71] Second, authority was unobtrusive but omnipresent. Repeatedly, the author notes that the abbot was obeyed after making an almost imperceptible hand motion.[72] Thus the magi in these lamaseries knew their place. And finally, a simple reading of world history informs the past and future of the place. The European past included a dark age, and again today (the end of World War II) doom threatens on every side.[73] But Shangri-la, "hidden behind the mountains in the valley of Blue Moon, [is] preserved as by a miracle for a new Renaissance. . . ."[74] The novel ends with the monks of Shangri-la as the messengers, the magi, of the (western) epiphany to come.

The breakdown of the ancient journey of the magi appears complete. Now those beset with feelings of alienation will find wisdom only abroad, in the desert orchard of a wise society of men. Jeffrey Masson describes himself as a "spiritual tourist . . . , going to meet sages" in *My Father's Guru*.[75] He visits gurus who do not eat, sleep, or speak, yet live to extreme ages (two to three hundred years). They do not die and certainly do not copulate. He visited one guru who considered all such claims, and all the adoration heaped on gurus, to be rubbish.[76] And yet, for all their seeming individualistic athleticism, in the telling these gurus are socially structured for the consumption of the western pilgrim. Masson twice notes that particular gurus were surrounded by impressive retinues, one by several hundred disciples, another indeed by thousands of them.[77] Like so many westerners, the writer had sought to escape the regimentation of the West, yet now found the magi, as in the West, surrounded by retinue. We recall the scholar of an earlier age opining that if the magi were really potentates, they were surely framed by great cortèges.

The historical evidence of the magi's dehistoricization lies before us. In the seventeenth century, the magi, already attacked as non-kings by Protestant Reformers, were for the first time imagined by Jacques d'Auzoles as deathless Jewish prophets residing in the Garden of Eden, high up and to the East. They were scarcely Christian, more wise than mighty, somehow less tangible than their predecessors.

Even as the historical magi were being redefined into non-history, they were becoming incredibly tangible for devotees. In the crèches of early modern Europe and then in the visions of Emmerich and Neumann, a

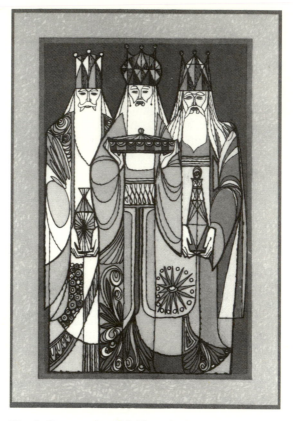

52. A Community Aid Abroad Christmas card

new type of miniaturized magi appeared, toys or dolls that in their fetish-
istic immediacy positively encouraged manipulation. The products of a
rural culture that resented modernity, these "childlike" figures, probably
even imagined as miniatures, become our children. No longer mighty
stone kings rooted in time, these playthings seem less in the business of
saving us from modernity than of giving us access to a dreamlike, simpli-
fied East or Other.

That did not mean that the magi's underlying symbolic content vanished. In modern urban life, to the contrary, the magi were found to be
still at work as communicators and social organizers. Here too, the magi
appear outside any specific historical context. But in the cities, they have
lost their identity as Christian figures, so that their social functionality
shines forth the more clearly. Thus their gifts are now a byword for luxury
gift giving in secular cultures, their act of gifting understood at times as
pure commercial transaction.

As different as Anna Emmerich and the organizer of a modern per-fumed gift bazaar may appear to be, the transformed character of the new if ever magi peers through. These are magi who are far away, in time as well as place. They belong to us all, not just Christians. With the exception of their ancient political roles, which have been assumed by other, more forceful instruments of the public weal, their fundamental social roles as images continues in modern cultures. They have become timeless exemplars, on the one hand the essence of "what is wrong" with modern Christmases, on the other the Western pilgrim's goal far to the East and out of time, a source of wisdom and of life worthwhileness.

A new, or rather inverted, adoration of the magi offers itself for our viewing. Now Westerners travel to these immobile figures of wisdom, wanting to "find a master," as they say, or rather, to find a father, as once the magi had sought a child. The magi or gurus or monks accommodate him on his arrival. The journey continues, even though, as pilgrims and sages all know, the answer "will be found within us."

CONCLUSION

Gustave Doré's (d. 1883) majestic drawing of the evangelical magi on their way to adore the infant (fig. 53) appears to us as in a dream. Mounted atop an enormous camel, the aged third and last of the wise men towers above his retinue of desert people. All move away from us, back toward the star shining luminously against the blackness of the desert night sky. Can it be that this image was produced scarcely a century ago? The wise man looks back as if beckoning us, one last time, to join his procession back into history. We have indeed made a long, if still unfinished, journey. When my father died a decade ago, I was drawn to build his eulogy around the image in Isaiah and in the psalm, of Matthew's magi in short, to postulate his redemption and resurrection for an audience of believers. In these last pages, I do the same for the magi themselves.

The story of the magi made its way into Matthew's Gospel as a way to legitimate the infant Jesus and his church. Quickly enough, the reverse also became possible. Individual Christians learned that they could justify their lives by showing that, like the magi, they too had given to God and his church. From early on, it seems, the gifts of the magi in the Christian tradition embodied, and acted out, the principle of exchange between Christians and their collectivities. But from the time that Constantine accepted Christianity as an ideological foundation of his empire, the magi, either as legates or putative kings and not just as wise men, began to lend living kings' approbation to the new religion. The ancient Roman triumph was taken up anew by Christianity. The magi were the only positive heraldic image in the Christian biblical tradition, and thus the one standard iconographic image by which the secular power could be shown continuingly to legitimate the infant Jesus and his church. In the great mosaics of Ravenna, the triumphal and legitimating meaning of the magi are echoed in the figures of Justinian and Theodora recognizing Jesus and vice versa at San Vitale, while at Sant'Apollinare Nuovo, the magi lead the eternal parade of martyrs and virgins in paradise. Exchange, legitimation, process: these three quanta of all human existence are anchored in the image of the magi in a way comparable to no other Christian picture. Little wonder why for so many centuries, in liturgy, in parades, in plays, and in crèches, their popularity has been so great. They speak about the organization of life in a way no other Christian image could.

The first part of this book concentrated on these different facets of the magi as a high social and political icon, establishing that political meaning

53. Gustave Doré, *Der Stern der Weisen*

in the first place, studying the emergence of the magi as a representational image in medieval Europe, and then dwelling on the actual content of these centuries of magi pageant. I argued that despite the fact that the kings were three, the message was often dualistic and polar in nature. Perhaps most significant, we found the tension between stability and eros repeatedly described in the differences between the solemn and immobile first and the volatile and narcissistic third kings.

The section of this book dealing with the application of the magi theme to the European missionary efforts in the Americas stands revealed as a type of bridge between the medieval and the modern worlds of the magi. What drew our attention was less tales of American magi than the

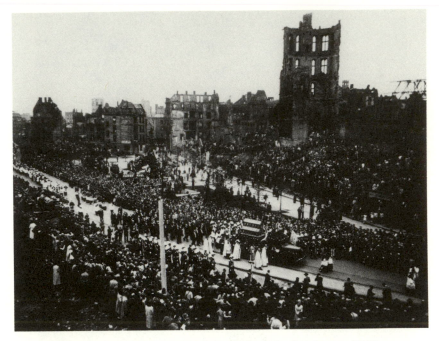

54. Procession on the Centenary of the Cathedral of Cologne, 1948

Europeans' behavioral application of the magi theme toward the processional reorganization of the various American tribes under the colonial
flags. The parades of the Tlaxomulcans, as well as those of the Hurons,
show cultures forced to play the magi within paradigms and affects pre-
scribed by the spiritual conquerors of these regions. Not surprisingly,
missionaries loved to write home about how docile and childlike such
peoples were.

   The sixteenth century brought a sea change in the way the magi were
represented in Europe. Generally speaking, men stopped playing them,
with poor children assuming the old roles. This change is best imaged,
and even explained, in Switzerland. Fribourg, we recall, boasted one of
the longest lived of European magi processions. Why did it continue this
municipal tradition so long? The answer lies in the fact that at the end of
the sixteenth century, the city inserted large military contingents into
what was from now on a parade, rather than a procession, to accompany
each of the three kings.[1] Elsewhere in Europe, the newfangled military
parades had little sacred patina, but in Fribourg they did. Elsewhere,
other forms of absolutist authority were taking over the streets to show
the force of the collectivity, or of the prince. In this Fribourg vestige we
see the link of the old to the new.

What was left elsewhere were children playing kings, and again, the Swiss evidence allows us to sense the transformation. Schärmeli describes magi festivals of several small towns around Fribourg in which, in the seventeenth century, the three magi had as part of their retinues one child each who played their sons.[2] At least representationally, these sons of the *roi-mages* may be related to the child kings who, elsewhere in Europe in the early years of the sixteenth century, became the only impersonators of the fabled three kings of the orient, who slowly fade away into the unfindable fastnesses of Asia.

Rulers no longer rely on fictional kings to legitimate their authority: the kings are infantile, poor, scruffy. Even as latter-day Christian visionaries view the magi in the mind's eye as miniatures and as childish, changing their clothes and twisting them into place in the family or convent crèche, and even as Spanish-speaking children imagine these friendly ghosts concealed behind a mountain, merchandisers use these toy talismans to market all those principles of exchange and social order that had made the fortune of the magi in the first place. Even as the familiar figurines are wrapped up for another holiday once the Twelve Nights are past, seekers set out to find the magi in the East, searching for masters who will show them how to behave or to pray as once did the evangelical magi, their ancestors.

The magi will come again, when the West needs to justify a new world order. Cologne was almost completely destroyed in 1948, when the city celebrated the anniversary of its cathedral. The relics of the three kings of Cologne were taken from their hiding places and processed through the smashed city center (fig. 54). Once again, the journey of the magi would culminate in resurrection.

NOTES

INTRODUCTION

1. Nicholas of Lyra (d. 1340), cited in G. Zappert, " 'Epiphania'. Ein Beitrag zur christlichen Kunstarchäologie," *Sitzungsberichte der philosophischen-histori-schen Classe der kaiserlichen Akademie der Wissenschaften*, 21 (a. 1856), Heft 2 (Vienna, 1857), 321f.

2. On such nativity astronomy, see H. Kehrer, *Die heiligen Drei Könige in Literatur und Kunst*, 2 vols. (reprint; Hildesheim, 1976), 1:2 ff. Further J. Campbell, *The Hero with a Thousand Faces* (Princeton, 1968); O. Rank et al., *In Quest of the Hero* (Princeton, 1990). For ancient examples, J. Deckers, "Die Huldigung der Magier in der Kunst der Spätantike," in *Die Heiligen Drei Könige: Darstellung und Verehrung* (Cologne, 1982), 24, 27.

3. See chap. 1 citation of the Song of Songs.

4. See the early tradition in U. Monneret de Villard, *Le leggende orientali sui magi evangelici* (Vatican City, 1952), 77, 107, 112, and 42, where Mary thought the magi wanted the infant himself in exchange for their gifts.

5. Unforgettable examples are the elaborate Neapolitan crèches in the Bavarian National Museum in Munich, Germany. In a personal communication, Hans Magnus Enzensberger recalled his father gathering moss for the family crèche each year and modifying the figures and positions within the crèche as the Twelve Days of Christmas (25 December-6 January) proceeded. See below, chap. 5.

6. 1 Tim. 3.7: "Oportet autem illum et testimonium habere ab his, qui foris sunt." For Latin text, I use the Vulgate version of the Bible; translations other than my own come from the Revised Standard Version of the Bible.

7. This is the so-called *Grosse Anbetung* of van Cleeve, which is accompanied in the Gallery by the *Kleine Anbetung*. Luke was thought to have been a painter as well as a writer, and was the usual patron of artists' guilds.

8. Mt. 2.1–16; Lk. 2.1–40. Neither Mark nor the Gospel attributed to John describes the nativity.

9. See the event in early antiphons, cited in N. King, *Mittelalterliche Drei-königsspiele: Eine Grundlagenarbeit zu den lateinischen, deutschen und franzö-sichen Dreikönigsspielen und spielszenen bis zum Ende des 16. Jahrhunderts* (Freiburg/S, 1979), 17, 199. The fusing of the two evangelists' stories, however, had already begun in the second century; R. Brown, *The Birth of the Messiah: A Commentary on the Infancy Narratives in Matthew and Luke* (Garden City, 1977), 176.

10. Mt. 2.11. Jesus, Mary, and Joseph in a cave or grotto, common in pictures, is apocryphal; for its Syriac origins, see Monneret de Villard, *Leggende*, 62ff.

11. Mt. 2.13–16; Lk. 2.21, 39–40.

12. "Omnis Hierosolyma" and "omnes principes sacerdotum et scribas [of the Jewish] populi" were party to the magi's arrival and query; Mt. 2.3–4. See chap. 1 below.

13. Brown, *Birth of the Messiah*, 197f.

14. See chap. 5.

15. See chap. 4, for the American evidence and chap. 5 for the European.

16. In addition to Kehrer and Zappert cited above, for general histories or overviews of the cult see H. Crombach, *Primitiae Gentium, seu Historia SS. Trium Regum Magorum* (Cologne, 1654); H. Hofmann, *Die heiligen Drei Könige: Zur Heiligenverehrung im kirchlichen, gesellschaftlichen und politischen Leben des Mittelalters* (Bonn, 1975). Among other standard works are G. Vezin, *L'adoration et le cycle des Mages dans l'art chrétien primitif: Étude des influences orientales et grecques sur l'art chrétien* (Paris, 1950); M. Élissagaray, *La légende des rois mages* (Paris, 1965); J. Hoster (ed.), "Achthundert Jahre Verehrung der heiligen Drei Könige in Köln, 1164–1964," *Kölner Domblatt: Jahrbuch des Zentral-Dombauvereins*, 23–24 (1964).

CHAPTER 1

1. K. Holl, "Der Ursprung des Epiphanienfestes," *Sitzungsberichte der königlich preussischen Akademie der Wissenschaften* 29 (1917), 401–38; for the first days of January, see M. Nilsson, "Studien zur Vorgeschichte des Weihnachtsfestes," *Archiv für Religionswissenschaft*, 19 (1916–19), 50–150; the linkage of this Egyptian feast to the later Byzantine celebration of 6 January is explored in F. Kampers, "Der Kosmokrator in einem altfranzösischen Märchen," *Historisches Jahrbuch*, 47 (1927), 467 seq.

2. The new order began only in the later fifth century; A. Renoux, "L'Épiphanie à Jérusalem au IV. et au V. siècles," *Lex Orandi* 40 (1967), 171–93.

3. Holl, "Ursprung," 403f. On the loaves and fishes, see H. Frank, "Zur Geschichte von Weihnachten und Epiphanie," *Jahrbuch für Liturgiewissenschaft*, 12 (1932), 145–55, and 13 (1933), 1–38.

4. The crucial change took place in 354; Kehrer, *Heiligen Drei Könige*, 1:25f.

5. Mt. 2.1–12, 16.

6. This remains the standard modern view; Brown, *Birth of the Messiah*, 167f. A list of the authorities choosing any one of the three locations I describe is found in V. De Waal, "Magier," in *Real-Encyklopädie der christlichen Alterthümer*, vol. 2 (Freiburg/Breisgau, 1886), 348.

7. Julian the Apostate (d. 363) held to this notion: "Rex [persarum] itaque nulla mora interjecta partem magorum, qui sub ipsius imperio erant, cum muneribus misit"; cited in C. Schoebel, *L'histoire des Rois Mages* (Paris, 1878), 78. John Chrysostom (d. 407) believed that the "legates from Egypt" mentioned in Psalm 68.32 referred to the magi; Crombach, *Primitiae gentium*, 56, with several references to the magi as legates. Augustine refers to the "magorum beata legatio"; *Patrologia cursus completus . . . Series latina* (hereafter *PL*), ed. J.-P. Migne, 221 vols. (Paris, 1844–64). 39:2012. See the Persian ruler Cyrus (!) dispatching the magi to find Jesus in an eleventh-century menologium of the monastery of Esphigmenou'; S.M. Pelekanidis et al, *The Treasures of Mount Athos: Illuminated Manuscripts*, vol. 2 (Athens, 1975), 236f.

8. H. Leseyre, "Mage," *Dictionnaire de la Bible*, vol. 4, part 1 (Paris, 1912), 543ff.

9. Mt. 1.22–23. Popular old testamental prophecies "confirming" the coming of Jesus are Is.7.14; Mic. 5.2; 2 Sam. 5.2.

10. Origen's dictum is in J. Gagé, *"Basiléia": Les Césars. Les rois d'Orient et les "Mages"* (Paris, 1968), 246f. Gagé emphasizes that again, Balaam, an outsider and non-Jew, legitimizes Jesus' fate. Philo, a contemporary of Jesus, had already labeled Balaam a magus; Brown, *Birth of the Messiah*, 193.

11. A man or scepter; Nu. 24.17.

12. Ps. 72.10–11. Tertullian's texts are in Kehrer, *Heiligen Drei Könige*, 1:13.

13. "Nam et magos reges habuit fere Oriens"; ibid.

14. 1 Kg. 10.1–13. See the three excellent articles on this visit in A. Chastel, *Fables, Formes, Figures*, vol. 1 (Paris, 1978).

15. The queen had had the gold shipped from Ophir to Jerusalem; 1 Kg. 10.11. She had entered the Nestorian liturgy as a type of the magi by 630; Kehrer, *Heiligen Drei Könige*, 1:30.

16. Ca. 3.6–11.

17. Ca. 4.5–7. A further source says frankincense came from Sheba; Je. 6.20.

18. Bernard of Clairvaux (d. 1153) does gloss these passages, but shame-facedly: The Star is equated with Solomon's lily; it smelled sweet and thus enticed the magi; *Sermones super Cantica Canticorum, 1–35*, ed. J. Leclercq et al. (Rome, 1957), 210 (sermon 70). My thanks to Rab Hatfield for this reference.

19. Monneret de Villard, *Leggende orientali*, 92.

20. G. Ryckmans, "De l'or (?), de l'encens et de la myrrhe," *Revue Biblique*, 58 (1951), 372–76; Monneret de Villard, *Leggende orientali*, 3f; however, see Brown, *Birth of the Messiah*, 176.

21. On the magi as doctors (*medici*), see Monneret de Villard, *Leggende orientali*, 7, 13, 91–97. The notion that the myrrh-bearing physicians SS. Cosmas and Damian provided retinue for the myrrh-gifting magus in Michelangelo's New Sacristy is, with Mary Lewis, in Trexler, *Church and Community, 1200–1600. Studies in the History of Florence and New Spain* (Rome, 1987), 201f.

22. More on this subject is below, chap. 3.

23. The fifth or sixth century *Opus Imperfectum* dwells on Isaiah 60; *Patrologia cursus completus . . . Series graeca* (hereafter *PG*), ed. J.-P. Migne, 166 vols. (Paris, 1857–66), 56:642.

24. Is. 60.1–7. On both Isaiah and Psalm 72 as implicitly cited by Matthew, see Brown, *Birth of the Messiah*, 187f.

25. T. Klauser, "Aurum Coronarium," *Reallexikon für Antike und Christentum*, vol. 1 (Stuttgart, 1950), 1012.

26. See the text in Kehrer, *Heiligen Drei Könige*, 1:34.

27. Monneret de Villard, *Leggende orientali*, 92–97. See Irenaeus (d. 202), cited in G. Wilpert, *I sarcofagi cristiani antichi*, 3 vols. (Rome, 1929–36), Text 2:284; for the gifts according to the Spaniard Prudentius (d. c.410), see J. Marsh-Edwards, "The Magi in Tradition and Art," *The Irish Ecclesiastical Record*, ser. 5, 85 (1956), 7. For a comparison of the magi's legation to Pompey's in the East, with verbal conceits on their mutual triumphs, see Crombach, *Primitiae gentium*, 57.

28. Brown, *Birth of the Messiah*, 180f. Condemnation of the Jewish savants in favor of the gentile magi is in the *opus imperfectum*; *PG*, 56:640. The shepherds

as Jews and magi as gentiles is in Fulgentius (d. 533), cited in H. Leclercq, "Mages," in *Dictionnaire d'archéologie chrétienne et de liturgie*, vol. 10, 1 (Paris, 1931), 986.

29. "Primitiae gentium"; Augustine, in *PL*, 39:2005ff; Kehrer, *Heiligen Drei Könige*, 1:34.

30. *PL*, 39:2012.

31. Ibid., 2008.

32. F. Cumont, "L'Adoration des mages et l'art triomphal de Rome," *Memorie della pontifica accademia romana di archeologia*, 3 (1922–23), 81–105, esp. 103; G. de Jerphanion, "L'ambon de Salonique: L'arc de Galère et l'ambon de Thèbes," ibid., 107–32; also A. Grabar, *L'empereur dans l'art byzantin* (Paris, 1936), 233.

33. Cumont, "L'adoration," 103ff. A summary of the relation between pre-Christian and Christian submission postures is in the article "Barbar II (ikonographisch)," in *Reallexikon für Antike und Christentum*, Supplement, volume 1 (Stuttgart, 1992), 944-forthcoming. E. Kantorowicz pursued the linkage between royal advents on earth and the entry of the soul into heaven; "The 'King's Advent,' and the Enigmatic Panels in the Doors of Santa Sabina," *Art Bulletin*, 26 (1944), 207–31. Without once considering the story of the magi, Kantorowicz believed that the entry of Jesus into Jerusalem on Palm Sunday was the prototype for receiving princes. Obviously, princes sought a heraldic model, and found it in the magi.

34. A. Dieterich, "Die Weisen aus dem Morgenlande. Ein Versuch," in *Albrecht Dieterich Kleine Schriften* (Leipzig, 1911), 272–89.

35. Dio Cassius reflected this ambiguity; cited in Dieterich, *Kleine Schriften*, 281.

36. "Magus ad eum Tiridates venerat Armeniacum de se triumphum adferens et ideo provinciis gravis"; Pliny, *Natural History*, vol. 8 (Cambridge, Mass., 1963), 288. Dieterich, *Kleine Schriften*, 282; see also Tacitus, cited in Gagé, *"Basiléia"*, 121, note 59.

37. Pliny; *Natural History*, 8:289; cited in Dieterich, *Kleine Schriften*, 282.

38. Gagé, *"Basiléia"*, 111, 114.

39. Ibid., 113ff, 123f.

40. One such deserves an attention it has not had, the so-called apocryphal "Testament of Job," kindly brought to my attention by my colleagues G. Kadish and J. Wilcox; J. Charlesworth (ed.), *The Old Testament Pseudepigrapha* (Garden City, 1983), 852f. Its particular interest is that Job and his three royal visitors compare precious stones, a leading gift given the magi by Jesus in the eastern tradition.

41. On this important object, see Klauser, "Aurum coronarium," especially 1013, where it is clear that the "wreath" was often commuted money. A quick process allowing masters of ceremonies to convert goods into money to determine their actual value was in place in late medieval Florence; Trexler, *Public Life*, 325f.

42. Ex. 23.15.

43. "Offeramus munera, quia nascenti regi semper publica paratur oblatio"; Peter Chrysologus (d. 450), cited in Klauser, "Aurum Coronarium," 1017.

44. See Nilsson, "Studien." Also M. Nilsson, "Kalendae Ianuariae," *Paulys Realencyclopädie der classischen Altertumswissenschaft*, 10, 2 (Stuttgart, 1931), 1563.

45. C. Miles, *Christmas Customs and Traditions. Their History and Significance* (New York, 1976), 166–69. Also M. Nilsson, "Strena," *Paulys Realencyclopädie der classischen Altertumswissenschaft*, 4. A. 1 (Stuttgart, 1931), 351ff.

46. For the frankincense *strena*, see *The Saturnalia*, in *The Works of Lucian*, vol. 6 (Cambridge, Mass., 1959), 110.

47. Suetonius, *The Lives of the Caesars* (Cambridge, Mass., 1944), 2 vols. *Life of Tiberius*, chap. 34 (1:342).

48. Suetonius, *Life of Augustus*, chap. 57 (1:212).

49. Suetonius, *Life of Tiberius*, chap. 42 (1:470).

50. M. Nilsson, "Strena."

51. Gagé, *"Basiléia"*, 104ff.

52. Ibid., 105, 121f. Further on Roman banquets in P. Veyne (ed.), *Histoire de la vie privée*, vol. 1 (Paris, 1985), 181–87.

53. Ibid., 105.

54. Ibid.

55. Augustine, cited in E. K. Chambers, *The Mediaeval Stage*, 2 vols. (Oxford, 1903), 2:293.

56. P. Saintyves, *Rondes enfantines et quêtes saisonniéres: Les Liturgies populaires* (Paris, 1919), 142f; text in Chambers, *Mediaeval Stage*, 2:295.

57. *PL*, 39:2002. The same custom occurs as a princely taxing custom of the Este family of Ferrara; see below, chap. 5.

58. Text in Chambers, *Mediaeval Stage*, 2:293; Saintyves, *Rondes enfantines*, 144.

59. "Dant illi strenas, date vos eleemosynas"; Chambers, *Mediaeval Stage*, 2:293.

60. Using the customary authority of Moses in Ex. 23.15.; J. Jungmann, *Missarum Solemnia*, 2 vols. (Vienna, 1952), 1:32; G. Ellard, "Bread in the Form of a Penny," *Theological Studies*, 4 (1943), 321, 336.

61. "Dignus est operarius mercede sua"; cited in Trexler, "The Bishop's Portion: Generic Pious Legacies in the Late Middle Ages in Italy," in my *Church and Community*, 293.

62. *PG*, 56:612f.

63. *PL*, 39:2007.

64. Ellard, "Bread," 328. Text of Fulgentius in Crombach, *Primitiae gentium*, 459.

65. Ellard, "Bread," 323.

66. Ibid., 343; O. von Simson, *Sacred Fortress: Byzantine Art and Statecraft in Ravenna* (Chicago, 1948), 94, 99.

67. Ellard, "Bread."

68. Simson, *Sacred Fortress*, 90; cf. Ellard, "Bread," 334.

69. See the story and elaboration in Wilpert, *Sarcofagi*, 259–84. Wilpert dates the images of these children to the third century; *Le pitture delle catacombe romane*, Text and Figure vols. (Rome, 1903), Text 181. See more recently

A. Nestori, *Repertorio topografico delle pitture delle catacombe romane* (Vatican City, 1975), especially 184, a list of adorations of the magi in many catacombs.

70. See such pictures in Wilpert, *Pitture*, Tavole 41, 57, 65, 93, 133.

71. Wilpert, *Pitture*, Text 176.

72. See especially the breakdown of styles in E. Baldwin Smith, *Early Christian Iconography and a School of Ivory Carvers in Provence* (Princeton, 1918), 162–86, especially 166, where the ages of the magi are first distinguished in the "oriental hellenistic," not the dominant hellenistic type.

73. Wilpert, *Pitture*, Tavole 13, 172. Indeed, Wilpert believed that the sculptural theme of the magi evolved directly from the three Chaldeans.

74. Augustine, in *PL*, 39: 2012. See also above.

75. See Wilpert, *Pitture*, Tavole 116, 207; *Sarcofagi*, Tavole 2:201, 249. On the arguments about Jesus' age at the time of the adoration, see Leclercq, "Mages," 990.

76. Typical among the mass of victory angels are those in Cumont, "L'adoration," Pl. 1, 1; 2, 3.

77. See, for example, Wilpert, *Pitture*, Tavole 239; further his *Sarcofagi*, Tavole 2:201.

78. Cumont, "L'adoration," 88ff, 100.

79. On the covered hands, a feature of Persian etiquette, see ibid., 93–98.

80. Kehrer, *Heiligen Drei Könige*, 1:33.

81. On plate at such Christian communions, see Ellard, "Bread," 338. On food products and the magi, see De Waal, "Magier," 350f.

82. Kehrer, *Heiligen Drei Könige*, 2:17; Klauser, "Aurum coronarium," 1016f.

83. Another example besides the one shown here is in Wilpert, *Sarcofagi*, Tavole, 225 (1 and 2); Wilpert also lists all such sarcophagues ibid., Text 2:285, note 5. See also *Pitture*, Text 177.

84. See the Arles sarcophague of the fourth century in *Die Heiligen Drei Könige: Darstellung und Verehrung* (Cologne, 1982), 20. Also Wilpert, *Sarcofagi*, Tavole 1:96; 2:219 (1), 225 (4). On late medieval grasping Jesuses in art, and the objections raised against them, see below, chap. 5.

85. On the linkage of the magi with death and funerals, see Von Simson, *Sacred Fortress*, 103–10; Trexler, "Triumph and Mourning in North Italian Magi Art," in *Art and Politics in Late Medieval and Early Renaissance Italy*, ed. C. Rosenberg (Notre Dame, 1990), 38–66.

86. On the lateness of a Passion canon, see A. Grabar, *Martyrium: Recherches sur le culte des reliques et l'art chrétien antique*, 2 vols. (Paris, 1946), 2:256.

87. Wilpert, *Sarcofagi*, Text 2:285. Examples other than that shown here are ibid., Tavole 2:177 (3), 185 (1), 222 (1); What may be a family playing the "fourth magus" is ibid., 2:219 (3), and for this theme, cf. Grabar, *Martyrium*, 2:96.

88. For Augustine, *PL*, 39:2013; Ambrose in Crombach, *Primitiae gentium*, 751; for Caesarius of Arles, *PL*, 39:2018.

89. See e.g. Wilpert, *Sarcofagi*, Tavole 2:224 (8). The same exchange mentality in "ut et pro bonis actibus vestris Deo gratias agatis, et mala vestra longe a vobis projiciatis"; from a sermon of Caesarius of Arles, in *PL*, 39:2018.

90. A. Grabar, *L'empereur*, 232f; F. Van Der Meer, *Maiestas Domini: Théophanies de l'apocalypse dans l'art chrétien* (Vatican City, 1938), figs. 18, 19, 66.

91. On his ascension as shown on coins, see Eusebius, *The Life of Constantine the Great* (New York, 1890), 559 (chap. 73); Grabar, *L'empereur*, 249–58.

92. Grabar, *L'empereur*, 95ff; see further Von Simson, *Sacred Fortress*, 32, 34. Replacing the Star with the Constantinian monogram in later art itself implied that Constantine had fulfilled prophetic promise.

93. The best preserved of the latter is in the catacomb of SS. Marcellino e Pietro; J. Wilpert, *Ein Cyclus christologischer Gemälde aus der Katakombe der heiligen Petrus und Marcellinus* (Freiburg/B., 1891), fig.; J. Decker, H. Seeliger, G. Mietke, *Die Katakombe Santi Marcellino e Pietro: Repertorium der Malereien* (Vatican City, 1987), 224, retain Wilpert's designation of these superimposed letters as "pre-Constantinian." I am myself inclined to think that in general, a physical star is shown before, letters of whatever kind after Constantine's vision. For all knees bending before the *name* of Jesus, and all mouths confessing Jesus Christ, see Ph 2.10.

94. Attention to the subtleties and difficulties of the sources is given by M. DiMaio, Jr., J. Zeuge, N. Zotov, "*Ambiguitas constantiniana*: the *Caeleste Signum Dei* of Constantine the Great," *Byzantion*, 58 (1988), 333–60, esp. 338, note 31, and 339; also H. Leclercq, "Labarum," *Dictionnaire d'archéologie chrétienne et de Liturgie*, 8, 1 (Paris, 1928), 940f.

95. Grabar, *L'empereur*, 227.

96. See Lactantius' text in DiMaio et al, "Ambiguitas," 338.

97. G. B. de' Rossi, in his *Bullettino di archeologia cristiana*, 1 (Rome, Oct. 1863), 76, 79; Wilpert, *Pitture*, Tavole 241; Testo 183; De Waal, "Magier," 350; Kehrer, *Heiligen Drei Könige*, 2:14.

98. Rossi, loc. cit., 79.

99. Wilpert, *Sarcofagi*, Tavole 1:73, and Text 153; H. Leclercq, "Chrisme," in *Dictionnaire d'archéologie chrétienne et de liturgie*, vol. 3, 1 (Paris, 1913), 1484.

100. Reproduced in Kehrer, *Heiligen Drei Könige*, 2:43.

101. Powerful men's habit of imposing their own pictures or symbols over or above what is conventionally adored, so that one cannot kneel before the one without adorning the other, is as old as images themselves and as new as television.

102. Kehrer, *Heiligen Drei Könige*, 1:15.

103. Ibid. This section of the lost book of Seth is preserved in the Opus Imperfectum; *PG*, 56:637f.; see the text in Monneret, *Leggende orientali*, 22.

104. Rossi, loc. cit., 79; Leclercq, "Labarum," 954f.

105. See, e.g., the large altarpiece by the Master of the Darmstadt Passion in the Dahlem Gallery, Berlin: the adoration of the magi is on the left panel, while on the right Constantine and Helena adore the true cross at the church door.

106. "Dominici sacramenti"; *PL*, 31:1052ff.

107. Ibid., 1053.

108. See, e.g., Roger van der Weyden's adoration in the Dahlem Gallery, Berlin, which shows Augustus' vision on the left, the adoration of the magi on the

right. See especially Domenico Ghirlandaio's *Adoration of the Shepherds*, reproduced in chap. 3.

109. See the excellent reproductions in H. Karpp, *Die frühchristliche und mittelalterliche Mosaiken in Santa Maria Maggiore zu Rom* (Baden-Baden, 1966).

110. Grabar, *L'empereur*, 214.

111. Ibid., 212.

112. The Pseudo Matthew was written in the fifth century; E. Baldwin Smith, *Early Christian Iconography*, 18ff.

113. With insight, Grabar, *L'empereur*, 228, notes that Jesus is actually making an *adventus*.

114. *PG*, 56:638; Monneret, *Leggende orientali*, 22,37,46.

115. Monneret de Villard, *Leggende orientali*, 63.

116. *PL*, 178:415.

117. On the cult and relics, see Miles, *Christmas Customs*, 107, 114f.

118. Grabar, *L'empereur*, 103. For the revisions carried out about 561, see G. Bovini, *Sant'Apollinare Nuovo in Ravenna* (Stuttgart, 1961), 24, and the standard work by Simson, *Sacred Fortress*, 81ff; Simson also provides a historical and ecclesiological background to the political meaning of these buildings; ibid., chap. 1.

119. Simson, *Sacred Fortress*, 89ff generally on the magi in the ancient church. Bovini, *Sant'Apollinare Nuovo*, 28, cautions that the upper bodies of the magi have been totally repainted at a much more recent date; this also explains the presence of their names above the figures, a high and late medieval innovation. Why the magi lead the female procession rather than the male one is uncertain. Perhaps it refers to the Byzantine habit of aristocratic women bringing the empress gifts when she gave birth; see chap. 2. Note also that in S. Vitale (see below), the magi appear on the garment of the empress, not the emperor. Paul Kaplan brought this to my attention.

120. Simson, *Sacred Fortress*, 121.

121. Peter Chrysologus (d. 450), cited in Klauser, "Aurum coronarium," 1017.

122. Simson, *Sacred Fortress*, 90.

123. Simson, *Sacred Fortress*, 117ff. Cf. Rev. 21.21.

124. Simson, *Sacred Fortress*, 92; Cf. such a mosaic of the fourth century in F. Van Der Meer and C. Mohrmann, *Atlas of the Early Christian World* (London, 1958), fig. 422 and text.

125. Simson, *Sacred Fortress*, 90.

126. Ibid., 110.

127. Ibid., 99f.

128. Ibid., 24.

129. On such Byzantine ceremonies, see below, chap. 2.

130. Grabar, *L'empereur*, 106.

131. This scholarly tendency has most recently taken the form of bestowing the fearful name "reception theory" on attempts like mine to determine what normal reactions to art works might have been. Obviously, such a name wants precisely to avoid its very subject.

132. "Illi magi tres reges dicuntur"; *PL*, 39:2018; Kehrer, *Heiligen Drei Könige*, 1:36.

133. For the case of St. William of Acquitaine (d. 804), see Wilpert, *Sarcofagi*, 3:26ff and Tavola 189.

134. Simson, *Sacred Fortress*, 182.

135. I owe my knowledge in this matter to E. Zürcher, whose detailed letter to me has proved invaluable. Further on the imperial dream in Zürcher, *Buddhist Conquest of China*, 2 vols. (Leiden, 1959), 1:22; H. Maspero, "Le songe et l'ambassade de l'empereur Ming: Étude critique des sources," *Bulletin de l'École d'Extrême Orient*, 10 (1910), 95–130.

136. Indeed, in the seventeenth century the Jesuits would maintain that the "golden man" in the dream was actually Jesus: The ambassadors mistook the devil Buddha for the God Jesus, who lay in Bethlehem much further on; P. Intorcetta, *Sinarum scientia politico-moralis* (Goa, 1669), postface (*Confucii vita*), 4.

137. Monneret de Villard, *Leggende*, 65.

138. A. Jackson, "The Magi in Marco Polo and the Cities in Persia from which they came to worship the infant Christ," *Journal of the American Oriental Society*, 26 (1905), 79–83; Monneret, *Leggende orientali*, 81.

139. C. Clermont-Ganneau, "La prise de Jérusalem par les Perses en 614," *Recueil d'archéologie orientale*, 2 (1899), 139f; Grabar, *Martyrium*, 2:243; Cumont, "L'adoration," 103. That this representation may rather have been on the apse inside is indicated in the next note.

140. On the famous treasure of sixth-century ampoules in northern Italy, see A. Grabar, *Les ampoules de Terre Sainte (Monza-Bobbio)* (Paris, 1958); Grabar, *Martyrium*, 2:174–77. The programs on these ampoules are sources for the study of apse programs in eastern churches, including that of the Nativity in Bethlehem; C. Ihm, *Die Programme der christlichen Apsismalerei vom vierten Jahrhundert bis zur Mitte des achten Jahrhunderts* (Wiesbaden, 1960), 52–55.

141. Kehrer, *Heiligen Drei Könige*, 1:68, more generally 64ff. Of special interest is the name "Melchior" coming from the Hebrew "king of light," as if to say that the magi had passed from darkness to light.

142. *PL*, 92:13.

143. *PL*, 92:15.

144. *PL*, 94:541. On this text, see R. McNally, "The Three Holy Kings in Early Irish Latin Writing," in *Kyriakon: Festschrift Johannes Quasten*, eds. P. Granfield and J. Jungmann, 2 vols. (Münster/Westf., 1970), 2:669f.

145. Baldwin Smith, *Early Christian Iconography*, 162, 166.

146. See the *opus imperfectum*, *PG*, 56:638, and further above.

147. Monneret de Villard, *Leggende orientali*, 35, also 77 for a similar group of visions.

148. Cf. Marco Polo ibid., 78.

149. *PG*, 56:637f; Monneret de Villard, *Leggende orientali*, 38–43.

150. Monneret, *Leggende orientali*, 122, 214 (see note 2 for much older references. On the "ducat of the three wise men" in Milan, see A. Arfwidsson, *Zeno oder die Legende von den Heiligen Drei Königen* (Lund, 1940), 13.

151. This very early story is traced in Monneret de Villard, *Leggende orientali*, 62ff; Baldwin Smith, *Early Christian Iconography*, 22.

152. Monneret, *Leggende orientali*, 152. The famous "Three Philosophers" or Magi of Giorgione has long fascinated art historians, because it relates in some way to this tale; S. Settis, *La 'Tempesta' interpretata. Giorgione, i commitenti, i soggetti* (Turin, 1978); J. Wilde, *Venetian Art from Bellini to Titian* (Oxford, 1974). The story seems to stem from Turkistan about the tenth century, to then be elaborated upon by Marco Polo in the late thirteenth.

153. Monneret de Villard, *Leggende orientali*, 105f.

154. Ibid., 108.

155. Ibid., 13–16.

156. Monneret, *Leggende orientali*, 70, 90. It is significant that this detail turns up in the famous *auto* or vernacular magi drama of medieval Spain, apparently making its way across the Mediterranean by way of southern France; see chap. 3.

157. On Caesarius and Arles at this time, see L. Stouff, *Arles à la fin du Moyen-Age*, 2 vols. (Aix-en-Provence, 1988), 1:63f, 68, 197.

158. J. Hubert et al., *Europe of the Invasions* (New York, 1969), fig. 298.

159. Ibid., 254; see also the figure on 247. Another beautiful magi scene from this period is studied in J. Beckwith, *The Adoration of the Magi in Whalebone* (London, 1966).

160. "Cum magna humilitate terrae prostratus"; *Le Liber pontificalis*, ed. L. Duchesne, 3 vols. (Paris, 1886–1957), 1:447.

161. "Aspersus cinere et indutus cilicio in terram prostratus, per misericordiam dei . . . obsecrat"; *Annales Mettenses*, in *Monumenta Germaniae Historica: Scriptores*, vol. 1 (Leipzig, 1925), 331.

162. Duchesne, *Liber*, 1:447. The meeting in fact probably stretched over two days; A. Cartellieri, *Die Zeit der Reichsgründungen, 382–911* (Munich, 1927), 159.

163. The text is in K. Reindel (ed.), *Die Kaiserkrönung Karls des Grossen* (Göttingen, 1970), 12f.

164. R. Folz, *Le couronnnement impérial de Charlemagne* (Paris, 1964), 172, argues against this view.

165. Monneret de Villard, *Leggende orientali*, 39. The source is the Cronicle of Zugnin, dated to before the eighth century. In the light of this source, which Folz did not know, the latter's reticence to accept Charlemagne's so-called *Festkrönung* is not persuasive.

166. Reindel, *Kaiserkrönung*, 13.

167. Ibid., 47.

CHAPTER 2

1. Liutprand of Cremona, *Legatio constantinopolitana*, in *Tutte le opere* (Milan, 1945), 233.

2. Unless otherwise indicated, in what follows I use the text vol. 1 of Constantin VII, Porphyrogénète, *Le livre des cérémonies*, ed. A. Vogt, 2 vols. (Paris, 1967). On Byzantine ceremony in this period, see S. MacCormack, *Art and Ceremony in Late Antiquity* (Berkeley, 1981).

3. Vogt, *Livre*, 1:30 (bk. 1, chap. 2).

4. Vogt, *Livre*, 1:32 (bk. 1, chap. 2); O. Treitinger, *Die oströmische Kaiser- und Reichsidee nach ihrer Gestaltung im höfischen Zeremoniell* (Bad Homburg vor der Höhe, 1969), 114.

5. Vogt, *Livre*, 1:33 (bk. 1, chap. 2).

6. See on this point *Annales Ecclesiastici*, ed. C. Baronius, vol. 1 (Lucca, 1738), anno 1, cc. 54v–55r.

7. See the references in chap. 1, above, note 7.

8. Vogt, *Livre*, 1:127ff (bk. 1, chap. 33); also ibid., *Commentaire*, 153f.

9. Vogt, *Livre*, 1:133 (bk. l, chap. 35).

10. Vogt, *Livre*, 1:130–35 (bk. 1, chap. 34).

11. At this time we find westerners toasting their saints on their feast days ("Bibe amorem S. Ioannis!"); Ekkehardi IV, "Casus S. Galli," in *Monumenta Germaniae Historia, Scriptores* vol. 2 (Hannover, 1829), 84. On the later convention of "Le roi boît," see further below, chap. 5.

12. Vogt, *Livre*, 1:36 (bk. l, chap. 3).

13. Perhaps significantly, in the mosaics of S. Maria Maggiore the magi adore Jesus who sits alone, his mother alongside him.

14. J. Ebersolt, *Constantinople* (Paris, 1951), 10f; C. Porphyrogenitus, *De cerimonibus aulae byzantinae*, vol. 1, in *Corpus scriptorum historiae byzantinae*, vol. 9 (Bonn, 1829), 615 (bk. 2, chap. 21).

15. Ibid., 618.

16. Ibid., 618f.

17. Treitinger believes that intent was probable; *Oströmische Kaiser*, 109; Ebersolt, *Constantinople*, ll, is certain; so is Grabar, *L'empereur*, 261.

18. E. Wellesz, "The Nativity Drama of the Byzantine Church," *The Journal of Roman Studies*, 37 (1947), 145–51.

19. Ibid., 147.

20. Ibid., 147. Joseph's unease can already be seen at work in Mt. 1.19.

21. Ibid., 150.

22. Joseph's fear of having been cuckolded is, for example, explicit in a *sacra rappresentazione* of the fifteenth-century Florentine playright Feo Belcari, and the so-called "Klatschgeschichte" can be seen whispered to Joseph in the London Adoration of P. Bruegel; on the subject, see W. Stechow, *Bruegel* (Cologne, 1974), 88.

23. Wellesz, "Nativity Drama," 148.

24. The 62nd Canon of the Council of Trullo is cited among the works of Theodore Balsamon (d. c. 1195), in *PG*, 137:726f. Balsamon's extensive commentary follows.

25. The following is from Theophanes Continuatus, bk. 4: *Michaelis Theofili F. Imperium*, in *Corpus scriptorum historiae byzantinae*, vol. 33 (Bonn, 1838), 200f.; E. Gibbon, *The Decline and Fall of the Roman Empire*, ed. J. Bury vol. 5 (London, 1901), 201; Chambers, *Mediaeval Stage*, l:327f.

26. This is a late festive incorporation; Treitinger, *Oströmische Kaiser*, 125f.

27. In Niceta Paphlagonis' *Life of Ignatius, Archbishop of Constantinople*, *PG*, 105:527.

28. Georgius Cedrenus, *Historiarum compendium*, 2 vols. (Bonn, 1839), 2:333. The text is actually Scylitzes'.

29. Balsamon, in *PG*, 137:727.

30. Ibid., 730f.

31. Ibid., 731.

32. Ibid., 727.

33. J. Frazer, *The Golden Bough*, 12 vols. (London, 1911–15).

34. Interesting observations regarding village election of kings in the late Middle Ages are in E. Schubert, "Erspielte Ordnung: Beobachtungen zur bäuerlichen Rechtswelt des späteren Mittelalters," *Jahrbuch für fränkische Landesforschung* 38 (1978), 51–65.

35. W. Volbach, "Il Cristo di Sutri e la venerazione del SS. Salvatore nel Lazio," *Rendiconti della pontificia accademia romana di archeologia* 27 (1940–41), 97–126.

36. On the Pfalzkapelle at Aachen, see H. Schnitzler, "Das Kuppelmosaik der Aachener Pfalzkapelle," *Aachener Kunstblätter*, 29 (1964), 14–24; E. Günther Grimme, "Novus Constantinus: Die Gestalt Konstantins des Großen in der imperialen Kunst der mittelalterlichen Kaiserzeit," *Aachener Kunstblätter*, 22 (1961), 11. On the elders, see Van der Meer, *Maiestas Domini*, especially for the Apocalypse of Trier, fig. 66.

37. A. von Euw, "Darstellungen der Heiligen Drei Könige im Kölner Dom und ihre ikonographische Herleitung," in *Achthundert Jahre Verehrung*, 309f; B. de Montesquiou-Fezensac, "L'arc de triomphe d'Einhardus," *Cahiers archéologiques*, 4 (1949), 79–103; Günther Grimme, "Novus Constantinus," 13.

38. Von Euw, "Darstellungen der heiligen Drei Könige," fig. 29; P. Schramm and F. Mütherich, *Denkmale der deutschen Könige und Kaiser* (Munich, 1962), fig. 107.

39. Schramm and Mütherich, *Denkmale*, fig. 297 (fig. 82); R. Deshman, "*Christus rex et magi reges*: Kingship and Christology in Ottonian and Anglo-Saxon Art," *Frühmittelalterlichen Studien*, 10 (1976), fig. 33.

40. The same Registrum Master inspired the Egberti magi as did the Chantilly representation; Deshman, "*Christus rex*," 382.

41. That is, an adoration of the magi is used to illustrate Psalm 72; Deshman, "*Christus rex*," 379, fig. 29.

42. I disagree at this point with Deshman, "*Christus rex*," 69.

43. Deshman, "*Christus rex*," 380.

44. Deshman missed this liturgical content; "*Christus rex*," 399.

45. Deshman, "*Christus rex*," 401.

46. That this is a church nave appears confirmed by the windows in the background; I. Forsyth, "Magi and Majesty: a Study of Romanesque Sculpture and Liturgical Drama," *Art Bulletin*, 50 (1968), 218, fig. 9; more cautiously in her *The Throne of Wisdom: Wood Sculptures of the Madonna in Romanesque France* (Princeton, 1972), 50.

47. Summary in Forsyth, "Magi and Majesty," 218, note 19.

48. These figures are based on a map in N. King, *Mittelalterliche Dreikönigsspiele*, 1:45. The vernacular play is the famous Castilian *auto de los reyes magos*; see below and W. Sturdevant, *The Misterio de los reyes magos. Its Position in the*

Development of the Medieval Legend of the Three Kings (Baltimore, 1927);
M. Doudoroff, "Sobre la naturaleza del 'Auto de los reyes Magos' en época moderna," *Revista de Dialectologia y Tradiciones Populares*, 29 (1973), 417–26.

49. Chambers, *Mediaeval Stage*, 2:301. The Parisian theologian Jean Beleth
(fl. 1180s) defined the *pueri* in his cathedral as "those who are less by age and
status" (*ordine*); *Rationale divinorum officiorum*, in *PL*, 202:79. For the kind of
activities to be expected, see the selection of texts in Chambers, *Mediaeval Stage*,
2:295–99.

50. Ekkehardi IV., *Casus S. Galli*, 84.

51. Ibid., 91 (917).

52. The late-medieval custom of taking prisoners on Epiphany is documented
in R. Vaultier, *Le folklore pendant la guerre de Cent Ans d'après les lettres de Remission du Trésor des Chartes* (Paris, 1965), 88.

53. J. Drumbl, *Quem Quaeritis. Teatro Sacro dell'alto medioevo* (Rome,
1981), 331, disagrees with this view of R. Stumpfl, *Kultspiele der Germanen als
Ursprung des Mittelalterlichen Dramas* (Berlin, 1936), 382f.

54. J. d'Avranches, *Liber de officiis ecclesiasticis*, in *PL*, 147:41f.

55. Chambers, *Mediaeval Stage*, 1:336–71.

56. Ibid., 1:355. The future would be rich in examples of the poor dressing
up as dignitaries and then begging; see chap. 5, below. In such giving to actors
can also be sensed one understanding of the gifts play magi will present to the
child: These gifts will not just be from the magi; they will also embody the "gifts"
given to the magi to do the Adoration; see chap. 5, below.

57. Ibid., 1:341; Letters 1119 and 1208 regarding the diocese of Paris, in *PL*,
212:73, 91.

58. "In quibusdam ecclesiis subdiaconi fortes & iuvenes faciunt hodie festum," referring to 1 January; Guielmus Durand, *Rationale divinorum officiorum*
(Antwerp, 1570), f. 280r.

59. In *PL*, 147:42f.

60. Referring to the feast of the "ypodiaconi" in *PL*, 202:79.

61. "Festum hypodiaconorum, quod vocamus stultorum"; ibid.

62. "Deposuit potentes de sede, et exaltavit humiles"; Chambers, *Mediaeval
Stage*, 1:276ff.

63. In *PL*, 212:73.

64. "Et debent esse scripti in tabula"; K. Young, *The Drama of the Medieval
Church*, 2 vols. (London, 1933), 2:437.

65. Text in King, *Mittelalterliche Dreikönigsspiele*, 47. Note the identification
of an *officium stellae* with the popular Herod evil figure, and not with the solemn
Three Kings or Mary figures. On which see further below.

66. Durand, *Rationale*, f. 280.

67. Thus in Chambers, *Mediaeval Stage*, 2:296. For Beleth, see *PL*, 202:79;
Durand, *Rationale*, ff. 279v-281v.

68. See Sturdevant, *Misterio*, 54f; also R. Donovan, *The Liturgical Drama in
Medieval Spain* (Toronto, 1958), 71ff. A key fact is that texts of liturgical dramas
of the magi are all but unknown in Spain; that contemporary liturgical plays
across the Pyrenees in France do not use the names of the Three Kings; but that
in the *auto*, each king has his name. Lastly, several of the earliest paintings of the

magi featuring these names are from Spain, probably influenced by this *auto*; for the Gerona Apocalypse, dating to the end of the tenth century, see the reproduction in D. Grivot, *Images de Noël à Autun et en d'autres lieux* (Autun, 1972), fig. 43, which shows the magi with names, but not as kings; and the Adoration in the early thirteenth-century altar piece of Espinelves, in the Episcopal Museum of Vich, Barcelona; reproduced in Cardini, *La stella*, fig. 24.

69. It is this narrative line which I earlier assumed Caesarius of Arles would have imbibed in his southern French monastery from the Syrian colony in Arles. See above, and for the *auto*, see Donovan, *Liturgical Drama*, 71.

70. I have brought together references to such customs in Florence, Italy, in my *Public Life*, index: "tribute." An excellent picture of debtors paying such dues to lords, with a large tapestry of the Adoration behind the receivers, is in an Eichstatt manuscript of ca. 1497 (2:23); F. Graus et al, *Eastern and Western Europe in the Middle Ages* (London, 1970), 173.

71. Beleth, in *PL*, 202:50.

72. Young, *Drama*, 2:32–43 for the earliest plays, performed at the offertory, and for Rouen, ibid., 43–46, especially 44.

73. Ibid., 40.

74. The historical dynamics of this movement are introduced by Young, *Drama*, 2:42–50.

75. "Puerorum festa colentes"; Chambers, *Mediaeval Stage*, 1:369.

76. For commentary on the picture, see Grimm, "Novus Constantinus," 18. The play: W. Meyer, "Der Ludus de Antichristo und Bemerkungen über die lateinischen Rythmen des XII Jahrhunderts," *Sitzungsberichte der philosophischen und historischen Classe der k. b. Akademie der Wisssenschaften zu München*, 1 (1882), 15f.

77. W. Lipphardt, "Liturgische Dramen," in *Die Musik in Geschichte und Gegenwart*, 8 (Kassel, 1960), 1023f; Lipphardt, "Das Herodesspiel von Le Mans nach den Handschriften Madrid, Bibl. Nac. 288 und 289 (11. und 12. Jh.)," in *Organicae Voces: Festschrift Joseph Smits van Waesbergher* (Amsterdam, 1963), 121f. For the expression "to out-Herod Herod," that is, to be wild, see Donovan, *Liturgical Drama*, 95.

78. See Young, *Drama*, 2:525 for Gerhoh of Reichersberg's reference to the *herodianam insaniam* in his monastery, presumably a clear indication that the heraldic part of the whole, in short, Herod's part, was what gave offense.

79. King, *Mittelalterlische Dreikönigsspiele*, 47; Young, *Drama*, 2:524f.

80. Young, *Drama*, 2:84; King, *Mittelalterliche Dreikönigsspiele*, 191.

81. Young, *Drama*, 2:34.

82. Ibid., 2:85.

83. Ibid., 2:38.

84. Chambers, *Mediaeval Stage*, 2:45f.

85. Cf. Young, *Drama*, 2:85.

86. As stated in Beleth, in *PL*, 202:50. See the Györ process in King, *Mittelalterliche Dreikönigsspiele*, 5.

87. A table showing the various forms of utensils carried by the magi in paintings is in S. Trocmé, *L'église de Villemards et sa 'Adoration des Mages'* (Paris, 1967), 22.

88. King, *Mittelalterliche Dreikönigsspiele*, 191.

89. Roughly: "We say that he reigns justly and holds the royal scepter. The name "king" is honored by him, because he decorates it with good morals"; Young, *Drama*, 2:75f.

90. Ibid., 2:97.

91. See, e.g., Ibid., 2:98.

92. Chambers, *Mediaeval Stage*, 2:56f; Stumpfl, *Kultspiele*, 376–83; J. Drumbl, *Quem Quaeritis*, 330–33.

93. Young, *Drama*, 2:81, 85; also 64, 76, 103.

94. Ibid., 60.

95. Ibid., 54.

96. Ibid., 69f.

97. Ibid., 70.

98. Ibid.

99. Ibid.

100. Ibid., 70, 87.

101. Ibid., 77f.

102. See in this chapter, above.

103. Ibid., 78f.

104. The best introduction to this theme is F. Büttner, *Imitatio Pietatis. Motive der christlichen Ikonographie als Modelle zur Verähnlichung* (Berlin, 1985), 19 seq.

105. King, *Mittelalterliche Dreikönigsspiele*, 5; for the image on the altar at Rouen, see Young, *Drama*, 2:437.

106. Ibid., 2:71, 437.

107. Ibid., 2:105.

108. Ibid., 40.

109. Julien de Vézelay, *Sermons*, vol. 1 (Paris, 1972), 66–85.

110. Ibid., 80.

111. Ibid., 80ff. Nor was this true only in the Middle Ages. In a recent performance of *Le Jeu d'Hérode* (ms. preserved in the Orléans library) at the abbey of Sylvanès, the performers "restored the medieval gestures" according to the recommendations of F. Garnier; *Le jeu d'Hérode: Drame liturgique du XIIe siècle* (Création par l'Ensemble Gilles Binchois . . . 12 aout 1988) (Paris, 1988). See further Garnier, *Le Langage de l'Image au Moyen Age*, 2 vols. (Paris, 1982–88). A review of Büttner, *Imitatio pietatis*, 19–32, shows how powerful the magi were as such a model, perhaps especially because they were assumed to be aristocrats. A twelfth-century, originally French text also urged the faithful to imitate the magi when praying or gifting; *The Lay Folks Mass Book, or The Manner of Hearing Mass*, ed. T. Simmons (London, 1879), 22f, brought to my attention by M. Rubin.

112. Young, *Drama*, 2:38.

113. "Ante maius altare; ibique flexis genibus offerunt sua munera cum coronis"; Young, *Drama*, 2:41.

114. See Trexler, "Träume der Heiligen Drei Könige." This article provides an overview of the different medieval visions of the magi.

115. "Tollentes coronas de capitibus suis, obtulerunt eas in manus ipsius, rursasque eas ab ipso reciperunt"; ibid., 67, note 12.

116. "Numisma aureum magnum, quasi imagine regia signatum"; ibid., note 14.

117. On the three churches at Besançon, see K. Young, "La procession des trois rois at Besançon," *Romanic Review*, 4 (1913), 76–83.

118. On such *Festkrönungen*, see in this chapter, above, and P. Schramm, *Herrschaftszeichen und Staatssymbolik*, vol. 3 (Stuttgart, 1956), 913–1014. A recent overview of the literature is in C. Brühl, "Kronen- und Krönungsbrauch im frühen und hohen Mittelalter," *Historische Zeitung*, 234 (1982), 6–12.

119. For the Canute story, see Deshman, "Christus Rex," 404. Bequeathing crowns to the church, often by placing them on the altar, was widespread; see an example in Brühl, "Kronen- und Krönungsbrauch," 10.

120. I wonder if such considerations explain those pictures where a king or kings move forward toward the infant, leaving their crown floating above them; see the Espinelves adoration referred to in this chapter, above, note 68, and Jacobello Alberegno's *Corteo dei magi*, in the Venetian Accademia.

121. King, *Mittelalterliche Dreikönigsspiele*, 49f; Young, *Drama*, 2:413.

122. Herrad of Hohenbourg, *Hortus deliciarum*, ed. R. Green et al (London, 1979), 492.

123. Text in Young, *Drama*, 2:525.

124. J.-P. Poly and E. Bournazel, *La mutation féodale: X-XII siècles* (Paris, 1991), 469.

125. On the *ducato dei tre re* at Milan, see A. Arfwidsson, *Zeno oder die Legende von den heiligen Drei Königen* (Lund, 1940), 13ff.

126. K. Meissen, *Die heiligen Drei Könige und ihr Festtag im Glauben und Brauch* (Cologne, 1945), 12.

127. Hofmann, *Heiligen Drei Könige*, 295f.

128. Durand, *Rationale*, f. 281r.

129. As found in the so-called Pseudo Bonaventura of the fourteenth century: Anonimo francescano, *Meditazioni sulla vita di Cristo* (Città Nuova, 1992), and then in Ludolphus de Saxonia, *Vita Jesu Christi* (Paris, 1865).

130. Julien de Vezelay, *Sermons*, 1:82. Of course there remain texts, like Jacopo da Voragine's *Golden Legend*, in which Mary follows the old eastern tradition and passes on the gifts to "the poor." Needless to say, by Mary we are also to understand the church, which must keep its breasts full.

131. The first inkling of a legend goes back to 1122, but the historian Otto of Freising made him a household word from the 1140s; P. Kaplan, *The Rise of the Black Magus in Western Art* (Ann Arbor, 1985), 45.

132. Mt. 2.1–12. For the whole passage, see Julien of Vezelay, *Sermons*, 1:68.

133. Mt.8.ll.

134. See *The Interpreter's Bible*, vol. 7 (New York, 1951), 341 (Mt. 8.11).

135. Albertus Aquensis, *Historia hiersolamitana* in *Recueil des historiens des croisades* (*Histoires Occidentaux*, vol. 4) (Paris, 1879), 536f.

136. Crombach, *Primitiae*, 164.

137. On Cologne at this juncture, see the collection by H. Stehkaemper (ed.), *Köln, das Reich und Europa* (Cologne, 1971).

138. On the canonization, see W. Kienast, *Deutschland und Frankreich in der Kaiserzeit*, 3 vols. (Stuttgart, 1974–75), continuing pagination 516–20. Recently on the (non-) events surrounding the alleged departure from Milan of the magi, in P. Geary, "I Magi e Milano," in *Il Millenio Ambrosiano*, ed. C. Bertelli (Milan, 1988), 274–87.

139. Bibliography on von Dassel as archbishop is in Hofmann, *Heiligen Drei Könige*, 302; also Kienast, *Deutschland und Frankreich*, 516–20.

CHAPTER 3

1. Cited in H. Kehrer, *Heiligen Drei Könige*, 1:39.

2. Young, *Medieval Drama*, 2:89. The line is common in magi plays.

3. Durand, *Rationale*, f. 279v.

4. R. Salvini, "La scultura romanica pistoiese," in *Il romanico pistoiese nei suoi rapporti con l'arte romanica dell'occidente* (Pistoia, 1979), 171; A. Chiappelli, *Pistoia nelle sue opere d'arte* (Florence, 1904), 27. The superior inscription reads: "Veniunt ecce magi, sidus regale secuti/ Falleris Herodes quod Christum perdere voles/ Melchior, Gaspar, Baltasar. Magos stella monet. Puero tria munera donant." There were several magian Journeys or Adorations on the architraves of pilgrimage churches in this part of Italy at the time, perhaps recalling the Kings' status as patrons of pilgrims; see the plates in R. Stopani, *Le vie di pellegrinaggio del Medioevo* (Florence, 1991).

5. "Non est credibile, cum illi reges fuerunt, quod tres soli venerint, imo potius multis comitatibus stipati fuerunt"; Crombach, *Primitiae*, 164.

6. On the coronation, see W. Kienast, *Deutschland und Frankreich in der Kaiserzeit*, 3 vols. (Stuttgart, 1974–75), continuous pagination, 516–20; R. Folz, *Le souvenir et la Légende de Charlemagne dans l'Empire germanique médiéval* (Paris, 1950), 197–205, with a list of monarchs sainted in these years. Others saw the two acts as part of one propaganda attack. O. Engels, "Die Reliquien der Heiligen Drei Könige in der Reichspolitik der Staufer," in *Die Heiligen Drei Könige—Darstellung*, 34.

7. In a list of tableaux presented by the bourgeoisie of the city, the "trois rois de Couloingne" and the "rois á fève" are found; Godefroy de Paris, in J. Buchon (ed.), *Collection des chroniques nationales françaises écrites en lange vulgaire de 13e. au 16e. siècle*, 47 vols. (Paris, 1826–29), 9:190.

8. P. Wapnewski, "Die Weisen aus dem Morgenland auf der Magdeburger Weihnacht (zu Walter von der Vogelweide 19,5)," in *Lebende Antike: Symposion für Rudolf Sühnel* ed. H. Meller and H. J. Zimmerman (Berlin, 1967), 87.

9. "Tres coronas de auro capitibus trium magorum imposuit"; Annals text of 1200, cited in H. Stehkämper, "Könige und Heilige Drei Könige," in *Die Heiligen Drei Könige—Darstellung*, 39, 48, note 37. At one time Otto's name could be read above this gold portrait; H. Hofmann, *Die Heiligen Drei Könige: Zur Heiligenverehrung im kirchlichen, gesellschaftlichen und politischen Leben des Mittelalters* (Bonn, 1975), 305.

10. Stehkämper, "Könige," 39.

11. "Magnus dominus avus suus, quia imperator romanus, magnus dominus pater, quia imperator et rex Sicilie, ipse maximus, quia imperator romanus, rex

Iherusalem et Sicilie. Profecto hii tres imperatores sunt quasi tres magi, qui venerunt cum muneribus deum et hominem adorare, sed hic est adolescentior illis tribus, super quem puer Ihesus felices manus posuit et brachiola sacrosancta." First printed by R. Kloos, "Nikolaus von Bari, eine neue Quelle zur Entwicklung der Kaiseridee unter Friedrich II," *Deutsches Archiv für Erforschung des Mittelalters* 11 (1954–55), 171; the laud's magi content was introduced into the magi literature by Büttner, *Imitatio Pietatis*, 27. Note the hint at anointing by laying on hands. It makes one wonder if Frederick's coronation in 1215 was being described.

12. Alternately, in the Wilton diptych of c. 1395 we see one dead ancestor and a dead patron saint commending one live King, Richard II of England, who was born on epiphany; M. Wilson, *The National Gallery London* (London, 1977), 31.

13. The first monarch of Germany to do so was Richard of Cornwall, in 1257; *Heiligen Drei Könige: Darstellung*, 40. On the magi's entry not just as *translatio* but as *adventus*, an *adventus* (23 July 1164) that would be commemorated in Cologne by the epiphany mass of 6 January being celebrated on that July day, see Hofmann, *Die Heiligen Drei Könige*, 140f.

14. Actually, the first king to come to Cologne after Aachen may have been the Englishman Richard of Cornwall, in 1257; Stehkämper, "Heiligung," 40. But Habsburg seems to have started the German practice.

15. See the texts in "Coronatio Aquisgranensis" in *Monumenta Germaniae Historica: Leges*, ed. G. Pertz, vol. 2 (Hannover, 1837), 384ff.

16. Ibid., 391f.

17. For the forks, see the recollection of the Florentine Benedetto Dei toward mid-fifteenth century: "Sono istato in detto anno nel Brabante e a Cholognia e o ttochato e' tre Magi chola forchete d'argiento"; *Biblioteca Nazionale di Firenze*, ms. II.ii.333 (Memorie di Benedetto Dei), f. 37.

18. "Henricus coronatur corone ferrea in Sancto Ambrosio die regum"; W. Bowsky, *Henry VII in Italy* (Lincoln, Nebraska, 1960), 234.

19. See, e.g., the sarcophagus of Severus (ca. 1365) in the church of St. Severus in Erfurt, Germany: his coronation and an Adoration are on opposite sides of the tomb; further, my "Triumph and Mourning." On papal coronations, see chap. 5, below. Debra Pincus brought the canon law illuminations to my attention.

20. H. Seitz, "Three Crowns as a European Symbol and as the Swedish Coat of Arms," in *V. Congrès international des sciences généalogique et héraldique* (Stockholm, 1961), 240–49. Note also the use of the term "the three crowns" in the fifteenth century to indicate a sense of totality. Thus, Dante, Boccaccio, and Petrarch were called the "three crowns of Florence"; H. Baron, *The Crisis of the Early Italian Renaissance* (Princeton, 1966), 332.

21. The following account is based largely on *Les grandes chroniques de France: Chronique des règnes de Jean II et de Charles V*, 2 vols. (Paris, 1916), 2:193–277, and to a lesser extent on Christine de Pisan, *Livre des fais et bonnes meurs* (*Collection complète des mémoires relatifs à l'histoire de France*, vol. 6) (Paris, 1819), 64–86.

22. See the Godefroy of Paris text regarding these "trois riches roys de grant afère" in Buchon, *Collection*, 9:178, 181f, 190f. It is this same document that

refers to the "trois rois de Couloingne," and to the "rois à feve et hommes souvages qui menoient grands rigolage." Re 1285: in that year the theologian Giles of Rome had completed his *de regimine principum*, which is said to have been dedicated to Philip just before the latter succeeded his father; *Recueil des historiens des Gaules et de la France*. vol. 21 (Paris, 1955), 7, 203.

23. "Eodem anno in epiphania domini natus est Ricardus rex Angliae apud Burdeywes, in cujus nativitate fuerunt iii. magi, scilicet rex Ispaniae, rex Navernie, et rex Portigalliae, qui quidem reges dederunt puero munera preciosa"; *Chronica W. Thorn. mon. S. Augustini Cantuarie*, in *Historiae anglicanae scriptores X . . .*, ed. R. Twysden (London, 1652), 2142. The story may be apocryphal; D. Gordon, *Making and Meaning: the Wilton Diptych* (London: The National Gallery, 1993), 57.

24. *Chronique . . . Jean II et . . . Charles V*, 2:193.

25. B. Guenée and F. Lehoux, in their excellent *Les entrées royales françaises de 1328 à 1515* (Paris, 1968), 13–18, state that "at the end of the fourteenth century everything encouraged the French to see in a royal entry only a Corpus Christi feast." However, in this case, the authors would have to have seen the magian overlay of the entry image.

26. *Chronique . . . Jean II et . . . Charles V*, 2:229ff. Doubtless the heralds did their euphemistic best. Cf. Christine, *Livre*, 79.

27. Christine, *Livre*, 75.

28. "Et quant ce vint à l'offrande, le Roy avoit fait appareillier trois peres de offrandes, d'or, d'encens et de mirre, pour offrir pour lui et pour l'Empereur, ainsi qu'il est acoustumé"; *Chronique . . . Jean II et . . . Charles V*, 2:233f. From what follows it is evident the writer meant what King Charles was used to doing himself. Cf. Christine, *Livre*, 80f. This custom was in place in England as well; see the image of Edward III (d. 1377) and his sons gifting the child in Hofmann, *Heiligen Drei Könige*, 396. In 1894, the royal offering was presented at the royal chapel in St. James' Palace, and consisted of spices plus 20 sovereigns. Prince Albert discovered one year that just one sovereign was in the box: The remainder "had been distributed in fees and perquisites to various persons who took part in the function and to some of the officials of the chapel"; *The International Herald-Tribune*, 6 January 1994.

29. Charles IV's magian credentials were, however, well established: he had been crowned king of the Lombards on Kings' Day, 1354; Stehkämper, "Könige," 40.

30. *Chronique . . . Jean II et . . . Charles V*, 2:234.

31. Christine, *Livre*, 83f; *Chronique . . . Jean II . . . et Charles V*, 239–42.

32. Contained in Fiamma's *De rebus gestis a . . . Vicecomitibus*, in *Rerum italicarum scriptores*, old ed., vol. 12 (Milan, 1728), 1017f.

33. Bonvesin de la Riva, *De magnalibus Mediolani* (Milan, 1974), 163; Trexler, "The Magi Enter Florence: the Ubriachi of Florence and Venice," in my *Church and Community, 1200–1600: Studies in the History of Florence and New Spain* (Rome, 1987), 75. Also Hofmann, *Heiligen Drei Könige*, 220.

34. On this matter, see Hofmann, *Heiligen Drei Könige*, 78–94, 176f.

35. "Ubi erat rex Herodes effigiatus cum scribis & sapientibus . . . , et responderunt . . ."; Fiamma, *De rebus gestis*, 1017f.

36. Although it is clear that a confraternity of three kings continued to flour-ish in the church; Hofmann, *Heiligen Drei Könige*, 155.

37. R. Hatfield, "The Compagnia de' Magi," *Journal of the Warburg and Courtauld Institutes*, 33 (1970), 107–61. See also my *Public Life*, 401–3, 423–24, 458–59.

38. Hatfield, "Compagnia," 110 (1417).

39. Ibid., 112.

40. Ibid., 114. The magi's almost uniform association with horses was, of course, emblematic of their nobility.

41. Cited in Hatfield, "Compagnia," 148ff.

42. To celebrate the election of a university rector, the doctors and scholars performed a *rappresentazione* of the Re Magi. Dressed appropriately, the kings were accompanied by "assai donzelli, mazzieri, e cavalieri, e seguiti da molto car-riaggio carico di valige e d'uccelli, e coperto di serici panni su' quali erano raffi-gurarte le armi di quei re"; A. Pezzana, *Storia di Parma*, 2 vols. (Parma, 1842), 2:157, who says this is the first but not the last *festa* of the magi encountered in the Parmese sources. Alas, Pezzana does not give us his primary source(s).

43. "Bellicula nuncupantur. Divident enim civitatem in partes duas . . . quarum unaquaque multas societates sive cohortes habet, que per singulas maiores parochias dividantur"; *Liber de laudibus civitatis Ticinae [Pavia]*, in *RIS*, vol. 11, part 1, 25.

44. See the texts in Hatfield, "Compagnia," 148.

45. Ibid., 118.

46. Ibid., 116.

47. Ibid., 116f. The broader social implications of this remark are in Trexler, *Public Life*, 368–87, esp. 384.

48. See the Egbert figure in chap. 2, above.

49. Actually, all the figures in this graveplate by Hermann Vischer are dead: the cardinal Friedrich Kasimir, and his presenters Pietrowin and St. Stanislaus; S. Meller, *Peter Vischer der Ältere und seine Werkstatt* (Leipzig, 1925), 130, 134f.

50. The engraving is reproduced in Trexler, "Träume," 57.

51. See my "Ritual Behavior in Renaissance Florence: The Setting," in Trex-ler, *Church and Community*, 19–21.

52. This fact of duality in many such paintings has been observed in any given painting by only one historian, to my knowledge; see the observation of W. Cook, "The Earliest Painted Panels of Catalonia (VI)," *Art Bulletin*, 10 (1928), 321.

53. For such male couples in early modern Italian art, see J. Manco, "Sacred vs. Profane: Images of Sexual Vice in Renaissance Art," *Studies in Iconography*, 13 (1990), esp. fig. 5. Note the phallic sword on the third king in the following figure.

54. On this illumination, see E. Spencer, "The First Patron of the *Très Belles Heures de Notre-Dame*," in *Miscellanea F. Lyna* (Gent, 1969), 146. Some other examples of the third king hanging back are the Adoration of Bartolomeo Viva-rini, at the Metropolitan Museum; of the Master of the Bartholomew Altar, (Col-lection of Mechtild Pankofer, Berg in Upper Bavaria); of Salamon Koninck in the

Mauritshaus, The Hague; of the church of Taganaro, Santa Cruz de Tenerife; of the Portuguese School, in Sé Evora. There are others where the third king is still mounted while the first two are kneeling, or where the third king is painted on a separate wing of the work.

55. Monneret de Villard, *Leggende orientali*, 78; L. Olschki, "The Wise Men of the East in Oriental Traditions," in *Semitic and Oriental Studies Presented to W. Popper* (Berkeley, 1951), 381–86.

56. For a list of these plays, see N. King, *Mittelalterliche Dreikönigsspiele*, 130 and note 203.

57. Ibid., 130f.

58. "Das ich wer alt"; ibid., 132.

59. Ibid.

60. "Anteaquam reges infantulum contingentes adorarent ter genu flexere, diuque ad invicem disputarunt, quis eorum prior adoraret: denique iunior primus accessit, pedes infantis exosculans, & quam capite gestabat coronam ante pedes infantuli solo reponens, quem Iesus infans benedixit. Sic quoque egere ceteri"; I. Isolano, "Vita b. Veronicae de Binasco virginis," in *Acta Sanctorum*, 107 vols. (Paris, 1863–1925) January I, 906.

61. My italics. "At reges specie corporis praestantes fuisse dicebat Veronica, aureis vestibus usque ad genua indutos, iunioremque regem, qui primus adoraverat, veluti effectum seniorem & unius aetatis cum reliquis duobus demirans intuita est"; ibid.

62. Perhaps only two kings wore masks, and they were identical, encouraging the perception that there was but one "old king."

63. G. A. Gilio (1564), *Degli errori e degli abusi de' pittori circa l'istoria* in P. Baronchi (ed.), *Trattati d'arte del cinquecento fra manierismo e controriforma*, 2 vols. (Bari, 1961), 2:45.

64. I have studied these conflicts in Florence; *Public Life*, 515–44.

65. N. Zemon Davis, *Society and Culture in Early Modern France* (Stanford, 1975), 97–123, 152–88.

66. One of the earliest Italian black servants is in the adoration of the Sienese pulpit by Nicola Pisano; see Kaplan, *Rise of the Black Magus*, fig. 3. Chronologically problematic, Kaplan finds the original inspiration for the appearance of blacks in magian format in their presence in Germany at the court of Frederick II; *Rise of the Black Magus*, 10. As inspiration for black Madonnas, see K. Schreiner, *Maria: Jungfrau, Mutter, Herrscherin* (Munich, 1994), 235.

67. The new style had been proceeded by a long tradition that showed a black Queen of Sheba visiting the white Salomon, and by a cult dating from the thirteenth century to the black St. Maurice; for examples, see Kaplan, *Rise of the Black Magus*, figs. 6, 9. The visit of the queen of Sheba was a standard old-testamental *typus* of the adoration of the kings.

68. L. Olschki argued that "true orientalism" was rare in Italian Renaissance art, but he missed the great Adoration cycle in the Bolognini chapel in S. Petronio, Bologna; "Asiatic Exoticism in Italian Art of the Early Renaissance," *Art Bulletin*, 26 (1944), 101; on the chapel, see I. Kloten, *Wandmalerei im Grossen Kirchenschisma: die Cappella Bolognini in San Petronio zu Bologna* (Heidelberg, 1986); Trexler, "Triumph and Mourning in North Italian Magi Art," in

Art and Politics in Late Medieval and Early Renaissance Italy, ed. C. Rosenberg (Notre Dame, 1990), 38–66.

69. Kaplan, *Rise of the Black Magus*, 95f.

70. Monneret de Villard, *Leggende orientali*, 217.

71. B. Hamilton, "Prester John and the Three Kings of Cologne," in *Studies in Medieval History Presented to R. H. C. Davis*, eds. H. Mayr-Harting and R. Moore (London, 1985), 177–91.

72. One possible exception is a Moor attributed to Juan de Flandre in the Adoration in Cervera de Pisuerga's parish church (ca. 1497); see I. Vandevivere, *El Cathédral et l'église paroissiale de Cervera de Pisuerga de Palencia* (Brussels, 1967), 104, pl. 190a. Because the painting may commemorate the fall of Granada to the Catholic kings in 1492, it could show the just-deposed Moorish king Boabdil.

73. Both are so adorned in the famous Prado Epiphany of H. Bosch, shown in J. Devisse and M. Mollat, *The Image of the Black in Western Art*, vol. 2, parts 1 and 2 (New York, 1979), 2, 2:180.

74. Giton "Oh, just splendid. . . . And while you're at it, please circumcise us too so we look like Jews, and bore our ears to imitate Arabians. . . ." Petronius, *Satyricon*, trans. W. Rouse (Cambridge, Mass., 1987), 245. See also the twelfth or thirteenth century mosaic of the Last Judgment in the cathedral of Torcello (Venezia); R. Polacco, *La cattedrale di Torcello* (Venice, 1984), 67, who characterizes these bearded men as those guilty of avarice, as one sees by the jewels (earrings) they wear. Marcello Fantoni kindly sent me a postcard of the same.

75. Including royals; see several of Van Dyck's paintings of Charles I of England. Needless to say, this monarch was thought to behave homosexually.

76. Cf. for instance the young king in the Adoration attributed to Filippo Lippi or a fra Angelico follower (ca. 1450) in the National Gallery of Art, Washington, D. C. (E. Morante [ed.], *L'opera completa dell'Angelico* Milano, 1970), 116 (no. 133), to the black king in a Mantegna Adoration; Devisse and Mollat, *Image of the Black*, 2, 2:140.

77. See for instance C. Bernis, "Modas moriscas en la sociedad cristiana española del siglo XV y principios del XVI," *Boletin de la real academia de la historia*, 144 (1959), 203f, and illustrations.

78. Kaplan, *Rise of the Black Magus*, 118.

79. Brown, *Birth of the Messiah*, 167ff.

80. *Wild Men and Moors*, tapestry, Alsace, about 1400; Boston, Museum of Fine Arts; reproduced in *The Image of the Black in Western Art*, vol. 2, parts 1 and 2 (New York, 1979), 2, part 2:14f.

81. J. Snyder, *Northern Renaissance Art* (New York, 1985), 402. Snyder's observation is of an adoration of the master of the Antwerp adoration in the Royal Fine Arts Museum in Antwerp. On the difference between dandyism and "effeminacy," see Garber, *Vested Interests*, 180. I prefer the term "effeminate" or "feminine" over the word "dandy" or "fop" because the latter is normally associated with adults, whereas the black, like the white, third king, is usually youthful.

82. Other examples of kings looking away are in the adoration of Konrad Laib in the Cleveland Museum; of the tympanon of the Liebfrauenkirche, Frankfurt

am Main; of the Bolognini chapel in San Petronio, Bologna; of Aurelio Lomi in the cathedral of Pisa; and of the Instituto de Valencia de don Juan, Madrid, where both the third and the second king swivel away and do not look at Jesus.

83. Cited in Garber, *Vested Interests*, 359.

84. Johannes of Hildesheim, *Liber de gestis et translacionibus trium regum*, in C. Horstmann, *The Three Kings of Cologne* (London, 1886), 257.

85. Kaplan Fahsel, *Die heiligen Drei Könige in der Legende und nach den Visionen der Anna Katharina Emmerich* (Basel, 1941), 11.

86. See her visions in chap. 5.

87. J. Wirth, "Sainte Anne est une sorciére," *Bibliothèque d'Humanisme et Renaissance* 40 (1978), 449–80.

88. C. Walker Bynum, *Jesus as Mother* (Los Angeles, 1982).

89. As in a sect studied by W. Doniger O'Flaherty, *Women, Androgynes and Other Mythical Beasts* (Chicago, 1982); I comment on the importance of this gender juxtaposition in my "Gendering Jesus Crucified," in *Iconography at the Crossroads*, ed. B. Cassidy (Princeton, 1993), 110.

90. L. Steinberg, *The Sexuality of Christ in Renaissance Art and in Modern Oblivion* (New York, 1983). In a review of Steinberg, Charles Hope maintains that, as the primary Christian cult figure, Mary was after all at the center of these Adorations; "Ostentatio genitalium," *The London Review of Books*, 13 November–6 December 1984, 19f. But in the adorations, Mary rarely interacts with anyone, including the infant, who regularly directs his attention (usually) to the first king. I know of only one painting in which, as in so many plays, the magi in any way greet Mary: the Herzebrock Altar from the studio of the Master of Liesborn, in which the black king, to (vainly) gain the attention of Mary, places his hand on her arm; reproduced in P. Pieper (ed.), *Die deutschen, niederländischen und italienischen Tafelbilder bis um 1530* (Münster, 1986), 251. On the other hand, paintings are not wanting that show the magi adoring a Jesus who is not held by Mary (as at S. Maria Maggiore, Rome, as described in chapter one) or ones in which Mary is not even present (as in the *Kostbares Evangeliar des hl. Bernward; Dom- und Diözesanmuseum Hildesheim*, DS. 187, f. 18r).

91. Steinberg, *Sexuality*, 67.

92. In its present form, it is thought to date from slightly after 1164; see the exhibition catalogue *Rhein und Maas: Kunst und Kultur 800–1400: eine Ausstellung . . .* (Cologne, 1972), 2:399f.

93. Reproduced in *Les très riches heures du duc de Berry* (Paris, 1970), f. 53r.

94. On the altar, see W. Beeh, "Mittelalterliche Abbilder als Legitimationsnachweis: Die Tafel mit der Anbetung der Könige in Lenzburg und der Ortenberger Altar," *Ulmer Verein: Kritische Berichte* 4 (1976), 4–18. In a later painting, preserved in the Museu Nacional de Arte Antiga in Lisbon, Holbein enlarged upon the same basic scene.

95. A. Chastel, "La Legend de la Reine de Saba," in his *Fables, Formes, Figures*, vol. 1 (Paris, 1978), 61–101.

96. On effeminacy, see the discussion in my *Sex and Conquest: Gendered Violence, Political Order, and the European Conquest of the Americas* (Cambridge and Ithaca, 1995), esp. 31–35.

97. D. Owen Hughes, "Earrings for Circumcision: Distinction and Purifica-

tion in the Italian Renaissance City," in R. Trexler (ed.), *Persons in Groups. Social Behavior as Identity Formation in Medieval and Renaissance Europe* (Binghamton, 1985), 155–182.

98. Third kings sometimes also wear liveried tights, inter alia, the one in the adoration of the Bolognini Chapel in the church of San Petronio, Bologna. Criticism of this and other types of "effeminate" or "feminine" clothing is in G. Klaniczay, *The Uses of Supernatural Power* (Oxford, 1990), 51–97. A legislative link of such male dress to the crime of sodomy is shown in R. Rainey, "Sumptuary Legislation in Renaissance Florence," (diss.: Columbia University, 1985), 577–83.

99. In Florence, the Uffizi Gallery.

100. A representative Bellange drawing, of John the Evangelist, is in H. Diane Russell (ed.), *Jacques Callot: Prints and Selected Drawings* (Washington, D.C., 1925), 163.

101. On the *velatio nuptialis*, see K. Stevenson, *Nuptial Blessing: a Study of Christian Marriage Rites* (New York, 1983), 27f, 37, 44. For the practice in same-sex unions, see J. Boswell, *Same-Sex Unions in Premodern Europe* (New York, 1994), 206f. It cannot be excluded that this wearing of a veil might be part of an initiation procedure of some type.

102. See at the head of this chapter.

103. For some sense of the range, see the figures in Hofmann, *Heiligen Drei Könige*, especially fig. 30, which shows Edward III of England, accompanied by his sons, making his annual epiphany offering to the infant, naturally in the form of an adoration. For King Charles V, see his image above, at note 57. For Emperor Charles IV, see Kaplan, *Rise of the Black Magus*, 88f.

104. For Ferdinand the Catholic as the first king, see Juan de Flandres' Adoration in Cervera de Pisuerga; J. Vandevivere, *Cathédral de Palencia*, pl. 192. The Emperor Sigismund is said to be the second king in Gentile da Fabriano's Strozzi Altarpiece; Kaplan, *Rise of the Black Magus*, 89. The elector Frederick the Wise of Saxony may be the second king in Baldung Grün's 1507 Adoration in the Dahlem Gallery in Berlin.

105. Hofmann, *Heiligen Drei Könige*, fig. 33.

106. See especially R. Hatfield, *Botticelli's Uffizi 'Adoration': a Study of Pictorial Content* (Princeton, 1976).

107. On this figure, see my "The Magi Enter Florence," in Trexler, *Church and Community*, pl. 2. The sculpture is in the Chiostro Grande of the convent of Santa Maria Novella, Florence. The fifteenth-century glass of a north choir chapel in the cathedral of Bourges features a "fourth magus," actually two young clerks being offered to the infant by a saint.

108. Simon Wynhoutsz Vries, *Adoration of the Magi*; reproduced in *Heiligen Drei Könige: Darstellung*, 240. Significantly, in copying his father's London adoration, Jakob Bruegel (see his adoration in the Vienna Art Museum) abandoned Peter's realistic kings for uninteresting, conventional royal types.

109. One need only mention the classic 1860 work of J. Burckhardt in this regard: *The Civilization of the Renaissance in Italy*.

110. On Marsilio Ficino's important work in these areas, including a 1490 treatise on the symbolic significance of the epiphany, see A. Chastel, *Art et hu-*

manisme à Florence au temps de Laurent le Magnifique (Paris, 1959), 246f; also *Marsile Ficin et l'art* (Geneva, 1975), and recently, S. Buhler, "Marsilio Ficino's *De stella magorum* and Renaissance Views of the Magi," *Renaissance Quarterly*, 43 (1990), 348–71.

111. Pompey refused to reveal the secrets of the Romans just as the magi went home by another way to avoid revealing Jesus' whereabouts to Herod; Crombach, *Primitiae gentium*, 57.

112. On the cases of Ercole d'Este of Ferrara, and Louis II, duke of Bourbon, see chap. 5 below.

113. After describing his "gift" to the crown, Samuel Pepys remarked: "Strange it was for me to see what a company of small fees I was called upon by a great many to pay there, which, I perceive, is the manner that courtiers do get their estates"; ibid. For France, see Vaultier, *Folklore*, 96.

CHAPTER 4

1. Paolo di Matteo Pietrobuoni, *Priorista, Biblioteca Nazionale, Firenze: Conventi religiosi soppressi* C.4.895, f. 109v (11 February).

2. *The Book of Ser Marco Polo the Venetian*, ed. G. Parks (New York, 1927); Hayton, Prince of Gorigos, *La flor de las ystorias de orient* (Chicago, 1934), 53, 111, 115. On Oderic, see H. Yule and H. Cordier, *Cathay and the Way Thither*, 4 vols. (London, 1913–16), 2:106; and Marignolli ibid., 3:267. On the general topic, see L. Olschki, *Marco Polo's Asia* (Berkeley, 1960).

3. Polo says that the kings of the lineage of Prester John "always obtain to wife either daughters of the Great Kahn or other princesses of his family"; *The Book of Ser Marco Polo the Venetian* (New York, 1927), 91 (chap. 59). See the end of this chapter for the same alleged marital norm governing the descendants of the Three Kings in Ethiopia.

4. The view that the magi did have descendants is found at the conclusion of this chapter.

5. *Mandeville's Travels: Texts and Translation*, ed. M. Letts (Nendeln, 1967); John of Hildesheim, *Liber de gestis et translacionibus trium regum*, in C. Horstmann, *The Three Kings of Cologne* (London, 1886). Kaplan notes that Hildesheim was never translated into Italian in this age, although it was widely translated into other languages; *Rise of the Black Magus*, 114, also 68.

6. Indeed in the seventeenth century it transpired that all the magi, not just one, had ended in Ethiopia as well; see the conclusion of this chapter. On this whole complex historical matter, see F. Rogers, *The Quest for Eastern Christians* (Minneapolis, 1962).

7. Cited in Kaplan, *Rise of the Black Magus*, 63.

8. Cited in C. de la Roncière, *Le decouverte de l'Afrique au moyen âge*, vol. 3 (Cairo, 1927), 84f.

9. One thinks of the black king in the carved Adoration of the Museo Diocesano, Covarribias, Spain, who wears the unmistakable iron cross of an Ethiopian Christian.

10. Andrea da Barberino, *Guerino il Meschino* (Milan, 1923), 155; trans. by Rogers, *Quest*, 96.

11. See the letters of 23 and 28 June 1402, in *Archivio Veneto*, 6 (1873), 323f.

12. Cited in Kaplan, *Rise of the Black Magus*, 12f.

13. Rogers, *Quest*, 38f (letter of 6 June 1438).

14. Ibid., 39.

15. Ibid., 41f.

16. L. Olschki fairly points out that there were already many "Mongolian" slaves living in Florence. But his downplaying of the exotic infusion brought on by the council is at odds with the impressed Florentine diarists of the period, whom Olschki did not know; "Asiatic Exoticism in Italian Art of the Italian Renaissance," *Art Bulletin*, 26 (1944), 95–106. See further I. Origo, "The Domestic Enemy: Eastern Slaves in Tuscany in the Fourteenth and Fifteenth Centuries," *Speculum*, 30 (1955), 321–66.

17. Cited in Kaplan, *Rise of the Black Magus*, 104.

18. Rogers, *Quest*, 149ff.

19. In *Le ciento novelle antike* of 1525; Rogers, *Quest*, 111. It is not said which of the three Fredericks was in question.

20. A. Bryer, "Ludovico da Bologna and the Georgian and Anatolian Embassy of 1460–1461," *Bedi Kartlisa*, 19–20 (1965), 190.

21. Ibid., 192.

22. An exception was the papal secretary Poggio Bracciolini. In writing up the report he received from Nicolò de' Conti of the latter's long travels, Poggio nowhere refers to Prester John, despite the fact that, as indicated above, Conti had almost certainly told Pero Tafur earlier that he had indeed been married by the Prester; Rogers, *Quest*, 48. Perhaps the humanist did not credit the whole legend.

23. J. Kirshner, "Eugenio IV e il Monte Comune," *Archivio storico italiano*, 127 (1969), 339–82. See further M. Mallett, *The Florentine Galleys in the Fifteenth Century* (Oxford, 1967).

24. Bartolommeo Del Corazza, "Diario fiorentino," ed. G. Corazzini, *Archivio storico italiano*, ser. 5, 14 (1894), 280 (21 April); also Pietrobuoni, ff. 122rv. Generally on Dom Pedro in fact and fiction, see F. Rogers, *The Travels of the Infante Dom Pedro of Portugal* (Cambridge, Mass., 1961).

25. Pietrobuoni, ff. 122rv.

26. Ibid., f. 158v.

27. These missions *ad prestandam obedientiam SS. D. N.* can be followed in the records of the papal Masters of Ceremonies; for oaths to Innocent VIII in 1484, e. g., see L. Thuasne (ed.), *Johannis Burchardi . . . Diarium sive rerum urbanorum commentarii (1483–1506)*, 3 vols. (Paris, 1883–85), 1:116, 129, 137–41, etc. For background on the Portuguese practice, see F. Rogers, *The Obedience of a King of Portugal* (Minneapolis, 1958).

28. The embassy of 1623–24, of which Galileo was a member, was described in this fashion by the poet Soldani; M. Biagioli, "Galileo's System of Patronage," *History of Science*, 28 (1990), 16. The suggestion that Botticelli's famous Uffizi Adoration commemorated the Florentine embassy to honor the new pope Sixtus IV, and thus that such a ritual was part of the political vocabulary of late medieval Adorations, is in my *Public Life*, 439.

29. Rogers, *Quest*, 69.

30. Ibid., 88.

31. Ibid., 129f.

32. Ibid., 130. On Leo X's existing association with the theme of the magi, see his coin in Trexler, "Two Captains," fig. 9. It puts him forward as "the true light that shines in the darkness."

33. Ibid., 147.

34. *The Voyage of Pedro Alvares Cabral to Brazil and India*, ed. W. Greenlee (Nendeln, 1967), 189.

35. Where no more is heard of it; ibid., 148. More probable is that indeed, the vestiges were recovered in 1523, as indicated by Rogers, *Quest*, 135.

36. Ibid.

37. The illumination has been attributed to Gregorio Lopes, and dated to 1538, when a certain coin (the *portugueses*) shown in the painting was minted; ibid., 214; see further X. da Cunha, *Noticia sobre Antonio José Colffs Guimaraes* (Coimbra, 1908), and especially R. Dos Santos, "Les principaux manuscrits à peintures conservés en Portugal," *Société française de reproductions de manuscrits à peintures*, 14 (1930), 22ff; also J. Barreira, *Arte Portuguesa: Pintura*, 204.

38. E. MacLagan, *The Jesuits and the Great Mogul* (New York, 1972), 234, 276.

39. Sanudo cites Pietro da Ca' da Pesaro: when the Portuguese expelled the Jews, God allowed the King of Portugal to discover the new route to India, "and God made him the King of Gold"; cited in B. Pullan, *Rich and Poor in Renaissance Venice* (Cambridge, Mass., 1971), 489. Priuli is cited in *Voyage of Pedro Alvares*, 132–37.

40. To my knowledge, the Magian angle on Columbus first entered the scholarly literature in 1982; R. Trexler, "La vie ludique dans la Nouvelle-Espagne: L'Empereur et ses Trois Rois," in *Les Jeux à la Renaissance*, ed. J.-C. Margolin and P. Ariès (Paris, 1982), 81–93, then in my *Church and Community*, 494. See now V. Flint, *The Imaginative Landscape of Christopher Columbus* (Princeton, 1992), 55, 123–26.

41. S. Morison (ed.), *Journals and Other Documents on the Life and Voyages of Christopher Columbus* (New York, 1963), 23; D. West and A. Kling (eds.), *The Libro de las Profecías of Christopher Columbus* (Gainsville, 1991), 69.

42. Morison, *Journals*, 133.

43. Ibid., 215f.

44. Ibid., 227f.

45. Ibid.

46. 1 Kg. 10; Morison, *Journals*, 244f. The latter reference of course is to Psalm 72.

47. West and Kling, *Libro*, 62; P. Martyr d'Anghera, *De orbe novo*, ed. F. MacNutt, 2 vols. (New York, 1912), 1:87f (dec. 1, chap. 3); also 114 (dec. 1, chap. 4).

48. Two treatises by Martin Lipens (fl. 1660) provide an overview of the previous literature: his *Dissertatio de Navigatio [sic] Salomonis*, and his *Dissertatio de Ophir*, in B. Ugolino (ed.), *Thesaurus antiquitatum sacrarum . . . opuscula . . .*, vol. 7 (Venice, 1747), respectively cccxliii-ccclix. and cclxi-ccccx. See esp. ccclxxv-ccclxxxii: "An Ophir sit Americana, et nominatim vel Hispaniolo, vel

Peru, vel Peru et Mexico simul?" The question of whether the Solomon Islands were not Ophir is also raised.

49. Antonio de la Calancha, *Cronica moralizada*, 6 vols. continuing pagination with index, (Lima, 1974–81), 722.

50. See J. Lafaye, *Quetzalcóatl et Guadalupe: La formation de la conscience nationale au Mexique (1531–1813)*, 242. On Thomas' marvelous imprint on the subcontinent, see Rogers, *Quest*, 133.

51. B. de Las Casas, *Historia de las Indias*, 3 vols. (Madrid, 1927), 2:92 (bk. 1, chap. 175). In his memoir published in 1557, the German Staden has an independent reference to a possible apostle in Brazil; A. Grafton, *New Worlds, Ancient Texts* (Cambridge, Mass., 1992), 142.

52. J. Hemming, *The Search for El Dorado* (London, 1978).

53. F. Vatable, *Biblia sacra, Hebraice, Graece, et Latine . . . cum annotationibus Francisci Vatable . . .* (Paris, 1586), 457.

54. The argument about the *ligna Almugim* is in B. Arias Montano Hispalensi, *Antiquitatum Iudaicorum libri IX* (Lyon, 1593), 20; further on this writer in Grafton, *New Worlds*, 149f.

55. Ibid. J. d'Auzoles Lapeyre, *La saincte Geographie, c'est à dire Exacte Description de la Terre et Veritable Demonstration du Paradis Terrestre . . .* (Paris, 1629), 217.

56. Thus Bento Pereyra, S.J., *Prior Tomus Commentariorum et Disputationum in Genesim* (Lyon, 1607), 337f, who, noting that there were no elephants in Peru, as in the biblical Ophir, and no mention in the Bible of Ophir being an ocean away, opted for the latter being near Palestine. See Lipens, *Dissertation*, ccclxxvii, for more argument and a list of authors who argued for the American Ophir.

57. B. de Las Casas, *Apologética Historia sumaria*, ed. E. O'Gorman, 2 vols. (Mexico City, 1967), 2: 632 (bk. 3, chap. 263); 1:649 (bk. 3, chap. 123).

58. J. Acosta, *Obras* (Madrid, 1954), 22, 24f.

59. Guaman Poma de Ayala, *El Primer Nueva Corónica y Buen Gobierno*, 3 vols. (Mexico City, 1980). Here as elsewhere in his chronicle, Guaman Poma means Americans by "Indians," not those from the Indian subcontinent.

60. Calancha, *Cronica*, 714, 734, 748f, 1267. He also tried to put to rest the claim that Lima, the "Ciudad de los Reyes," had been named after the magi, ibid., 539–44. "Los Reyes" meant simply the Spanish monarchs Charles I and his mother. Unaware of Calancha's critique, historians continue to make this error, most recently T. Cummins in *Converging Cultures: Art and Identity in Spanish America*, ed. D. Fane (New York, 1996), 158f.

61. The theme of the four continents, however, often preserved strong echoes of its magian ancestry. See the striking *Triumph of Christ the King with the Four Continents*, an eighteenth-century Cuzco painting in which the three "old" continents are shown as the three magi, while the fourth—America—stands apart, a woman! *Converging Cultures*, 235 (fig. 90). On the emerging theme of the Four Continents, see S. Boorsch, "America in Festival Presentations," in *First Images of America*, eds. F. Chiappelli, 2 vols. (Berkeley, 1976), 503–15.

62. Jacques d'Auzoles Lapeyre, *Saincte Geographie*, and his *L'Epiphanie, ou Pensées nouvelles à la Gloire de Dieu touchant les trois Mages* (Paris, 1638).

63. For biting criticism of this and other points of view of "Peter" d'Auzoles, see Melchior Inchofer, *Tres Magi Evangelici* (Rome, 1639), 146ff.

64. Arias Montano, whom d'Auzoles had consulted, shows Siberia and Alaska united in his map of 1593; Grafton, *New Worlds*, 150. D'Auzoles thought that Sem's descendants had peopled America from Asia, and that "Tartarie orientale" was "forte proche" to North America; d'Auzoles, *Saincte Geographie*, 201, 217; and *L'Epiphanie*, 150, where "l'Amerique estoit anciennement contigué et attachie à l'Asie." This union existed before the biblical flood. Note that d'Auzoles does not draw the conclusion from his acceptance of a land bridge that an American magus had visited Bethlehem. It is Guaman Poma de Ayala who implicitly closes that circle.

65. A further painting preserved in the University at Salamanca (Spain) should be mentioned. In this Adoration by Juan Correa De Vivar from the mid-sixteenth century, the third king may be meant to be an Inca. As occasionally happens, the second king points the Star out to the third in what appear a missionary gesture; reproduced in C. Post, *A History of Spanish Painting*, vol. 9, part 1 (Cambridge, Mass., 1947), 322.

66. T. Gisbert, *Iconografía y Mitos Indíginas en el Arte* (La Paz, 1980), 77f. J. de Mesa, "Diego de la Puente: Pintor flamenco en Bolivia, Peru y Chile," *Arte y arqueología*, 5 (1978), 197f. On the importance of Juli as a center of indigenous culture, under the Jesuits since 1576, see M. Beyersdorff, *La Adoración de los Reyes Magos* (Cuzco, 1988), 20–24.

67. See Trexler, "We Think, They Act: Clerical Readings of Missionary Theatre in Sixteenth Century Mexico," in my *Church and Community*, 575–613. In this article, I neglected an important document regarding such early ethnographic theater: a 1555 performance of eight Comedies regarding pre-Christian Peruvian history in the Bolivian center of Potosí; cf. Beyersdorff, *Adoración*, 20f.

68. J. de Torquemada, *Monarquia Indiana*, 3 vols. (Mexico City, 1969), 1:380f (bk. 4, chap. 14).

69. J. Rojas Garcidueñas, *El Teatro de Nueva España en el siglo XVI* (Mexico City, 1935), 209.

70. Andrés Pérez de Ribas, *Historia de los Triunfos de N. S. Fe entre Gentes las mas barbaras y fieras del Nuevo Orbe*, 3 vols., (Mexico City, 1944), 2:207. See further 2:157. Shepherd plays in Spain probably inspired those in the Americas. They were part of a broad movement in European representational life toward showing the bucolic or rather "ridiculous" parts of the population.

71. J. Lafaye, *Quetzalcóatl et Guadalupe*, 221f, 251f, stresses that this notion tended to legitimate creole, not native or peninsular culture. Still, Lafaye to the contrary, it must be stressed that the idea that Thomas was in Mexico was late (1685) and thoroughly literary in nature, with no obvious sign of popularity.

72. Antonio de Ciudad Real, *Tratado curioso y docto de las grandezas de la Nueva España*, 2 vols. (Mexico City, 1976), 1:470.

73. The event and propagation is described in extenso in Trexler, *Church and Community*, 578ff. I have yet to encounter one of these pictures; perhaps they fell during the anti-Cortés phobia of the early twentieth century.

74. Ibid., 579.

75. J. McAndrew, *The Open-Air Churches of Sixteenth-Century Mexico* (Cambridge, Mass., 1965), 372. The "provinces" were the calpullis or wards of Aztec Tenochtitlan.

76. Toribio Motolinía, *Memoriales e Historia de los Indios de la Nueva España* (Madrid, 1970), 50, 232. The printed text actually reads "las provincias" rather than "las primicias de los gentiles," but this is almost certainly an editing error. The self-serving character of Motolinía's words hardly need noting; there is no evidence that native Americans felt this way.

77. Ibid., 49f, 230. On the triumphal arches, see V. Fraser, "Architecture and Imperialism in Sixteenth-Century Spanish America," *Art History*, 9 (1986), 325–34, and McAndrew, *Open-Air Churches*, 418ff. In America as well as in Flanders, locals called crèches (contemporary Spanish: pessebre) "Bethlehems"; A. Van Gennep, *Manuel de folklore français contemporain*, tome 1, 8 vols. (Paris, 1937–88), 8:3292; see also McAndrew, *Open-Air Churches*, 418, and the quote of Thomas Gage, below.

78. The following is drawn from Antonio de Ciudad Real, *Tratado curioso*, 2:100–103 (chap. 79).

79. Pérez de Ribas, *Historia de los triunfos*, 3:155.

80. Ciudad Real, *Tratado curioso*, loc. cit.

81. Geronimo Mendieta, *Historia eclesiástica indiana* (Mexico City, 1971), 498f (bk. 4, chap. 32).

82. T. Gage, *A New Survey of the West Indies, 1648*, ed. A. P. Newton (New York, 1929), 261f. On crèches in general as objects, see the work of R. Berliner, *Die Weihnachtskrippe* (Munich, 1955); the author alas does not discuss the sociology or tributary character of the crèche.

83. See chap. 5. These plays are the basis of my study "La vie ludique dans la Nouvelle-Espagne," in Trexler, *Church and Community*, 493–510. They are mentioned by J. Lockhart, *The Nahuas after the Conquest: A Social and Cultural History of the Indians of Central Mexico, Sixteenth Through Eighteenth Centuries* (Stanford, 1992), 406f.

84. Trexler, *Church and Community*, 507. But note as well the echo of Aztec sacrifice, in which those to be offered up received preferential treatment while alive.

85. "Tú, pobre, haz todo tu esfuerzo con motivo de mi querido hijo único, que, ultimadamente, nunca descansarás con el trabajo, y tus hijos por siempre serán pobres, trabajarán; haz todo tu esfuerzo, buen Melchor"; attributed to Agustin de la Fuente, *Comedia de los Reyes*, trans. F. del Paso y Troncoso (Florence, 1902), 122; Trexler, *Church and Community*, 508.

86. Trexler, *Church and Community*, 509.

87. The text is taken from Claude Dablon, "Relation de ce qui s'est passé de plus remarquable dans la mission des pères de la Compagnie de Jésus en la Nouvelle France en l'année 1679," in *Travels and Explorations of the Jesuit Missionaries in New France, 1610–1791*, ed. R. Gold Thwaites, vol. 61 (Cleveland, 1900), 112–21 ("Of the Huron and Algonquin Missions which are at St. Ignace, at Missilimakinac"). My italics. M. Walsh draws attention to this episode: "A Three Kings Pageant at Michilmackinac, 1679," *Michigan Academician*, 26 (1994), 19–27.

88. In earlier times, the practice was widespread in France as well. Today, in highland Peru, but also in Portugal and Spain, one may still witness the arrival of these statues. They are welcomed at the doors of houses, "fed," and freed from the dirt of the road, in short given hospitality, before moving on to another home. I have myself seen the practice in Cuzco and in Seville. On the German practice, see chap. 5.

89. The Mitla (Oaxaca) celebration was still done, by children, ca. 1920, as it was in many other places in Mexico; E. Clews Parsons, *Mitla, Town of the Souls, and other Zapotec-Speaking Pueblos of Oaxaca, Mexico* (Chicago, 1936), 239. On the classical miracle play in Popayán at mid-century, see *Americas*, 1, no. 9 (November 1949), 46, with a list of performances in the hemisphere at this time; a magi play with a Hispanic emphasis is a feature of the parishes of San Felipe de Neri and of San José, in Albuquerque, New Mexico; *The Catholic Communicator: An Official Communication of the Archdiocese of Santa Fe*, 20, no. 30 (7 January 1990); a sample of Pueblo celebration is in C. Lange, "King's Day Ceremonies at a Rio Grande Pueblo, (January 6, 1940)," 58 (1951), 398–406. More than any other script, it was "la Adoración de los santos Reyes a Jesu-Christo" by Gaspar Fernández y Avila that was used in Latin America and in Spain from the eighteenth century forward; Gaspar Fernández y Avila, *La infancia de Jesu-Christo: Zehn spanische Weihnachtsspiele von . . .*, ed. M. Wagner (Halle, 1922), 86–115.

90. See the excellent article by F. Ortiz, "Los Cabildos Afro-Cubanos," *Revista Bimestre Cubana*, 16 (1921), 6–39.

91. For the operational details of secular and ecclesiastical cabildos in America, both native and Spanish, see C. Gibson, *The Aztecs Under Spanish Rule* (Stanford, 1964), 166–93.

92. N. Ross Crumrine, *Le Ceremonial de Pascua y la Identidad de los Mayos de Sonora* (Mexico City, 1974), 57f., 141, 144; a comparable situation in Mitla; Clews Parsons, *Mitla*, 202.

93. Trexler, *Church and Community*, 610; M. Pazos, "El teatro franciscano en Méjico durante el siglo XVI," *Archivo Ibero-Americano*, ser. 2, 11 (1951), 138.

94. See chap. 5, below.

95. F. Ortiz, *La Antigua Fiesta Afrocubana del "Dia de Reyes"* (Havana, 1960), 10ff, 27f.

96. Cited in Trexler, *Church and Community*, 508.

97. "A 24 del mes de septiembre pasado tuve aviso de como los negros tenian elegido un Rey, y concertado entrellos de matar á todos los españoles, y alzarse con la tierra, y que los indios eran tambien en ello"; *Colección de documentos ineditos relativos al descubrimiento, conquista y organización de las antiguas posesiones españoles de América y Oceanía, sacado de los archivos del reino y muy especialmente del de Indias*, eds. J. Pacheco and F. de Cárdinas, vol. 2 (Madrid, 1864), 198.

98. B. Diaz del Castillo, *Historia verdadera de la conquista de la Nueva España*, 2 vols. (Mexico City, 1904), 2:420f (chap. 148). On this ambivalence, see Trexler, *Public Life*, 340.

99. Torquemada, *Monarquia Indiana*, 1:759 (bk. 5, chap. 70). Torquemada

reports on another conspiracy of blacks in Mexico City in the late 1530s or 1540s, but it could be the same one mentioned by the viceroy in his letter; see ibid., 616 (bk. 5, chap. 11).

100. *Chronicle of Colonial Lima: the Diary of Josephe and Francisco Muga-bura, 1640–1697*, ed. R. Ryal Miller (Norman, 1975), 108–9.

101. G. Foster, *Culture and Conquest: America's Spanish Heritage* (Chicago, 1960), 187.

102. Luis de Urreta, *Historia Eclesiastica, politica, natural, y moral de los grandes y remotos Reynos de la Etiopia, Monarchia del Emperador llamado Preste Juan de las Indias* (Valencia, 1610), 168–74, 628–53.

103. Pedro Paez, *Historia Aethiopiae*, 2 vols. (Rome, 1905–06), 1:xxx, 3, 5–11, 161–64.

104. Manuel de Almeida, *Some Records of Ethiopia, 1593–1646, Being Records of the History of High Ethiopia or Abasinia* . . . (Nendeln, 1967), 71. Presumably this excluded as well their identification as the "magian *kings*."

CHAPTER 5

1. The following is based on the sermon of 5 January 1531, in M. Luther, *Werke*, vol. 34 (Weimar, 1980), 21–31. Further Luther texts on the subject are in R. Bainton, ed., *The Martin Luther Christmas Book* (Philadelphia, 1948), 53–65.

2. "Das nyemant gelauben schol, dacz das chind Christus hab nach dem opher griffen, als etleich maler malent"; cited in P. Mück (ed.), *Volkskultur des Europäischen Spätmittelalters* (Stuttgart, 1987), 155. Klaus Schreiner kindly passed this on; see now his *Maria: Jungfrau, Mutter, Herrscherin* (Munich, 1994), 291. A modern complaint that such grasping Jesuses were "in bad taste" and thus not found among "the best pictures" is in Mrs. (A.) Jameson, *Legends of the Madonna as Represented in the Fine Arts* (London, 1891), 217.

3. Luther also suggested they might be "Westphalian farmers"; K. Lutz, "Dreikönigliches und Reformationsgeschichtliches in und um Speyrer Chroniken des 13.-16. Jahrhunderts," *Blätter für Pfälzische Kirchengeschichte und religiöse Volkskunde* 33 (1966), 30.

4. Luther, *Werke*, 22.

5. See the end charts of both historical and contemporary *Sternsingen* in Germany in H. Wetter, *Heischebrauch und Dreikönigsumzug im deutschen Raum* (diss., Univ. Greifswald, Wiesbaden, 1933); also the end map in Hofmann, *Heiligen Drei Könige*.

6. The following is drawn from K. Young, "La procession des Trois Rois at Besançon," *Romanic Review*, 4 (1913), 83; A. Castan, "Les origines du Festin des Rois à Besançon," *Mémoires de la société d'émulation du Doubs*, ser. 5, 3 (1878), 287–312. Young did not hazard a guess at the date of his early materials, but Castan did not hesitate to assign it to the thirteenth century.

7. J.-B. Bullet, *Du festin du Roi-Boît* (Besançon, 1762), 4ff.

8. Castan, *Origines*, 295f.

9. Y. Schärmeli, *Königsbrauch und Dreikönigsspiele im welschen Teil des Kantons Freiburg* (Freiburg/S, 1988).

10. Schärmeli, *Königsbrauch und Dreikönigsspiele*, 146. This may be thought of as a commutation of an earlier obligation to furnish the clerks a banquet.

11. King, *Mittelalterliche Dreikönigsspiele*, 8ff.

12. Schärmeli, *Königsbrauch und Dreikönigsspiele*, 156f.

13. Ibid., 138.

14. Ibid., 123.

15. Ibid., 166.

16. Ibid., 157.

17. Ibid., 97.

18. Ibid., 174.

19. On these famous military parades that accompanied the three kings, including the blackfaced squadron of the blackfaced king, see ibid., 152f, and further below in this chapter.

20. Ibid., 31. The author remarks how little information there is for such a structure.

21. Ibid., 51.

22. Ibid., 145. Recall that a Herod play included a large cavalcade.

23. On this movement, see Y. Bercé, *Fête et Révolte* (Paris, 1976).

24. Castan, "Origins," 299f.

25. The same is true for the sudden disappearance of magi dramatic celebrations, if not of magi evocations, in Florence; see R. Trexler with M. Lewis, "Two Captains and Three Kings, 205–13.

26. Presumably they exist, but have escaped my attention; a group of Habsburg magi are pictured in Hofmann, *Heiligen Drei Könige*, 397–401.

27. Many are reproduced in L. Voet, *Antwerp: the Golden Age* (Antwerp, 1973).

28. *Les Fêtes de la Renaissance*, ed. J. Jacquot and E. Koenigson, 3 vols. (Paris, 1956–75), 2:444. It is tempting to wonder if there is any connection between the morphology of this feast of the magi and those that were to have followed the one celebrated in 1336 and described above, in chap. 3.

29. See above, chap. 3, note 53. The engraving is reproduced in Trexler, "Träume," 57.

30. M. Pericoli, *Il trionfo della passione e resurrezione a Todi nella Pasqua 1563* (Todi, 1963), 19–22.

31. *Relación de los fechos del mui magnifico e mas virtuoso señor don Miguel Lucas [de Iranzo], Condestable de Castilla* (Madrid, 1855), 75f; for 1463, ibid., 108; trans. in P. Meradith and J. Tailley, *The Staging of Religious Drama in Europe in the Later Middle Ages* (Kalamazoo, 1983), 250. Henry IV Trastamara was the father of Queen Isabella. Note how "Mary" was placed among a group of women.

32. Ibid., 165–68.

33. I shall soon explain this practice in detail.

34. A. Chabot, *La fête des Rois dans tous les pays* (Paris, 1908), 116ff.

35. *Les très riches heures*, f. 1v. In the commentary there, a guess has been hazarded that the battle scene represents the Trojan War.

36. E. Henster, "Das Königreich zu Mainz: Ein Bild aus frohen Tagen der kurmainzischen Kanzlei," in *Studien aus Kunst und Geschichte; Friederich Schnei-*

der zum siebzigsten Geburtstag (Freiburg/B., 1906), 393–410, with extensive extracts from the "Wirtschaft" or banquet records. Rather than offices being won by the bean, at Mainz one drew lots for them. On these "Three Kings' Tickets," see further below.

37. His chronicler was Jean Cabaret d'Orville, who wrote in 1429; for the following, see Bullet, *Festin*, 7f; Chabot, *Fête*, 111; van Gennep, *Manuel*, 8:3551,3573 for Moulins and Montluçon.

38. W. Gundersheimer, *Ferrara: the Style of a Renaissance Despoty* (Princeton, 1973), 186f. Neither chronicler however assumes that the goods were turned over to the poor; see the anonymous *Diario ferrarese*, in the *Rerum italicarum scriptores*, 24, 7, 1 (Bologna, 1966), 83f, 277; and Bernardino Zambotti, *Diario ferrarese*, ibid., 2 (Bologna, 1969), each 5 January.

39. Zambotti, *Diario*, 302.

40. Ibid., 295.

41. The selection and publication of offices took place between 6 and 11 January; see Zambotti, *Diario*, 30, 231, 278, 295 ("dati segondo hè consueto ognianno"), 302.

42. Zambotti, *Diario ferrarese*, 311f, note; *Diario ferrarese*, 277.

43. On the collecting of gifts at doors in antiquity, see Saintyves, "Rondes," 137. In a writing attributed to Augustine but more probably of Caesarius of Arles, it is said that on 1 January, country people put at their door tables of food for passersby, persuaded that such liberality assures good luck in the whole year; Miles, *Christmas Customs*, 170. Miles also cites similar customs in Rome in a letter of Boniface to Pope Zacharias in 742 on Roman customs.

44. Gundersheimer, *Ferrara*, 187. In his review of Gundersheimer's work, A. Molho commented on the author's reading of the sources for this custom, in *Journal of Modern History*, 47 (1975), 353f.

45. On this momentous shift in royal identity, see A. Guery, "Le roi dépensier: Le don, la contrainte, et l'origine du système financier de la monarchie française d'Ancien Régime," *Annales E.S.C.*, 39 (1984), 1241–69.

46. See the analysis of the Florentine gifting of Emperor Frederick III in 1452 in my *Public Life*, 324f.

47. H. Moser, *Volksbräuche im geschichtlichen Wandel* (Munich, 1985), 72. Even modern visionaries have noted that the magi always were surrounded by a retinue precisely because they afforded them ongoing gifts; see chapter six, below.

48. Schärmeli, *Königsbrauch*, 177; H. Moser, *Volksbräuche*, 69.

49. H. Wetter, *Heischbrauch*, 54.

50. There are however exceptional cases where the magi appear in the streets well before the feast of the epiphany; see the modern cases of the magi out during Advent in Van Gennep, *Manuel*, 7:2916 (Swiss canton of Lure) and 2924f (Gascogne); the slim evidence linking the *quête* of the magi to the feast of St. Lucy (13 December) is in Moser, *Volksbräuche*, 69 (1549 in Weilheim).

51. On Spanish gift-giving traditions, see G. Foster, *Culture and Conquest: America's Spanish Heritage* (Chicago, 1960), 168ff. For the general problem of so-called "popular culture," see P. Burke, *Popular Culture in Early Modern Europe* (London, 1978); N. Z. Davis, "Some Tasks and Themes in the Study of

Popular Religion," in *The Pursuit of Holiness in Late Medieval and Renaissance Religion*, ed. C. Trinkaus with H. Oberman (Leiden, 1974), 307–36; Trexler, "Historiography Sacred or Profane? Reverence and Profanity in the Study of Early Modern Religion," in *Religion and Society in Early Modern Europe,1500–1800*, ed. K. von Greyerz (London, 1984), 243–69.

52. See two cases where this is arguable, in J. Drumbl, *Quem quaeritis*, 330f.

53. In the eighteenth century, there was a heated campaign to suppress the custom, which some called pagan. Thus, the bibliography on the custom is large; see, e.g., Castan, "Origines," 287–312, which summarizes the old debate. As early as the fifteenth century, an ecclesiastical document from Mainz claimed that the origin of the roi-boît came from the three kings watching Jesus suck Mary, whereupon they let out this cry; Van Gennep, *Manuel*, 8:3536f. Certainly this tale was only an attempt to give a Christian slant to a traditional secular practice.

54. R. Vaultier, *Le folklore*, 100 (1412, 1414).

55. Vaultier, *Le folklore*, 93f; Foster, *Culture and Conquest*, 126. The etimology of the word remains uncertain; it is however possible that the words "l'an neuf," the new year, form part of it.

56. The Steen painting apparently shows these cards being held by different participants. On the custom, see Van Gennep, *Manuel*, 3541, also 3556; further L. Van Puyvelde, *Jordaens* (Paris, 1953), 135f, for the custom in early modern Antwerp. Such cards were also used in the *Königsreich* at Mainz; Henster, *Königsreich zu Mainz*, 394.

57. Van Gennep, *Manuel*, 3538–73 (a historical review). See this boy in the figure of the Queen of the Bean, just above.

58. M. Höfler, "Die Gebäcke des Dreikönigstages," *Zeitschrift des Vereins für Volkskunde*, 14 (1904), esp. 272, shows how the King of Beans was imported into Germany.

59. Several are reproduced in Puyvelde, *Jordaens*, figs. 7–8, 86–87, 90–91; also R.-A. d'Hulst, *De Tekeningen von Jakof Jordaens* (Brussels, 1956). See further "Bean Feasts" by Gabriel Metsu and by Jan Gerritsz Van Bronchorst in F. Robinson, *Gabriel Metsu (1629–1667)* (New York, 1974), 110.

60. Thus in modern Thionville, Lorraine, a domestic who was drawn as king had his kingdom repurchased from him, the definitive king always being a family member *strictu sensu*. But in lots made to elect a black king, all had the right to participate; Van Gennep, *Manuel*, 8:3544, and further below.

61. Evidence that in some areas the father automatically became the household king is in Van Gennep, *Manuel*, 3551 (modern Posanges, Burgundy).

62. J. Amades, *Costumàri Català*, 2 vols. (Barcelona, 195), 1:431. The author adds that during the family banquet that apparently followed the Adoration, this king was greeted with the cry "le roi boît!" (*el rei beu, el rei beu!*).

63. The most scholarly study, summarizing the earlier literature, is by R. Berliner, *Die Weinachtskrippe* (Munich, 1955).

64. See the reproduction of the five surviving pieces (minus the missing virgin and child), made for the church of S. Maria Maggiore in Rome, in R. Berliner, *Denkmäler der Krippenkunst*, 12 fascicules (Augsburg, 1926–29), 8:1–2. The oldest crèche in a private home known to Berliner was documented in 1567; Berliner, *Weinachtskrippe*, 62.

65. One could also construct a crèche of multiple parts, so that during the season, one could simply replace or add new parts to represent the next feast. Or, to correct for the calendar, the images might simply be redressed. For such devotional implications, see Berliner, *Weinachtskrippe*, 60, 174, 185, 217.

66. Berliner, *Weinachtskrippe*, 44, 59. Eugenio Battisti kindly told me of the church's later decision to separate these stations' space from the devotees who came to see them. An important Florentine inspiration for Michelangelo's use of magian space is the audience room of the Medici-Ricciardi Palace, where Gozzoli's Journey of the Magi on three walls surrounds those in the room. On the New Sacristy, see Trexler with M. Lewis, "Two Captains," in Trexler, *Church and Community*, 214f.

67. Léopold Dor, cited in Berliner, *Weinachtskrippe*, 188.

68. For such criticism, see ibid., 38–41.

69. Such payments are documented ibid., 41, 190. On the automatons, ibid., 65ff.

70. Van Gennep, *Manuel*, 8:3546.

71. See my "The Bishop's Portion: Generic Pious Legacies in the Late Middle Ages in Italy," *Traditio* 28 (1972), 397–450.

72. Thus Boemus and Sebastian Franck in the sixteenth century both mention an epiphany cake, though here hiding a coin rather than a bean; cited in W. Brandmüller (ed.), *Handbuch der bayerischen Kirchengeschichte*, vol. 2 (St. Ottlien, 1993), 875; Moser, *Volksbräuche*, is cited often in what follows.

73. Moser, *Volksbräuche*, 1–34.

74. Moser, *Volksbräuche*, 62 (a. 1583), 66 (1634), etc., although most of the singing took place *vor den Häusern*; e.g. ibid., 65 (1635). For Berry in the nineteenth century, where the inhabitants feigned resistance "before permitting [the visitors] to seat themselves at the banquet of the cake," that is, so that they would get the *part à Dieu*, see Van Gennep, *Manuel*, 7:2889.

75. For the massive bibliography, start with B. Pullan, *Rich and Poor in Renaissance Venice*; J.-P. Gutton, *La société et les pauvres en Europe (XVIè-XVIIIè siècles)* (Paris, 1974), 93–121.

76. Van Gennep, *Manuel*, 7:2879.

77. Moser, *Volksbräuche*, 69.

78. Van Gennep, *Manuel*, 7:2899.

79. E.g., Van Gennep, *Manuel*, 7:2896, 2910f, 2920f.

80. Van Gennep, *Manuel*, 7:2897; for good wishes, see ibid, 7:2894–2981, and Moser, *Volksbräuche*, 64 (1609).

81. Moser, *Volksbräuche*, 63 (1598), 67f (1678), 70 (1687).

82. See, e.g., Van Gennep, *Manuel*, 7:2882. Note that child kings sometimes played the magi in these centuries; see the ten-year old Louis XIII of France adoring Mary and Jesus in an almanac engraving of 1611, shown in Vloberg, *Noëls de France*, 28.

83. The best document of this type is a Jesuit appeal in Innsbruck of 1568, and another done between 1571 and 1619, protocolled in Moser, *Volksbräuche*, 60f.

84. Thus a church meal for the poor was financed "von dem Gelde, so sie

mit recordation und stern zu Weihnachten ersungen haben"; Moser, *Volksbräuche*, 80.

85. Angers: Van Gennep, *Manuel*, 7:2883f, repeated in 1688. Moser, *Volksbräuche*, 62 (1582). See the complaint ibid., 89 (1789).

86. Moser, *Volksbräuche*, 82 (1646).

87. See the example in Moser, *Volksbräuche*, 68 (1697), where soldiers either get what they want or "sie gleich mit Abrennen und anderem sehr bedrohlich sind," and ibid., 87, for German soldiers bringing the custom to Denmark in the Thirty Years War.

88. Van Gennep, *Manuel*, 7:2893. For a case of children having a queen who taught them how to beg and threaten, see ibid., 7:2955 (modern).

89. Thus from Munich to Innsbruck and north to Abensberg; Moser, *Volksbräuche*, 79, 61 (1577), 62 (1595), 62f (1596), 64 (1609). On the country-city polarity, Van Gennep, *Manuel*, 7:2889.

90. Ibid., 8:3545, citing various letters of pardon; see in general J.-C. Schmitt and J. Le Goff (eds.), *Le Charivari* (Paris, 1981). The following French terms all refer to the black-faced king in the sources cited by Van Gennep: *noircir, brousser, barbouiller, bronquer, mâchurer*, the latter being linked as well to the notion of disguise; ibid., 3543.

91. Van Gennep, *Manuel*, 8:3544 (modern Lorraine), with a description of how the blackened king was made as hideous in appearance as possible.

92. E. Theodore, "Notes sur un ornement en étain, d'une couronne de roi de la fève au XV. siècle, et sur quelques médailles religieuses," *Bulletin de la commission départementale des monuments historiques du Pas-de-Calais*, 5 (1932), 692. Then the black king had to remain black as long as the reign of the King of the Bean; Amades, *Costumàri Català*, 1:432. Van Gennep, *Manuel*, 8:3541 (Flanders, for several centuries); ibid., 3545f (modern Saint-Père, Ille-et-Vilaine); ibid., 3551 (modern Burgundy).

93. Moser, *Volksbräuche*, 88 (1621 Cologne); Van Gennep, 7:2944 (modern Moselle area); ibid., 7:2920 (1899 Franche-Compté). In the Fribourg festival, the cortège of the black king wore black uniforms and had their face and hands blackened; P. Wagner, "Das Dreikönigspiel zu Freiburg in der Schweiz," *Freiburger Geschichtsblätter*, 10 (1903), 79 (sixteenth century).

94. Thus two kings' cheeks were painted red, but the third king was made black with soot: Van Gennep, 7:2944 (modern Moselle area). R. Stumpfl, *Kultspiele der Germanen*, 357, assures us that all three Kings were "often" black-faced, but mentions only one, in northeastern Germany. Moser, *Volksbräuche*, 66 (1652), cites a Tyrolian case of "drei Käspar" all black.

95. Kaplan, *Rise of the Black Magus*, 95–101.

96. A classic is E. Mâle, "Les rois mages et le drame liturgique," *Gazette des beaux arts*, ser. 4, 4 (1910), 261–70.

97. C. Naselli, "I re magi nella religiosità popolare," in *La religiosità popolare nella valle padana. Atti del II Convegno di studi sul folklore padano (Modena, 19–20–21 marzo 1965* (Modena, 1966), 293. Van Gennep, *Manuel*, 7:2944 (modern German-speaking Moselle area); ibid, 2920 (1899 Franche-Comté), where the black king was the usual beggar, "en secouant sa tirelire ou en présentant un panier."

98. Foster, *Culture and Conquest*, 169.

99. On "Kasper," see J. Grimm, *Deutsches Wörterbuch*, vol. 5 (Leipzig, 1873), 258f; cf. King, *Mittelalterliche Dreikönigsspiele*, 128f. "Caspar" is the name of the black king in scores of songs and poems, so that the puppet figure easily derived from the former. But as always, that black king could also be Balthazar or Melchior, so it remains best to refer respectively to the first, second, or third king.

100. Van Gennep, *Manuel*, 7:2915 (Flanders, after 1930).

101. See in general Devisse and Mollat, *Image of the Black*, vol. 2, parts 1 and 2.

102. For blackface as disguise, see Van Gennep, *Manuel*, 8:3543, note 52; Amades, *Costumàri Català*, 1:432 ("d'emmascarar-li la cara amb un suro crémat o amb altra sutzura que la hi deixés ben negra en càstig del seu poc respecte"). Blackface, as Belmont points out, is the simplest mask of all; "Fonction de la dérision et symbolisme du bruit dans le charivari," in Le Goff and Schmitt, *Charivari*, 19. See also A. Burguière, "Pratique du charivari et répression religieuse dans la France d'Ancien Régime," ibid., 185f.

103. Moser, *Volksbräuche*, 66 (1652), and Stumpfl, cited above.

104. For Paris, see Van Gennep, *Manuel*, 8:3545. One is reminded of the festive habit in the United States of naming the day before a festival "devils' night," "soap night," and the like.

105. Van Gennep, *Manuel*, 8:3543.

106. Van Gennep, *Manuel*, 8:3545. In the Vosges in the nineteenth century, a *roi blanc* was elected on the eve of epiphany, then a *roi noir* one week later on this *jour des rois noirs*; ibid., 7:2941. The identical procedure was widespread in the province of Lorraine at this time; ibid., 8:3562.

107. In the early eighteenth century a narrator, telling a traveller about the Chichimecas or free natives of New Mexico, states: " Además, tienen la costumbre de pintarse el cuerpo, como los frailes que van a Belén"; G. F. Gemelli Careri, *Viaje a la Nueva España* (Mexico City, 1976), 70. I can think of no other explanation of this practice than that offered here. Celebrating 6 January in this same region today, the Pueblan natives remain fascinated by blackface, which they still employ with reference to one of the magi; C. Lange, "King's [sic] Day Ceremonies at a Rio Grande Pueblo, January 6, 1940," *El Palacio*, 58, no. 12 (December, 1951), 404, 406. Blackfaced kings in contemporary Europe are referred to in chap. 6, below.

108. Ortiz, *La Antigua Fiesta*, 17.

109. Y. Lange, "The Household Wooden Saints of Puerto Rico," 2 vols. (diss., Univ. of Penna., 1975), 2:549. The kings perform a dance in front of each house, and then solicit contributions. At the end of the day, according to Lange, they gave this money to their church.

110. In addition to the work by Bercé, *Fête et Revolte*, cited above, see as a practical example of this suppression Joseph II's actions in Austria; U. Mayerhofer, "Bekleidete Prozessionsfiguren in Tirol. Ein Beitrag zur Kult-Funktion von Bildern," *Jahrbuch für Volkskunde*, n. f. 8 (1985), 107–20.

111. Voltaire, "Épiphanie," in his *Questions sur l'Encyclopédie par des amateurs*, vol. 5 (Paris, 1771), 225–28; cited in C. Schoebel, *L'Histoire des Rois Mages* (Paris, 1878), 98f.

112. Poli, "Royauté," 5.

113. Van Gennep, *Manuel*, 8:3548.

114. Ibid.

115. The so renamed Hotel Drei Könige am Blumenrain is mentioned in the contemporary Baedeker Guide to *Basel*, Switzerland, 53.

116. Chabod, *La fête*, 116.

CHAPTER 6

1. On d'Auzoles, see above, chap. 4.

2. *The Encyclopedia of Religions*, ed. M. Eliade, 16 vols. (New York, 1987), 5:93, referring specifically to Enoch. There was in fact no sound reason to include Melchizedek among those who had escaped death.

3. *Melchisedech, ou Discours auquel on voit qui est ce grand Prestre-Roy, et comment il est encores aujourd'hui vivant, en corpus et en ame, bien qu'il y aye plus de trois mil sept cens ans qu'il donna sa benediction à Abraham* (Paris, 1622).

4. D'Auzoles, *L'Epiphanie*, 243ff. In 1631, d'Auzoles in Paris published an attack on the Jesuit Denis Petau regarding the genealogy of Job: *Le disciple des temps: Avec 100 remarques chronologiques contre ses animadversions sur St. Epiphane, et quelques eschertillons des deffauts de sa chronologie*. I have been unable to consult this work.

5. ". . . Puis s'en retournerent au Paradis terrestre leur pays et demeure perpetuelle"; ibid., 276–82.

6. Ibid., 284ff. D'Auzoles does admit that the people buried there might be holy men; they were just not the magi. Crombach, cited *infra*, leaves no doubt about the revolutionary nature of the "novator's" claims.

7. M. Inchofer, *Tres magi evangelici* (Rome, 1639), 146ff.

8. D'Auzoles also showed that the twelfth-century documentary tradition gives little sustenance to the whole notion of the magi's translation from Milan to Cologne; see D'Auzoles, *L'Epiphanie*, 284–89; Crombach, *Primitiae gentium*, 870–79.

9. On which see L. Thorndike, *A History of Magic and Experimental Science*, 4 vols. (New York, 1923–34), 4:267, 323, 566.

10. D'Auzoles, *Saincte Geographie*, itself subtitled *Exacte Description de la Terre et Veritable Demonstration du Paradis Terrestre*, 14, 23–28, 89, 103ff, 165f (on printed maps of the earthly paradise), and his table of authorities, provides an introduction to such literature.

11. P. Sartori, *Sitte und Brauch*, 3 vols. (Leipzig, 1910–14), 3:77.

12. See F. Yates, *Giordano Bruni and the Hermetic Tradition* (New York, 1964); A. Fields, *The Origins of the Platonic Academy of Florence* (Princeton, 1989); E. Cochrane, *Tradition and Enlightenment in the Tuscan Academies, 1690–1800* (Chicago, 1962); D. Roche, *Le siècle des lumières en province: Académies et académiciens provinciaux, 1680–1789*, 2 vols. (Paris, 1989).

13. This city is west of Lhassa, the official residence of the Dalai-Lama; the latter was first entered by the Jesuits Johan Grueber and d'Orville in 1662; M. Jan (ed.), *Le voyage en Asie centrale au Tibet* (Paris, 1992), xiii; F. de Filippi (ed.), *An Account of Tibet: the Travels of Ippolito Desideri of Pistoia, S.J., 1712–1727*

(London, 1932), 23 (introduction by C. Wessels). The letter of Cacella (4 October) is in C. Wessels, *Early Jesuit Travellers in Central Asia, 1603–1721* (The Hague, 1924), esp. 327f.

14. The 781 Nestorian inscription in both Syriac and Chinese was found on a stone at Chou-chih (Si-ngan-fu), 50 miles southwest of Sian Prefecture in China; a detailed text is in E. Gibbon, *The Decline and Fall of the Roman Empire*, ed. J. Bury, vol. 5 (London, 1901), 520ff.

15. A. Tomas, *Shambhala: Oasis of Light* (London, 1977); the film by S. Aernecke and M. Görden, *Shambhala* (1993); and M. Görden, *Shambhala: Auf der Suche nach dem verborgenen Herz Asiens* (Munich, 1994).

16. See W. Frühwald, *Das Spätwerk Clemens Brentanos (1815–1842): Romantik im Zeitalter der Metternich'schen Restauration* (Tübingen, 1977).

17. Generally on her life, see the useful apologia of J. Steiner, *Theres Neumann von Konnersreuth: Ein Lebensbild nach authentischen Berichten, Tagebüchern und Dokumenten* (Munich, 1988). Steiner is also the editor of *Visionen der Therese Neumann*, 2 vols. (Munich, 1977).

18. Frühwald, *Spätwerk*, 148, 273.

19. Neumann was not badly served, however. Her original biographer was Fritz Gerlich, erstwhile Munich newspaper editor and *Staatsarchivrat*; he died in the concentration camp at Dachau. See his *Die stigmatisierte Thérèse Neumann von Konnersreuth*, 2 vols. (Munich, 1929), written soon after he converted from Calvinism under Neumann's influence. The source for many of Neumann's visions was the parish priest Naber.

20. See *Die Reiche der heiligen drei Könige, ihr Sterndienst, ihre Reise nach Bethlehem, etc. Nach den Gesichten der gottseligen Katharina Emmerich*, ed. A. Urbas (Laibach, 1884); W. Hümpfner, *Clemens Brentanos Glaubwürdigkeit in seinen Emmerick-Aufzeichnungen* (Würzburg, 1923); also Hümpfner, "Coup d'Oeil sur les publications relatives à Anne Catherine Emmerick," *Revue d'ascétique et de mystique*, 5 (1924), 349–80; K. Fahsel, *Die heiligen Drei Könige in der Legende und nach den Visionen der Anna Katharina Emmerich* (Basel, 1941). For the fraud evident in Neumann's visions, see C. M. Staehlin, *Apariciones* (Madrid, 1954), 206–27. He shows that even before she died, she was disappearing from standard reference works published by the Catholic house of Herder.

21. At times, Emmerich/Brentano claimed an earlier date for the epiphany than 6 January, and so the visions occurred somewhat earlier. See Hümpfner, *Clemens Brentanos Glaubwürdigkeit*, 573.

22. *Clemens Brentano Religiöse Schriften*, ed. W. Oehl, 2 vols. (Munich, 1913), 2:323f.

23. Ibid., 272. For Emmerich/Brentano's outbursts against modern husbands who try to keep their wives from spending much time in church, see ibid., 279.

24. Ibid., 263, 292, 308. This sentiment may have implications for understanding the early modern custom of the *Dreikönigssingen*. After all, the poor children dressed as kings can be thought of as soliciting the real kings—homeowners—on 5–6 January.

25. Fahsel, *Heiligen Drei Könige*, 144.

26. Gerlich, *Die stigmatisierte Therese Neumann*, 1:190.

27. Steiner, *Visionen*, 1:126–29. Recall that John of Hildesheim had them lifelong virgins. Fahsel says that the first mention of a magi wife is contained in the so-called German Passional printed in Augsburg by Günther Zainer in 1471; Fahsel, *Heiligen Drei Könige*, 11.

28. Steiner, *Visionen*, 1:126f.

29. As I could confirm by an examination of my friend W. Christian's collection of holy post cards. For the medieval visual imagination, see W. Christian, *Apparitions in Late Medieval and Renaissance Spain* (Princeton, 1981), and for the modern, his *Visionaries: the Spanish Republic and the Reign of Christ* (Berkeley, 1996).

30. Steiner, *Visionen*, 1:124.

31. Brentano, *Religiöse Schriften*, 2:255.

32. Ibid., 269.

33. Ibid., 303f.

34. Ibid., 324f.

35. "Ich sah immer die Könige gen Bethlehem kommen, wenn ich im Kloster das Krippchen aufrichtete"; ibid., 253.

36. E. Hobsbawm and T. Ranger, *The Invention of Tradition* (Cambridge, 1972).

37. For this type of trio, see the picture in Berlin's *Der Tagesspiegel*, 30 December 1993, and the *Liechtensteiner Volksblatt*, 5 January 1994. A picture of queens raising money to get women into the Swiss *Bundesrat* is in the Bern section of *Der Bund*, 7 January 1994.

38. See the picture in the Chur, Switzerland *Bündner Zeitung*, 6 January 1994. The bakers make the cakes or sweets hiding the bean.

39. See especially the pictures of the crowned elders in G. Arsenault, "Le Gâteau des Rois à l'Ile-du-Prince-Édouard," in *En r'montant la tradition: Hommage au père Anselme Chiasson* (Moncton, 1982), 39–56, with that island's celebrations recorded in Tignish, Summerside, Charlottetown, etc.; information on seventeenth-century celebrations of Christmas and New Years, if not the Epiphany, in these parts, is in R. Montpetit, *Le temps des Fêtes au Québec* (Montreal, 1978), 46f.

40. V. Reda, "Cohoes: A Door to Franco-American past," *Albany Times Union*, 6 January 1984.

41. The feast is sponsored by the Franco-American and Quebec Heritage Series of the Department of French, State University of New York at Albany; Reda, "Cohoes"; R. Purvin, "Cohoes Canadians kick up their clogs," *The Times Record*, 6 January 1984. My thanks to Prof. Eloise Brière and Louis Dupont for information on this celebration.

42. A. Oman, "And Finally, on the 12th Night," *Washington Post*, 3 January 1986, with a recipe for the *galette* and a cartoon of a young boy elected *roi*. The Cohoes recipe "from Michel Fiat, a French baker in Massachusetts," is in the *Albany Times Union*, 2 January 1985.

43. My account is based on personal observation of several processions. For pictures of the same, see the *New York Times*, 7 January 1984; 7 January, 1986; 7 January 1991.

44. A picture of one of the kings in Spain listening to what a child wants as a gift on epiphany—just as Santa Claus or Father Nikolaus listens to other children, is in the magazine of Madrid's *ABC*, 5 January 1994.

45. The Museo often houses displays of the *santeros* or wooden saints' statues from the American Southwest, a major theme of which are the three kings.

46. See these representative articles: "12th Night: Theatrics and Roast Pig," *New York Times*, 6 January 1984; J. Dunning, "12th Night: 9 Ways to Celebrate," ibid., 4 January 1985.

47. See above, chap. 4.

48. My source for much of this information is Prof. Mildred Semple. She recalls in detail the participation of her children in these plays, and their goals. Children at St. Mary's Orthodox Catholic Church in Endicott still dress up as the magi and carol on 6 January, as they have for more than half a century; see the picture in the *Binghamton Press and Sun Bulletin*, 7 Jan. 1988.

49. Vinho Espumante Natural: Magos. José Marques Agostinho, Filhos and Cia.

50. For the nativity scene featuring 16-inch high clay figurines of the Reagans, Pertini, and Andropov, see the picture in the *Binghamton Sunday Press*, 25 December 1983. In Palermo, Italy in 1993–94, figures in the crèches included anti-mafia heroes, and the magi instead of their normal gifts offered "Work, Decency, and Justice"; *Frankfurter Rundschau*, 22 December 1993.

51. See the *3 Wise Men Dream Book*, the *Three Wise Men Almanac and Encyclopedia*, the *Three Wise Men Daily Lottery*, and the *Three Wise Men Rundowns & Workouts*, all by (the pseudonomous) Professor A. Z. Hitts and available from the Sneaky Pete Group in Rockville, Maryland.

52. Original Design by John Richard Allen, in a card of the Recycled Paper Products, Inc.

53. Design by Lynne Weising, of Recycled Paper Products, Inc.

54. Cartoon by Viv Quillan, of Cath Tate Cards of London.

55. *The New Yorker*, 21 December 1992.

56. Mehta, pride of the Parsis, who followed Zoroaster, who were descendants of the magi; *New York Times*, 26 September 1984. Michael Rocke sent me the publicity sheet for *il Vernacoliere* of Livorno (December 1988).

57. Sold by the Conception Abbey in Missouri.

58. I have seen such merchandizing myself, but I am again indebted to the aforementioned Mildred Semple for her specialized knowledge and experience in this area.

59. J. Miller, "Oman's Perfume With a Gold Price Tag," *New York Times*, 27 February 1985, kindly passed to me by Elizabeth Cropper.

60. T. Abercrombie, "Arabia's Frankincense Trail," *National Geographic Magazine* (October, 1985), 474–513.

61. The telephone number of Majan Research, Inc., was 1–800–321-MAJI. It has since been disconnected.

62. Examples: M. Tournier, *The Four Wise Men* (New York, 1984); H. van Dyke, *The Story of the Other Wise Man* (New York, 1985); H. Erlau, *Die Legende vom Vierten König* (Freiburg/B, 1979); W. Atiyeh, *The Fourth Wise Man* (New York, 1959).

63. Virginia Yans-McLaughlin of Rutgers University was kind enough to send me the poem, which she found in a letter of late 1941 from the sociologist Leo Srole to Margaret Mead. Srole took it as an example of contemporary pro-German propaganda in upstate New York.

64. The group sometimes met in conjunction with other "Magical Societies"; *The Magi*, no. 2 (June, 1910). C. Jackson's history of "Oriental" religions' influence on American thought ends with a chapter on the World Parliament; *The Oriental Religions and American Thought* (Westport, Conn., 1981), 243–58.

65. Jan, *Le voyage*, vi, citing Julien Gracq. The "Center Out There" is an expression used by V. Turner to designate the pilgrims' goal; Turner, "The Center Out There: Pilgrim's Goal," *History of Religions*, 12 (1972), 191–230.

66. A. Tomas, *Shambhala*, 11, 57, 82. A direct link to the evangelical magi is ibid., 85.

67. Ibid., 86f, 99 seq. On the "mythical kingdom of Shambhala," characterized as an earthly paradise or Eden, see *The Encyclopedia of Religion*, 14:502.

68. J. Hilton, *Lost Horizon* (Bern, 1945), 113. It is later revealed that the monks had gold mines.

69. Ibid., 88.

70. Ibid., 187.

71. Ibid., 119.

72. Thus ibid., 156, 158, 173 etc.

73. Ibid., 188, 234.

74. Ibid., 235.

75. J. Masson, *My Father's Guru: A Journey through Spirituality and Disillusion* (London, 1993), 111. I wish to thank Masson for discussing such matters with me during our stay in Berlin, 1993–94.

76. Ibid., 115–18, 123f. One who died anyway was said to have "changed planes" (ibid., 118).

77. Ibid., 116, 118.

CONCLUSION

1. As a comparison, Machiavelli wished to make the military parade a feature of carnival celebrations in Florence in the early sixteenth century; Trexler, *Public Life*, 511.

2. Schärmeli, *Königsbrauch*, 105, 107, 133, 167.

BIBLIOGRAPHY

Abercrombie, T. "Arabia's Frankincense Trail." *National Geographic Magazine* (October 1985), 474–513.

Achthundert Jahre Verehrung der Heiligen Drei Könige, 1164–1964, in *Kölner Domblatt: Jahrbuch des Zentral-Dombauvereins*, 23–24 (1964).

Aernecke, S. and M. Görden, *Shambhala* (1993 motion picture).

Agustin de la Fuente (attrib.). *Comedia de los Reyes*, trans. F. del Paso y Troncoso (Florence, 1902).

Albertus Aquensis, *Historia hiersolamitana* in *Recueil des historiens des croisades* (*Histoires Occidentaux*, vol. 4) (Paris, 1879).

Almeida, M. de. *Some Records of Ethiopia, 1593–1646, Being Records of the History of High Ethiopia or Abasinia . . .* (Nendeln, 1967).

Amades, J. *Costumàri Català*, 2 vols. (Barcelona, 1950–56).

Andrea da Barberino, *Guerino il Meschino* (Milan, 1923).

Annales Ecclesiastici. Ed. C. Baronius, vol. 1 (Lucca, 1738).

Annales Mettenses, in *Monumenta Germaniae Historica: Scriptores*, vol. 1 (Leipzig, 1925).

Anonimo francescano. *Meditazioni sulla vita di Cristo* (Città Nuova, 1992).

Arfwidsson, A. *Zeno oder die Legende von den heiligen Drei Königen* (Lund, 1940).

Arias Montano Hispalensi, B. *Antiquitatum Iudaicorum libri IX* (Lyon, 1593).

Arsenault, G. "Le Gâteau des Rois à l'Ile-du-Prince-Édouard." In *En r'montant la tradition: Hommage au père Anselme Chiasson* (Moncton, 1982), 39–56.

Atiyeh, W. *The Fourth Wise Man* (New York, 1959).

Bainton, R. (ed.). *The Martin Luther Christmas Book* (Philadelphia, 1948).

Baldwin Smith, E. *Early Christian Iconography and a School of Ivory Carvers in Provence* (Princeton, 1918).

Baron, H. *The Crisis of the Early Italian Renaissance* (Princeton, 1966).

Barreira, J. *Arte Portuguesa: Pintura* (Lisbon, 1948).

Beckwith, J. *The Adoration of the Magi in Whalebone* (London, 1966).

Beeh, W. "Mittelalterliche Abbilder als Legitimationsnachweis: Die Tafel mit der Anbetung der Könige in Lenzburg und der Ortenberger Altar." *Ulmer Verein: Kritische Berichte* 4 (1976), 4–18.

Beleth, Jean. *Rationale divinorum officiorum*, in *PL*, 202.

Bercé, Y. *Fête et Révolte* (Paris, 1976).

Berliner, R. *Denkmäler der Krippenkunst*, 12 fascicules (Augsburg, 1926–29).

———. *Die Weihnachtskrippe* (Munich, 1955).

Bernard of Clairvaux. *Sermones super Cantica Canticorum, 1–35*, ed. J. Leclercq et al. (Rome, 1957).

Bernis, C. "Modas moriscas en la sociedad cristiana española del siglo XV y principios del XVI." *Boletin de la real academia de la historia*, 144 (1959), 199–226.

Beyersdorff, M. *La Adoración de los Reyes Magos* (Cuzco, 1988).

Biagioli, M. "Galileo's System of Patronage." *History of Science*, 28 (1990), 1–62.

Boorsch, S. "America in Festival Presentations." In *First Images of America*, ed. F. Chiappelli, vol. 2 (Berkeley, 1976), 503–15.

Boswell, J. *Same-Sex Unions in Premodern Europe* (New York, 1994).

Bovini, G. *Sant'Apollinare Nuovo in Ravenna* (Stuttgart, 1961).

Bowsky, W. *Henry VII in Italy* (Lincoln, Nebraska, 1960).

Brandmüller, W. (ed.). *Handbuch der bayerischen Kirchengeschichte*, vol. 2 (St. Ottlien, 1993).

Brown, R. *The Birth of the Messiah: A Commentary on the Infancy Narratives in Matthew and Luke* (Garden City, 1977).

Brühl, C. "Kronen- und Krönungsbrauch im frühen und hohen Mittelalter." *Historische Zeitung*, 234 (1982), 6–12.

Bryer, A. "Ludovico da Bologna and the Georgian and Anatolian Embassy of 1460–1461." *Bedi Kartlisa*, 19–20 (1965), 178–98.

Buchon, J. (ed.), *Collection des chroniques nationales françaises écrites en lange vulgaire de 13e. au 16e. siècle*, 47 vols. (Paris, 1826–29).

Buhler, S. "Marsilio Ficinos *De stella magorum* and Renaissance Views of the Magi," *Renaissance Quarterly*, 43 (1990), 348–71.

Bullet, J.-B. *Du festin du Roi-Boît* (Besançon, 1762).

Burckhardt, J. *The Civilization of the Renaissance in Italy* (New York, 1958).

Büttner, F. *Imitatio Pietatis. Motive der christlichen Ikonographie als Modelle zur Verähnlichung* (Berlin, 1985).

Bynum, C. Walker. *Jesus as Mother* (Los Angeles, 1982).

Calancha, Antonio de la. *Cronica moralizada*, 6 vols. (Lima, 1974–81).

Campbell, J. *The Hero with a Thousand Faces* (Princeton, 1968).

Cartellieri, A. *Die Zeit der Reichsgründungen, 382–911* (Munich, 1927).

Castan, A. "Les origines du Festin des Rois à Besançon." *Mémoires de la société d'émulation du Doubs*, ser. 5, 3 (1878), 287–312.

Catholic Communicator: An Official Communication of the Archdiocese of Santa Fe, The. 20, no. 30 (7 January 1990).

Chabot, A. *La fête des Rois dans tous les pays* (Paris, 1908).

Chambers, E. K. *The Mediaeval Stage*, 2 vols. (Oxford, 1903).

Charlesworth, J. (ed.), *The Old Testament Pseudepigrapha* (Garden City, 1983).

Chastel, A. *Art et humanisme à Florence au temps de Laurent le Magnifique* (Paris, 1959).

———. *Fables, Formes, Figures*, 2 vols. (Paris, 1978).

———. "La Legend de la Reine de Saba." In *Fables, Formes, Figures*, vol. 1 (Paris, 1978), 61–101.

———. *Marsile Ficin et l'art* (Geneva, 1975).

Chiappelli, A. *Pistoia nelle sue opere d'arte* (Florence, 1904).

Christian, W. Jr. *Apparitions in Late Medieval and Renaissance Spain* (Princeton, 1981).

———. *Visionaries: the Spanish Republic and the Reign of Christ* (Berkeley, 1996).

Christine de Pisan. *Livre des fais et bonnes moeurs (Collection complète des mémoires relatifs à l'histoire de France,* vol. 6) (Paris, 1819), 64–86.

Ciudad Real, A. de. *Tratado curioso y docto de las grandezas de la Nueva España,* 2 vols. (Mexico City, 1976).

Clemens Brentano Religiöse Schriften, ed. W. Oehl, 2 vols. (Munich, 1913).

Clermont-Ganneau, C. "La prise de Jérusalem par les Perses en 614." *Recueil d'archéologie orientale,* 2 (1899), 138–140.

Cochrane, E. *Tradition and Enlightenment in the Tuscan Academies, 1690–1800* (Chicago, 1962).

Colección de documentos ineditos relativos al descubrimiento, conquista y organización de las antiguas posesiones españoles de América y Oceanía, sacado de los archivos del reino y muy especialmente del de Indias, eds. J. Pacheco and F. de Cárdinas, vol. 2 (Madrid, 1864).

Cook, W. "The Earliest Painted Panels of Catalonia (VI)." *Art Bulletin,* 10 (1928), 305–22.

"Coronatio Aquisgranensis." In *Monumenta Germaniae Historica: Leges,* ed. G. Pertz, vol. 2 (Hannover, 1837).

Crombach, H. *Primitiae Gentium, seu Historia SS. Trium Regum Magorum* (Cologne, 1654).

Crumrine, N. Ross. *Le Ceremonial de Pascua y la Identidad de los Mayos de Sonora* (Mexico City, 1974).

Cumont, F. "L'Adoration des mages et l'art triomphal de Rome." *Memorie della pontifica accademia romana di archeologia,* 3 (1922–23), 81–105.

D'Auzoles Lapeyre, J. *Le disciple des temps: Avec 100 remarques chronologiques contre ses animadversions sur St. Epiphane, et quelques eschertillons des deffauts de sa chronologie* (Paris, 1625).

————. *L'Epiphanie, ou Pensées nouvelles à la Gloire de Dieu touchant les trois Mages* (Paris, 1638).

————. *Melchisedech, ou Discours auquel on voit qui est ce grand Prestre-Roy, et comment il est encores aujourd'hui vivant, en corpus et en ame, bien qu'il y aye plus de trois mil sept cens ans qu'il donna sa benediction à Abraham* (Paris, 1622).

————. *La saincte Geographie, c'est à dire Exacte Description de la Terre et Veritable Demonstration du Paradis Terrestre . . .* (Paris, 1629).

D'Hulst, R.-A. *De Tekeningen von Jakof Jordaens* (Brussels, 1956).

Da Cunha, X. *Noticia sobre Antonio José Colffs Guimaraes* (Coimbra, 1908).

Davis, N. Zemon. *Society and Culture in Early Modern France* (Stanford, 1975).

————. "Some Tasks and Themes in the Study of Popular Religion." In *The Pursuit of Holiness in Late Medieval and Renaissance Religion,* ed. C. Trinkaus with H. Oberman (Leiden, 1974), 307–36.

De Mesa, J. "Diego de la Puente: Pintor flamenco en Bolivia, Peru y Chile." *Arte y arqueología,* 5 (1978), 197–98.

De Jerphanion, G. "L'ambon de Salonique: L'arc de Galère et l'ambon de Thèbes." *Memorie della pontifica accademia romana di archeologia,* 3 (1922–23), 107–32.

De la Riva, Bonvesin. *De magnalibus Mediolani* (Milan, 1974).

De la Roncière, C. *Le decouverte de l'Afrique au moyen âge,* 3 vols. (Cairo, 1927).

De Waal, V. "Magier," in *Real-Encyklopädie der christlichen Alterthümer*, vol. 2 (Freiburg/Breisgau, 1886), 340–51.

Deckers, J. "Die Huldigung der Magier in der Kunst der Spätantike." In *Die Heiligen Drei Könige: Darstellung und Verehrung*, 20–32.

Deckers, J., H. Seeliger, G. Mietke. *Die Katakombe "Santi Marcellino e Pietro: Repertorium der Malereien* (Vatican City, 1987).

Del Corazza, Bartolomeo. "Diario fiorentino," ed. G. Corazzini, *Archivio storico italiano*, ser. 5, 14 (1894), 233–98.

Deshman, R. "*Christus rex et magi reges*: Kingship and Christology in Ottonian and Anglo-Saxon Art." *Frühmittelalterlichen Studien*, 10 (1976).

Devisse, J. and M. Mollat. *The Image of the Black in Western Art*, vol. 2, parts 1 and 2 (New York, 1979).

Diario ferrarese, in *Rerum italicarum scriptores*, 24, 7, 1 (Bologna, 1966).

Díaz del Castillo, B. *Historia verdadera de la conquista de la Nueva España*, 2 vols. (Mexico City, 1904).

Die Heiligen Drei Könige: Darstellung und Verehrung (Cologne, 1982), 20.

Dieterich, A. "Die Weisen aus dem Morgenlande: Ein Versuch." In *Albrecht Dieterich Kleine Schriften* (Leipzig, 1911), 272–89.

DiMaio, Jr., M., J. Zeuge, N. Zotov. "*Ambiguitas constantiniana*: the *Caeleste Signum Dei* of Constantine the Great." *Byzantion*, 58 (1988), 333–60.

Doniger O'Flaherty, W. *Women, Androgynes and Other Mythical Beasts* (Chicago, 1982).

Donovan, R. *The Liturgical Drama in Medieval Spain* (Toronto, 1958).

Dos Santos, R. "Les principaux manuscrits à peintures conservés en Portugal." *Société française de reproductions de manuscrits à peintures*, 14 (1930), 22–25.

Doudoroff, M. "Sobre la naturaleza del 'Auto de los reyes Magos' en época moderna." *Revista de Dialectologia y Tradiciones Populares*, 29 (1973), 417–26.

Drumbl, J. *Quem Quaeritis. Teatro Sacro dell'alto medioevo* (Rome, 1981).

Duchesne, L. (ed.). *Le Liber pontificalis*, 3 vols. (Paris, 1886–1957).

Durand, Guilelmus. *Rationale divinorum officiorum* (Antwerp, 1570).

Ebersolt, J. *Constantinople* (Paris, 1951).

Ekkehard IV. "Casus S. Galli." In *Monumenta Germaniae Historia, Scriptores* vol. 2 (Hannover, 1829).

Élissagaray, M. *La légende des rois mages* (Paris, 1965).

Ellard, G. "Bread in the Form of a Penny." *Theological Studies*, 4 (1943), 319–46.

Encyclopedia of Religions, The. ed. M. Eliade, 16 vols. (New York, 1987).

Engels, O. "Die Reliquien der Heiligen Drei Könige in der Reichspolitik der Staufer." In *Die Heiligen Drei Könige—Darstellung*, 33–6.

Erlau, H. *Die Legende vom Vierten König* (Freiburg/B, 1979).

Eusebius. *The Life of Constantine the Great* (New York, 1890).

Euw, A. von. "Darstellungen der Heiligen Drei Könige im Kölner Dom und ihre ikonographische Herleitung." In *Achthundert Jahre Verehrung*, 293–339.

Fahsel, Kaplan. *Die heiligen Drei Könige in der Legende und nach den Visionen der Anna Katharina Emmerich* (Basel, 1941).

Fane, D. (ed.) *Converging Cultures: Art and Identity in Spanish America* (New York, 1996).

Fernández y Avila, G. *La infancia de Jesu-Christo: Zehn spanische Weihnachtsspiele von . . .*, Ed. M. Wagner (Halle, 1922).

Fiamma, Galvano. *De rebus gestis a . . . Vicecomitibus*, in *Rerum italicarum scriptores*, old ed., vol. 12 (Milan, 1728), 1017–1018.

Fields, A. *The Origins of the Platonic Academy of Florence* (Princeton, 1989).

Filippi, F. de (ed.). *An Account of Tibet: the Travels of Ippolito Desideri of Pistoia, S.J., 1712–1727* (London, 1932).

Flint, V. *The Imaginative Landscape of Christopher Columbus* (Princeton, 1992).

Folz, R. *Le souvenir et la Légende de Charlemagne dans l'Empire germanique médiéval* (Paris, 1950).

———. *Le couronnnement impérial de Charlemagne* (Paris, 1964).

Forsyth, I. "Magi and Majesty: a Study of Romanesque Sculpture and Liturgical Drama." *Art Bulletin*, 50 (1968), 215–22.

———. *The Throne of Wisdom: Wood Sculptures of the Madonna in Romanesque France* (Princeton, 1972).

Foster, G. *Culture and Conquest: America's Spanish Heritage* (Chicago, 1960).

Frank, H. "Zur Geschichte von Weihnachten und Epiphanie." *Jahrbuch für Liturgiewissenschaft*, 12 (1932), 145–55, and 13 (1933), 1–38.

Fraser, V. "Architecture and Imperialism in Sixteenth-Century Spanish America." *Art History*, 9 (1986), 325–34.

Frazer, J. *The Golden Bough*. 12 vols. (London, 1911–15).

Frühwald, W. *Das Spätwerk Clemens Brentanos (1815–1842): Romantik im Zeitalter der Metternich'schen Restauration* (Tübingen, 1977).

Gage, T. *A New Survey of the West Indies, 1648*. Ed. A. P. Newton (New York, 1929).

Gagé, J. *"Basiléia": Les Césars. Les rois d'Orient et les "Mages"* (Paris, 1968).

Garber, M. *Vested Interests* (New York, 1992).

Garnier, F. *Le Langage de l'Image au Moyen Age*, 2 vols. (Paris, 1982–88).

———. (ed.). *Le jeu d'Hérode: Drame liturgique du XIIe siècle* (Création par l'Ensemble Gilles Binchois . . . 12 aout 1988) (Paris, 1988).

Geary, P. "I Magi e Milano," in *Il Millenio Ambrosiano*. Ed. C. Bertelli (Milan, 1988), 274–87.

Gemelli Careri, G. F. *Viaje a la Nueva España* (Mexico City, 1976).

Georgius Cedrenus. *Historiarum compendium*, 2 vols. (Bonn, 1839).

Gerlich, F. *Die stigmatisierte Thérèse Neumann von Konnersreuth*, 2 vols. (Munich, 1929).

Gibbon, E. *The Decline and Fall of the Roman Empire*. Ed. J. Bury, vol. 5 (London, 1901).

Gibson, C. *The Aztecs under Spanish Rule* (Stanford, 1964).

Gilio, G. A. *Degli errori e degli abusi de' pittori circa l'istoria*. In P. Baronchi (ed.), *Trattati d'arte del cinquecento fra Manierismo e Controriforma*, vol. 2 (Bari, 1961).

Gisbert, T. *Iconografía y Mitos Indígenas en el Arte* (La Paz, 1980).

Gold Thwaites, R. (ed.). *Travels and Explorations of the Jesuit Missionaries in New France, 1610–1791*, vol. 61 (Cleveland, 1900).

Görden, M. *Shambhala: Auf der Suche nach dem verborgenen Herz Asiens* (Munich, 1994).

Gordon, D. *Making and Meaning: the Wilton Diptych* (London: The National Gallery, 1993).

Grabar, A. *L'empereur dans l'art byzantin* (Paris, 1936).

Grabar, A. *Martyrium: Recherches sur le culte des reliques et l'art chrétien antique*, 2 vols. (Paris, 1946).

Grabar, A. *Les ampoules de Terre Sainte (Monza-Bobbio)* (Paris, 1958).

Grandes chroniques de France: Chronique des règnes de Jean II et de Charles V, Les. 2 vols. (Paris, 1916).

Grafton, A. *New Worlds, Ancient Texts* (Cambridge, Mass., 1992).

Graus, F., et al. *Eastern and Western Europe in the Middle Ages* (London, 1970).

Grimm, J. *Deutsches Wörterbuch*, vol. 5 (Leipzig, 1873).

Grivot, D. *Images de Noël à Autun et en d'autres lieux* (Autun, 1972).

Guenée, B. and F. Lehoux (eds.). *Les entrées royales françaises de 1328 à 1515* (Paris, 1968).

Guery, A. "Le roi dépensier: Le don, la contrainte, et l'origine du système financier de la monarchie française d'Ancien Régime." *Annales E.S.C.*, 39 (1984), 1241–69.

Gundersheimer, W. *Ferrara: the Style of a Renaissance Despoty* (Princeton, 1973).

Günther Grimme, E. "Novus Constantinus: Die Gestalt Konstantins des Großen in der imperialen Kunst der mittelalterlichen Kaiserzeit." *Aachener Kunstblätter*, 22 (1961), 7–20.

Gutton, J.-P. *La société et les pauvres en Europe (XVIè–XVIIIè siècles)* (Paris, 1974).

Hamilton, B. "Prester John and the Three Kings of Cologne," in *Studies in Medieval History Presented to R.H.C. Davis*. Ed. H. Mayr-Harting and R. Moore (London, 1985), 177–91.

Hatfield, R. "The Compagnia de' Magi." *Journal of the Warburg and Courtauld Institutes*, 33 (1970), 107–61.

———. *Boticelli's Uffizi 'Adoration': a Study of Pictorial Content* (Princeton, 1976).

Hayton, Prince of Gorigos. *La flor de las ystorias de orient* (Chicago, 1934).

Die Heiligen Drei Könige: Darstellung und Verehrung (Cologne, 1982).

Hemming, J. *The Search for El Dorado* (London, 1978).

Henster, E. "Das Königreich zu Mainz: Ein Bild aus frohen Tagen der kurmainzischen Kanzlei." In *Studien aus Kunst und Geschichte; Friederich Schneider zum siebzigsten Geburtstag* (Freiburg/B., 1906), 393–410.

Herrad of Hohenbourg. *Hortus deliciarum*. Ed. R. Green et al. (London, 1979).

Hilton, J. *Lost Horizon* (Bern, 1945).

Hitts, A. Z. *Three Wise Men Almanac and Encyclopedia* (Rockland, Maryland).

———. *Three Wise Men Daily Lottery* (Rockland, Maryland).

———. *Three Wise Men Rundowns & Workouts* (Rockland, Maryland).,

———. *3 Wise Men Dream Book* (Rockville, Maryland).

Hobsbawm, E., and T. Ranger. *The Invention of Tradition* (Cambridge, 1972).

Höfler, M. "Die Gebäcke des Dreikönigstages." *Zeitschrift des Vereins für Volkskunde*, 14 (1904), 257–78.

Hofmann, H. *Die heiligen Drei Könige: Zur Heiligenverehrung im kirchlichen, gesellschaftlichen und politischen Leben des Mittelalters* (Bonn, 1975).

Holl, K. "Der Ursprung des Epiphanienfestes." *Sitzungsberichte der königlich preussischen Akademie der Wissenschaften* 29 (1917), 401–38.

Hope, C. "Ostentatio genitalium." *The London Review of Books*, 13 November-6 December 1984, 19–20.

Hubert, J., et al. *Europe of the Invasions* (New York, 1969).

Hughes, D. Owen. "Earrings for Circumcision: Distinction and Purification in the Italian Renaissance City." In R. Trexler, *Persons in Group*, 155–82.

Hümpfner, W. "Coup d'Oeil sur les publications relatives à Anne Catherine Emmerick." *Revue d'ascétique et de mystique* 5 (1924), 349–80.

Hümpfner, W. *Clemens Brentanos Glaubwürdigkeit in seinen Emmerick-Aufzeichnungen* (Würzburg, 1923).

Ihm, C. *Die Programme der christlichen Apsismalerei vom vierten Jahrhundert bis zur Mitte des achten Jahrhunderts* (Wiesbaden, 1960).

Inchofer, M. *Tres Magi Evangelici* (Rome, 1639).

Interpreter's Bible, The. Vol. 7 (New York, 1951).

Intorcetta, P. *Sinarum scientia politico-moralis* (Goa, 1669).

Isolano, I. "Vita b. Veronicae de Binasco virginis." In *Acta Sanctorum*, 107 vols. (Paris, 1863–1925), January I, 904–6.

Jackson, A. "The Magi in Marco Polo and the Cities in Persia from Which They Came to Worship the Infant Christ." *Journal of the American Oriental Society*, 26 (1905), 79–83.

Jackson, C. *The Oriental Religions and American Thought* (Westport, Conn., 1981).

Jacquot, J. and E. Koenigson (eds.). *Les Fêtes de la Renaissance*, 3 vols. (Paris, 1956–75).

Jameson, Mrs. (A.). *Legends of the Madonna as Represented in the Fine Arts* (London, 1891).

Jan, M. (ed.). *Le voyage en Asie centrale et au Tibet* (Paris, 1992).

Jean d'Avranches. *Liber de officiis ecclesiasticis*, in *PL*, 147.

Johannes of Hildesheim. *Liber de gestis et translacionibus trium regum*. In *The Three Kings of Cologne*, ed. C. Horstmann (London, 1886).

Julien de Vézelay. *Sermons*, 2 vols. (Paris, 1972).

Jungmann, J. *Missarum Solemnia*, 2 vols. (Vienna, 1952).

Kampers, F. "Der Kosmokrator in einem altfranzösischen Märchen." *Historisches Jahrbuch*, 47 (1927), 457–72.

Kantorowicz, E. "The 'King's Advent,' and the Enigmatic Panels in the Doors of Santa Sabina." *Art Bulletin*, 26 (1944), 207–31.

Kaplan, P. *The Rise of the Black Magus in Western Art* (Ann Arbor, 1985).

Karpp, H. *Die frühchristliche und mittelalterliche Mosaiken in Santa Maria Maggiore zu Rom* (Baden-Baden, 1966).

Kehrer, H. *Die heiligen Drei Könige in Literatur und Kunst*, 2 vols. (reprint: Hildesheim, 1976).

Kienast, W. *Deutschland und Frankreich in der Kaiserzeit*, 3 vols. (Stuttgart, 1974–75).

King, N. *Mittelalterliche Dreikönigsspiele: Eine Grundlagenarbeit zu den lateinischen, deutschen und französichen Dreikönigsspielen und -spielszenen bis zum Ende des 16. Jahrhunderts* (Freiburg/S, 1979).

Kirshner, J. "Eugenio IV e il Monte Comune." *Archivio storico italiano*, 127 (1969), 339–82.

Klaniczay, G. *The Uses of Supernatural Power* (Oxford, 1990).

Klauser, T. "Aurum Coronarium." *Reallexikon für Antike und Christentum*, vol. 1 (Stuttgart, 1950), 1010–20.

Kloos, R. "Nikolaus von Bari, eine neue Quelle zur Entwicklung der Kaiseridee unter Friedrich II." *Deutsches Archiv für Erforschung des Mittelalters* 11 (1954–55), 166–90.

Kloten, I. *Wandmalerei im Grossen Kirchenschisma: die Cappella Bolognini in San Petronio zu Bologna* (Heidelberg, 1986).

Lafaye, J. *Quetzalcóatl et Guadalupe: La formation de la conscience nationale au Mexique (1531–1813)*.

Lange, C. "King's [sic] Day Ceremonies at a Rio Grande Pueblo, January 6, 1940." *El Palacio*, 58, no. 12 (December, 1951), 398–406.

Lange, Y. "The Household Wooden Saints of Puerto Rico," 2 vols. (diss., Univ. of Penna., 1975).

Las Casas, Bartolomé de. *Historia de las Indias*, 3 vols. (Madrid, 1927).

———. *Apologética Historia sumaria*. Ed. E. O'Gorman, 2 vols. (Mexico City).

Lay Folks Mass Book, or The Manner of Hearing Mass, The. Ed. T. Simmons (London, 1879).

Leclercq, H. "Labarum," *Dictionnaire d'archéologie chrétienne et de liturgie*, 8, 1 (Paris, 1928), 927–62.

———. "Mages." In *Dictionnaire d'archéologie chrétienne et de liturgie*, vol. 10, 1 (Paris, 1931), 980–1067.

———. "Chrisme." In *Dictionnaire d'archéologie chrétienne et de liturgie*, vol. 3, 1 (Paris, 1913), 1481–1534.

Leseyre, H. "Mage." *Dictionnaire de la Bible*, vol. 4, part 1 (Paris, 1912), 543–45.

Liber de laudibus civitatis Ticinae (Pavia), in *RIS*, vol. 11, part 1.

Lipens, Martin. *Dissertatio de Navigatio* [sic] *Salomonis*, and his *Dissertatio de Ophir*, in B. Ugolino (ed.), *Thesaurus antiquitatum sacrarum . . . opuscula . . .*, vol. 7 (Venice, 1747), respectively cccxliii–ccclix. and cclxi–ccccx.

Lipphardt, W. "Liturgische Dramen." In *Die Musik in Geschichte und Gegenwart*, 8 (Kassel, 1960).

Lipphardt, W. "Das Herodesspiel von Le Mans nach den Handschriften Madrid, Bibl. Nac. 288 und 289 (11. und 12. Jh.)." In *Organicae Voces: Festschrift Joseph Smits van Waesbergher* (Amsterdam, 1963).

Liutprand of Cremona. *Legatio constantinopolitana*. In *Tutte le opere* (Milan, 1945).

Lockhart, J. *The Nahuas after the Conquest: A Social and Cultural History of the Indians of Central Mexico, Sixteenth through Eighteenth Centuries* (Stanford, 1992).

Lucian. *The Saturnalia*. In *The Works of Lucian*, vol. 6 (Cambridge, Mass., 1959).

Ludolphus de Saxonia. *Vita Jesu Christi* (Paris, 1865).

Luther, M. *Werke*, vol. 34 (Weimar, 1980).

Lutz, K. "Dreiköngliches und Reformationsgeschichtliches in und um Speyrer

Chroniken des 13.-16. Jahrhunderts." *Blätter für Pfälzische Kirchengeschichte und religiöse Volkskunde* 33 (1966), 18–32.

MacCormack, S. *Art and Ceremony in Late Antiquity* (Berkeley, 1981).

MacLagan, E. *The Jesuits and the Great Mogul* (New York, 1972).

Mâle, E. "Les rois mages et le drame liturgique." *Gazette des beaux arts*, ser. 4, 4 (1910), 261–70.

Mallett, M. *The Florentine Galleys in the Fifteenth Century* (Oxford, 1967).

Manco, J. "Sacred vs. Profane: Images of Sexual Vice in Renaissance Art." *Studies in Iconography*, 13 (1990), 145–90.

Mandeville's Travels: Texts and Translation. Ed. M. Letts (Nendeln, 1967).

Marco Polo the Venetian, The Book of Ser. Ed. G. Parks (New York, 1927).

Marsh-Edwards, J. "The Magi in Tradition and Art." *The Irish Ecclesiastical Record*, ser. 5, 85 (1956), 1–9.

Maspero, H. "Le songe et l'ambassade de l'empereur Ming: Étude critique des sources." *Bulletin de l'École d'Extrême Orient*, 10 (1910), 95–130.

Masson, J. *My Father's Guru: A Journey through Spirituality and Disillusion* (London, 1993).

Mayerhofer, U. "Bekleidete Prozessionsfiguren in Tirol. Ein Beitrag zur Kult-Funktion von Bildern." *Jahrbuch für Volkskunde*, n. f. 8 (1985), 107–20.

McAndrew, J. *The Open-Air Churches of Sixteenth-Century Mexico* (Cambridge, Mass., 1965).

McNally, R. "The Three Holy Kings in Early Irish Latin Writing." In *Kyriakon: Festschrift Johannes Quasten*, ed. P. Granfield and J. Jungmann, 2 vols. (Münster/Westf., 1970).

Meissen, K. *Die heiligen Drei Könige und ihr Festtag im Glauben und Brauch* (Cologne, 1945).

Meller, S. *Peter Vischer der Ältere und seine Werkstatt* (Leipzig, 1925).

Mendieta, G. *Historia eclesiástica indiana* (Mexico City, 1971).

Meredith, P., and J. Tailley. *The Staging of Religious Drama in Europe in the Later Middle Ages* (Kalamazoo, 1983).

Meyer, W. "Der Ludus de Antichristo und Bemerkungen über die lateinischen Rythmen des XII Jahrhunderts." *Sitzungsberichte der philosophischen und historischen Classe der k. b. Akademie der Wissenschaften zu München*, 1 (1882), 1–40.

Migne, J.-P. (ed.). *Patrologia cursus completus . . . Series graeca* (*PG*), 166 vols. (Paris, 1857–66).

———. (ed.). *Patrologia cursus completus . . . Series latina* (*PL*), 221 vols. (Paris, 1844–64).

Miles, C. *Christmas Customs and Traditions: Their History and Significance* (New York, 1976).

Miller, J. "Oman's Perfume with a Gold Price Tag." *New York Times*, 27 February 1985.

Monneret de Villard, U. *Le leggende orientali sui magi evangelici* (Vatican City, 1952).

Montesquiou-Fezensac, B. de. "L'arc de triomphe d'Einhardus." *Cahiers archéologiques*, 4 (1949), 79–103.

Montpetit, R. *Le temps des Fêtes au Québec* (Montreal, 1978).

264 BIBLIOGRAPHY

Morante, E. (ed.). *L'opera completa dell'Angelico* (Milano, 1970).

Morison, S. (ed.). *Journals and Other Documents on the Life and Voyages of Christopher Columbus* (New York, 1963).

Moser, H. *Volksbräuche im geschichtlichen Wandel* (Munich, 1985), 72.

Motolinía, Toribio de Benevento, called. *Memoriales e Historia de los Indios de la Nueva España* (Madrid, 1970).

Mück, P. (ed.). *Volkskultur des Europäischen Spätmittelalters* (Stuttgart, 1987).

Mugabura, J. and F. *Chronicle of Colonial Lima: The Diary of Josephe and Francina M.* Ed. R. Ryal Miller (Norman, 1975).

Naselli, G. "I re magi nella religiosità popolare." In *La religiosità popolare nella valle padana. Atti del II Convegno di studi sul folklore padano (Modena, 19–20–21 marzo 1965)* (Modena, 1966), 289–99.

Nestori, A. *Repertorio topografico delle pitture delle catacombe romane* (Vatican City, 1975).

Nilsson, M. "Studien zur Vorgeschichte des Weihnachtsfestes." *Archiv für Religionswissenschaft*, 19 (1916–19), 50–150.

Nilsson, M. "Kalendae Ianuariae," *Paulys Realencyclopädie der classischen Altertumswissenschaft*, 10, 2 (Stuttgart, 1931), 1562–64.

Nilsson, M. "Strena," *Paulys Realencyclopädie der classischen Altertumswissenschaft*, 4. A. 1 (Stuttgart, 1931), 351–53.

Olschki, L. "Asiatic Exoticism in Italian Art of the Italian Renaissance." *Art Bulletin*, 26 (1944), 95–106.

———. *Marco Polo's Asia* (Berkeley, 1960).

———. "The Wise Men of the East in Oriental Traditions." In *Semitic and Oriental Studies Presented to W. Popper* (Berkeley, 1951).

Oman, A. "And Finally, on the 12th Night." *Washington Post* (3 January 1986).

Origo, I. "The Domestic Enemy: Eastern Slaves in Tuscany in the Fourteenth and Fifteenth Centuries." *Speculum*, 30 (1955), 321–66.

Ortiz, F. *La Antigua Fiesta Afrocubana del "Dia de Reyes"* (Havana, 1960).

———. "Los Cabildos Afro-Cubanos." *Revista Bimestre Cubana*, 16 (1921), 6–39.

Paez, P. *Historia Aethiopiae*, 2 vols. (Rome, 1905–06).

Parsons, E. Clews. *Mitla, Town of the Souls, and other Zapotec-Speaking Pueblos of Oaxaca, Mexico* (Chicago, 1936).

Pazos, M. "El teatro franciscano en Méjico durante el siglo XVI." *Archivo Ibero-Americano*, ser. 2, 11 (1951), 129–89.

Pelekanidis, S. M., et al. *The Treasures of Mount Athos: Illuminated Manuscripts*, vol. 2 (Athens, 1975).

Pereyra, B., S.J. *Prior Tomus Commentariorum et Disputationum in Genesim* (Lyon, 1607).

Pérez de Ribas, A. *Historia de los Triunfos de N. S. Fe entre Gentes las mas barbaras y fieras del Nuevo Orbe*, 3 vols. (Mexico City, 1944).

Pericoli, M. *Il trionfo della passione e resurrezione a Todi nella Pasqua 1563* (Todi, 1963).

Petronius. *Satyricon*, trans. W. Rouse (Cambridge, Mass., 1987).

Petrus Martyr d'Anghera. *De orbe novo*, ed. F. MacNutt, 2 vols. (New York, 1912).

Pezzana, A. *Storia di Parma*, 2 vols. (Parma, 1842).

Pieper, P. (ed.). *Die deutschen, niederländischen und italienischen Tafelbilder bis um 1530* (Münster, 1986).

Pliny. *Natural History*, vol. 8 (Cambridge, Mass., 1963).

Polacco, R. *La cattedrale di Torcello* (Venice, 1984).

Poly, J.-P. and E. Bournazel. *La mutation féodale: X-XII siècles* (Paris, 1991).

Poma de Ayala, G. *El Primer Nueva Corónica y Buen Gobierno*, 3 vols. (Mexico City, 1980).

Porphyrogenitus, Constantin VII. *De cerimonibus aulae byzantinae*, vol. 1, in *Corpus scriptorum historiae byzantinae*, vol. 9 (Bonn, 1829), 615 (bk. 2, chap. 21).

———. *Le livre des cérémonies*, ed. A. Vogt, 2 vols. (Paris, 1967).

Post, C. *A History of Spanish Painting*, vol. 9, part 1 (Cambridge, Mass., 1947).

Pullan, B. *Rich and Poor in Renaissance Venice* (Cambridge, Mass., 1971).

Purvin, R. "Cohoes Canadians kick up their clogs." *The Times Record* (6 January 1984).

Rainey, R. "Sumptuary Legislation in Renaissance Florence" (diss.: Columbia University, 1985).

Rank, O., et al. *In Quest of the Hero* (Princeton, 1990).

Recueil des historiens des Gaules et de la France. vol. 21 (Paris, 1955).

Reda, V. "Cohoes: A Door to Franco-American past." *Albany Times Union* (6 January 1984).

Reindel, K. (ed.). *Die Kaiserkrönung Karls des Grossen* (Göttingen, 1970).

Relación de los fechos del mui magnifico e mas virtuoso señor don Miguel Lucas [de Iranzo], Condestable de Castilla (Madrid, 1855).

Renoux, A. "L'Épiphanie à Jérusalem au IV. et au V. siècles." *Lex Orandi* 40 (1967), 171–93.

Rerum italicarum scriptores (RIS).

Rhein und Maas: Kunst und Kultur 800–1400: eine Ausstellung. 2 vols. (Cologne, 1972).

Robinson, F. *Gabriel Metsu (1629–1667)* (New York, 1974).

Roche, D. *Le siècle des lumières en province: Académies et académiciens provinciaux, 1680–1789*, 2 vols. (Paris, 1989).

Rogers, F. *The Obedience of a King of Portugal* (Minneapolis, 1958).

———. *The Quest for Eastern Christians* (Minneapolis, 1962).

———. *The Travels of the Infante Dom Pedro of Portugal* (Cambridge, Mass., 1961).

Rojas Garcidueñas, J. *El Teatro de Nueva España en el siglo XVI* (Mexico City, 1935).

Rossi, G. B. de'. *Bullettino di archeologia cristiana*, 1 (Rome, Oct. 1863).

Russell, H. Diane (ed.). *Jacques Callot: Prints and Selected Drawings* (Washington, D.C., 1925).

Ryckmans, G. "De l'or (?), de l'encens et de la myrrhe." *Revue Biblique*, 58 (1951), 372–76.

Saintyves, P. *Rondes enfantines et quêtes saisonniéres: Les Liturgies populaires* (Paris, 1919).

Salvini, R. "La scultura romanica pistoiese." In *Il romanico pistoiese nei suoi rap-porti con l'arte romanica dell'occidente* (Pistoia, 1979), 165–73.

Sartori, P. *Sitte und Brauch*, 3 vols. (Leipzig, 1910–14).

Schärmeli, Y. *Königsbrauch und Dreikönigsspiele im welschen Teil des Kantons Freiburg* (Freiburg/S, 1988).

Schmitt, J.-C. and J. Le Goff (eds.). *Le Charivari* (Paris, 1981).

Schnitzler, H. "Das Kuppelmosaik der Aachener Pfalzkapelle." *Aachener Kunst-blätter*, 29 (1964), 14–24.

Schoebel, C. *L'histoire des Rois Mages* (Paris, 1878).

Schramm, P. *Herrschaftszeichen und Staatssymbolik*, 3 vols. (Stuttgart, 1956).

Schramm, P. and F. Mütherich. *Denkmale der deutschen Könige und Kaiser* (Munich, 1962).

Schreiner, K. *Maria: Jungfrau, Mutter, Herrscherin* (Munich, 1994).

Schubert, E. "Erspielte Ordnung: Beobachtungen zur bäuerlichen Rechtswelt des späteren Mittelalters." *Jahrbuch für fränkische Landesforschung* 38 (1978), 51–65.

Seitz, H. "Three Crowns as a European Symbol and as the Swedish Coat of Arms." In *V. Congrès international des sciences généalogique et héraldique* (Stockholm, 1961), 240–49.

Settis, S. *La 'Tempesta' interpretata. Giorgione, i committenti, i soggetti* (Turin, 1978).

Simson, O. von. *Sacred Fortress: Byzantine Art and Statecraft in Ravenna* (Chi-cago, 1948).

Snyder, J. *Northern Renaissance Art* (New York, 1985).

Spencer, E. "The First Patron of the *Très Belles Heures de Notre-Dame*." In *Mis-cellanea F. Lyna* (Gent, 1969), 145–49.

Speyer, W. and I. Opelt. "Barbar II (ikonographisch)." In *Reallexikon für Antike und Christentum*, Supplement, volume 1 (Stuttgart, 1992), 944–59 and forth-coming fascicule.

Staehlin, C. *Apariciones* (Madrid, 1954), 206–27.

Stechow, W. *Bruegel* (Cologne, 1974).

Stehkaemper, H. (ed.). *Köln, das Reich und Europa* (Cologne, 1971).

———. "Könige und Heilige Drei Könige." In *Die Heiligen Drei Könige—Darstellung*, 37–50.

Steinberg, L. *The Sexuality of Christ in Renaissance Art and in Modern Oblivion* (New York, 1983).

Steiner, J. *Theres Neumann von Konnersreuth: Ein Lebensbild nach authentischen Berichten, Tagebüchern und Dokumenten* (Munich, 1988).

———. (ed.). *Visionen der Therese Neumann*, 2 vols. (Munich, 1977).

Stevenson, K. *Nuptial Blessing: a Study of Christian Marriage Rites* (New York, 1983).

Stopani, R. *Le vie di pellegrinaggio del Medioevo* (Florence, 1991).

Stouff, L. *Arles à la fin du Moyen-Age*, 2 vols. (Aix-en-Provence, 1988).

Stumpfl, R. *Kultspiele der Germanen als Ursprung des Mittelalterlichen Dramas* (Berlin, 1936).

Sturdevant, W. *The Misterio de los reyes magos: Its Position in the Development of the Medieval Legend of the Three Kings* (Baltimore, 1927).

Suetonius, *The Lives of the Caesars* (Cambridge, Mass., 1944).

Theodore, E. "Notes sur un ornement en étain, d'une couronne de roi de la fève au XV. siècle, et sur quelques médailles religieuses," *Bulletin de la commission départementale des monuments historiques du Pas-de-Calais*, 5 (1932), 687–98.

Theophanes Continuatus. *Michaelis Theofili F. Imperium* (bk. 4), in *Corpus scriptorum historiae byzantinae*, vol. 33 (Bonn, 1838).

Thorn, G. *Chronica W. Thorn. mon. S. Augustini Cantuarie*. In *Historiae anglicanae scriptores X . . .*, ed. R. Twysden (London, 1652).

Thorndike, L. *A History of Magic and Experimental Science*, 4 vols. (New York, 1923–34).

Thuasne, L. (ed.). *Johannis Burchardi . . . Diarium sive rerum urbanorum commentarii (1483–1506)*, 3 vols. (Paris, 1883–85).

Tomas, A. *Shambhala: Oasis of Light* (London, 1977).

Torquemada, J. de. *Monarquia Indiana*, 3 vols. (Mexico City, 1969).

Tournier, M. *The Four Wise Men* (New York, 1984).

Treitinger, O. *Die oströmische Kaiser- und Reichsidee nach ihrer Gestaltung im höfischen Zeremoniell* (Bad Homburg vor der Höhe, 1969).

Très riches heures du duc de Berry, Les. (Paris, 1970).

Trexler, R. "The Bishop's Portion: Generic Pious Legacies in the Late Middle Ages in Italy." *Traditio* 28 (1972), 397–450.

———. *Church and Community, 1200–1600. Studies in the History of Florence and New Spain* (Rome, 1987).

———. "Gendering Jesus Crucified." In *Iconography at the Crossroads*, ed. B. Cassidy (Princeton, 1993), 107–20.

———. "The Magi Enter Florence: The Ubriachi of Florence and Venice." In R. Trexler, *Church and Community*, 75–168.

———. (ed.). *Persons in Groups. Social Behavior as Identity Formation in Medieval and Renaissance Europe* (Binghamton, 1985).

———. *Public Life in Renaissance Florence* (New York, 1980; Ithaca, 1991).

———. "Ritual Behavior in Renaissance Florence: The Setting." In R. Trexler, *Church and Community*, 11–36.

———. *Sex and Conquest: Gendered Violence, Political Order and the European Conquest of the Americas* (Cambridge and Ithaca, 1995).

———. "Träume der Heiligen Drei Könige." In *Träume im Mittelalter: Ikonologischen Studien*, ed. A. Paravicini Bagliani and G. Stabile (Stuttgart, 1989), 55–71.

———. "Triumph and Mourning in North Italian Magi Art." In *Art and Politics in Late Medieval and Early Renaissance Italy*, ed. C. Rosenberg (Notre Dame, 1990), 38–66.

———. "La vie ludique dans la Nouvelle-Espagne: L'Empereur et ses Trois Rois." In *Les Jeux à la Renaissance*, ed. J.-C. Margolin and P. Ariès (Paris, 1982), 81–93.

———. "We Think, They Act: Clerical Readings of Missionary Theatre in Sixteenth Century Mexico." In R. Trexler, *Church and Community*, 575–613.

Trexler, R., with M. Lewis, "Two Captains and Three Kings: New Light on the Medici Chapel." In R. Trexler, *Church and Community*, 169–244.

Trocmé, S. *L'église de Villemards et sa 'Adoration des Mages'* (Paris, 1967).

Turner, V. "The Center Out There: Pilgrim's Goal." *History of Religions*, 12 (1972), 191–230.

Urbas, A. (ed.). *Die Reiche der heiligen drei Könige, ihr Sterndienst, ihre Reise nach Bethlehem, etc. Nach den Gesichten der gottseligen Katharina Emmerich* (Laibach, 1884).

Urreta, L. de. *Historia Eclesiastica, politica, natural, y moral de los grandes y remotos Reynos de la Etiopia, Monarchia del Emperador llamado Preste Juan de las Indias* (Valencia, 1610).

Van Puyvelde, L. *Jordaens* (Paris, 1953).

Van Gennep, A. *Manuel de folklore français contemporain*, tome 1, 8 vols. (Paris, 1937–88).

Van Der Meer, F. *Maiestas Domini: Théophanies de l'apocalypse dans l'art chrétien* (Vatican City, 1938).

Van Der Meer, F. and C. Mohrmann. *Atlas of the Early Christian World* (London, 1958).

Van Dyke, H. *The Story of the Other Wise Man* (New York, 1985).

Vandevivere, I. *El Cathédral et l'église paroissiale de Cervera de Pisuerga de Palencia* (Brussels, 1967).

Vatable, F. *Biblia sacra, Hebraice, Graece, et Latine ... cum annotationibus Francisci Vatable ...* (Paris, 1586).

Vaultier, R. *Le folklore pendant la guerre de Cent Ans d'après les lettres de Remission du Trésor des Chartes* (Paris, 1965).

Veyne, P. (ed.). *Histoire de la vie privée*, vol. 1 (Paris, 1985).

Vezin, G. *L'adoration et le cycle des Mages dans l'art chrétien primitif: Étude des influences orientales et grecques sur l'art chrétien* (Paris, 1950).

Voet, L. *Antwerp: The Golden Age* (Antwerp, 1973).

Volbach, W. "Il Cristo di Sutri e la venerazione del SS. Salvatore nel Lazio." *Rendiconti della pontificia accademia romana di archeologia* 27 (1940–41), 97–126.

Voltaire. *Questions sur l'Encyclopédie par des amateurs*, vol. 5 (Paris, 1771).

Voyage of Pedro Alvares Cabral to Brazil and India, The. Ed. W. Greenlee (Nendeln, 1967).

Wagner, P. "Das Dreikönigspiel zu Freiburg in der Schweiz." In *Freiburger Geschichtsblätter*, 10 (1903), 77–101.

Walsh, M. "A Three Kings Pageant at Michilmackinac, 1679." In *Michigan Academician*, 26 (1994), 19–28.

Wapnewski, P. "Die Weisen aus dem Morgenland auf der Magdeburger Weihnacht (zu Walter von der Vogelweide 19,5)," In *Lebende Antike: Symposion für Rudolf Sühnel*, ed. H. Meller and H. J. Zimmerman (Berlin, 1967), 74–94.

Wellesz, E. "The Nativity Drama of the Byzantine Church." *The Journal of Roman Studies*, 37 (1947), 145–51.

Wessels, C. *Early Jesuit Travellers in Central Asia, 1603–1721* (The Hague, 1924).

West, D. and A. Kling (eds.). *The Libro de las Profecías of Christopher Columbus* (Gainesville, 1991).

Wetter, H. *Heischebrauch und Dreikönigsumzug im deutschen Raum* (diss., Univ. Greifswald; Wiesbaden, 1933).

Wilde, J. *Venetian Art from Bellini to Titian* (Oxford, 1974).

Wilpert, G. *Ein Cyclus christologischer Gemälde aus der Katakombe der heiligen Petrus und Marcellinus* (Freiburg/B., 1891).

_____. *Le pitture delle catacombe romane*, 2 vols. (Text and Figures) (Rome, 1903).

_____. *I sarcofagi cristiani antichi*, 3 vols. (Rome, 1929–36).

Wilson, M. *The National Gallery London* (London, 1977).

Wirth, J. "Sainte Anne est une sorciére." *Bibliothèque d'Humanisme et Renaissance* 40 (1978), 449–80.

Yates, F. *Giordano Bruni and the Hermetic Tradition* (New York, 1964).

Young, K. *The Drama of the Medieval Church*, 2 vols. (London, 1933).

_____. "La procession des trois rois at Besançon." *Romanic Review*, 4 (1913), 76–83.

Yule, H. and H. Cordier. *Cathay and the Way Thither*, 4 vols. (London, 1913–16).

Zambotti, B. *Diario ferrarese*, *RIS* 24, 7, 2 (Bologna, 1969).

Zappert, G. "'Epiphania'. Ein Beitrag zur christlichen Kunstarchäologie." *Sitzungsberichte der philosophischen-historischen Classe der kaiserlichen Akademie der Wissenschaften*, 21 (a. 1856), Heft 2 (Vienna, 1857), 291–373.

Zürcher, E. *Buddhist Conquest of China*, 2 vols. (Leiden, 1959).

INDEX

About the Author

RICHARD C. TREXLER is Professor of History at the State University of New York, Binghamton. He is the author of *Public Life in Renaissance Florence* and *Sex and Conquest: Gendered Violence, Political Order, and the European Conquest of the Americas.*